Contemporary Issues in Accounting

Elaine Conway · Darren Byrne
Editors

Contemporary Issues in Accounting

The Current Developments in Accounting Beyond the Numbers

palgrave
macmillan

Editors
Elaine Conway
Derby Business School
University of Derby
Derby, Derbyshire, UK

Darren Byrne
College of Business, Accounting Department
University of Derby
Derby, Derbyshire, UK

ISBN 978-3-030-08181-2 ISBN 978-3-319-91113-7 (eBook)
https://doi.org/10.1007/978-3-319-91113-7

Softcover re-print of the Hardcover 1st edition 2018

Cover image: © bjdlzx
Cover design: Tom Howey

Printed on acid-free paper

This Palgrave Macmillan imprint is published by the registered company Springer International Publishing AG part of Springer Nature
The registered company address is: Gewerbestrasse 11, 6330 Cham, Switzerland

Preface

The foundation for this book lies in conversations the authors had which recognised that graduate accountants need a wider appreciation of broader contemporary issues in the accounting field and wider business environment. Most university accounting courses cover technical subjects such as financial accounting, management accounting, audit, tax, strategy and operations, and there is already a wealth of text books to support these technical areas. The focus of most accounting courses is to align to the requirements of professional accounting exam syllabuses. Whilst these syllabuses may cover 'contemporary' issues, they are often 'light touch' in content, as their focus is more on the immediate changes in the technical areas of accounting, including developments in standards. Hence this book is not about the implications of day-to-day changes in accounting or audit standards or tax rates. Whilst the accountant needs to understand these issues, we wanted to broaden the scope of thinking about the big, even 'wicked' problems and issues that the profession is likely to face in the future and which go 'beyond the numbers'. Most students studying accounting now will be working in a very dynamic and changing business environment as soon as they graduate, so it is critically important that they are appraised of current developments in some depth, so that they can prepare themselves to adapt to the changes effectively and support their future employers to do the same.

In designing this book, the authors asked themselves the question—what would we like to tell future accountants about what is happening in the world of work beyond the technical accounting knowledge which could impact on their careers? This book is the result of that thought process. There is a danger in writing a book called *Contemporary Issues in Accounting* that it is no longer 'contemporary' by the time it is published. However, after a lot of painstaking research about what industry thinkers consider will change the accounting profession over the next decade, the authors are confident that the broad themes covered in this book will be 'hot topics' for the foreseeable future. Over the next several years, there will an imperative to move to sustainable business models, including those based on the circular economy; to respond and contribute to changing technology; to develop responsible tax strategies; to adopt more narrative reporting; to improve the quality of audit; to get performance management 'right' for an organisation and perhaps most importantly, to be aware of the need to develop individual self-leadership and soft skills to meet the challenges of this complex world.

We want our students to be ready for anything when they graduate and we hope this book helps them prepare for whatever their career throws at them.

Derby, UK
March 2018

Elaine Conway
Darren Byrne

Contents

Notes on Contributors

Darren Byrne is a Senior Lecturer in Accounting and Finance and the Programme Leader for Business Accounting at the University of Derby, UK. He teaches on numerous modules covering managerial theory, project management and other disciplines that support the Business Accountant. His teaching philosophy is to draw upon his own professional experience and to help to apply ideas contextually for the benefit of students' own learning. His research interests are currently project management skills, business ethics and with the perception of professionalism within the international context. He is a Fellow of the Higher Education Academy.

Elaine Conway is a Senior Lecturer in Accounting and Finance at the Derby Business School, University of Derby, UK. She is a Fellow of the Higher Education Academy and the Chartered Institute of Management Accountants. She is also a Member of the Chartered Institute of Marketing, the Chartered Institute of Public Finance and Accountancy and the Chartered Management Institute. She has an MBA from Duke University, USA. Prior to entering academia, Elaine spent 17 years in various managerial roles in the automotive industry. Her research interests are corporate social responsibility, sustainable business and financial reporting.

Hilary Coyle is a Senior Lecturer in Management Accounting at the Derby Business School, University of Derby, UK. She is a Fellow of the Higher Education Academy and has been an Associate of the Chartered

Institute of Management Accountants for over 20 years. She is interested in the public sector and has been an elected member of her local district council for seven years. Her research interests include performance measurement in local government.

Liz Crookes is a Lecturer in Accounting and Finance at the University of Derby, UK. She is an Associate of the Chartered Institute of Management Accountants and a Fellow of the Higher Education Authority. She has a degree in mathematics and statistics from the University of Sheffield and spent several years analysing the costs of aircraft engines before finding her passion and settling into life as a lecturer. She has worked with publishers to develop accounting and finance questions for books and for on-line delivery. Her research interests span teaching, learning and assessment methods and data analytics.

Prof. Jose Arturo Garza-Reyes is Head of the Centre for Supply Chain Improvement, at Derby Business School, University of Derby, UK. He has published over 100 articles in leading international journals and conferences, and four books in the areas of operations and innovation management, quality management systems and manufacturing performance measurement systems. He is Co-founder and Editor of the *Int. J. of Supply Chain and Operations Resilience* (IJSCOR), Associate Editor of the *Int. J. of Operations and Production Management* (IJOPM) and *J. of Manufacturing Technology Management* (JMTM) as well as Editor-in-Chief of the *Int. J. of Industrial Engineering and Operations Management* (IJIEOM). Prof. Garza-Reyes has participated as a Guest Editor for special issues in various highly ranked international journals. His research interests include general aspects of operations and manufacturing management, operations and quality improvement, and supply chain improvement.

Denise Glanville is a Senior Lecturer in Accounting and Finance at the University of Derby, UK. She delivers financial modules specialising in management accounting aimed at developing knowledgeable managers and accountants. Denise is a Chartered Management Accountant and a Fellow of the Higher Education Academy. Her research interests include project management, business decision-making, incentive schemes in addition to the circular economy model and sustainability. Previous business experience included management positions within design, purchasing, production, sales and marketing. Her previous accounting roles were within the textile, clothing and engineering industries.

Juliet Hogsden is a Senior Lecturer of Accounting and Finance at the Derby Business School, University of Derby, UK. A Fellow of the Higher Education Authority, Juliet is also a member of both the ICAEW and the Chartered Institute of Taxation. She has an MRes from Derby University and is in the final stage of her Ph.D. Her research interests include the issues charities encounter generating adequate resources, as well as a range of contemporary taxation issues.

Parminder Johal is Head of Accounting and Finance Division at Derby Business School at the University of Derby, UK. She is a member of the Chartered Institute of Management Accountants and Fellow of the Higher Education Academy. Her research interests are Accounting Education, Management Accounting Practices in SMEs/emerging markets and Financial Analysis/Reporting. She also actively engages with external organisations in the capacity of an independent governor, mentor and trustee.

Dave Lees is a Senior Lecturer in Leadership and Management at Derby Business School and Derby Management School. With an MBA from the University of Derby he is a Senior Fellow of the Higher Education Academy, an Academic Member of the CIPD and a Member of the Association for Coaching. He has published on aspects of feedback for students on assignments and is a freelance writer for Pearson. He is currently working towards a Ph.D. on alternative understanding of leadership at York St. John University.

Simon Peter Nadeem is a Ph.D. candidate at the University of Derby and has been teaching at university level since 2013. He has earned his Executive MBA from Preston University and an MBA from American University of Central Asia and is now pursing Ph.D. with a focus on Circular Economy and Operations Management. Prior to his academic career, he has enriched experience of business management by working with International organisations, mainly in the health sector. As a growing academic, he has presented and published in international academic conferences and is also active in contributing to scientific academic journals in the area of Circular Economy, Operations Management, Lean, Logistics and Supply Chain Management.

David Thompson is a Senior Lecturer in Accounting and Finance at the University of Derby, UK. He is a Fellow of the Higher Education Academy and the Association of Chartered Certified Accountants. He has worked in the education sector for eight years delivering professional and higher education courses at both undergraduate and postgraduate level. He has worked for a number of Chartered Accountancy firms, gaining experience in general practice and specialising in audit. His research interests include audit and governance.

List of Figures

List of Tables

CHAPTER 1

Introduction

Darren Byrne

1.1 Introduction

Numbers are traditionally the accountant's domain. Businesses trust that professional accountants and auditors will maintain, monitor and deliver the required figures to report their activities. But increasingly a mastery of numbers is not the only task expected of the modern accountant or finance professional. Business decision-makers need to have confidence in the data that they use to make decisions, but they also need to understand what is behind the headline figures. They need to follow the trends to anticipate new business markets and opportunities, to be aware and mindful of the environment in which they operate and have confidence in the ability of their accountants to step up and contribute to a range of contemporary issues.

In this book, we seek to go 'Beyond the Numbers'; we consider a range of current developments in accounting that can help accounting and finance professionals to be well placed to contribute to the future of businesses, to the economy, and to our collective social welfare.

This book explores the developing challenges and opportunities within the business world which are likely to impact on the accounting profession in the foreseeable future. It outlines several approaches

D. Byrne (✉)
Derby Business School, University of Derby, Derby, UK

E. Conway and D. Byrne (eds.), *Contemporary Issues in Accounting*,
https://doi.org/10.1007/978-3-319-91113-7_1

to ensure that the accountants of the future are equipped with a useful awareness of some of the key topic areas that are quickly becoming a reality.

In this sense, the book helps to bridge the gap between academia and practice and thus equips students with the knowledge to discuss and contribute to topical issues within the profession and to be able to then implement this knowledge skilfully and appropriately. It will also appeal to practitioners who may be looking for concise introductions to several contemporary issues which are likely to impact upon their profession in the future. Many of these chapters outline the changing external business environment and updates on several important developing issues. Many of the authors also demonstrate a range of the accounting industry's responses to these changes within their specialist area of expertise.

Although we cannot claim to predict the future; we have made reasonable speculation of the issues that are seen to be contemporary, and we have been able to objectively observe what we see happening within our industry, all to provide the reader with that knowledge. All the contributors have researched the literature and made use of their considerable experience within finance or accounting to extrapolate the near future and to support readers' awareness with our expectations of the future.

What is meant by 'contemporary'? Merriam-Webster (2018) define contemporary as simply, 'marked by characteristics of the present period: modern, current'. Therefore, it is what is modern and it is what is happening now. In this book, 'Contemporary Issues in Accounting', we discuss our observations on accounting issues that are emerging or are already having some impact on the accounting profession.

Our experiences are wide—many of the contributing authors here have had long, interesting and challenging careers in accounting and finance—and they talk objectively about issues both present and future within their profession as they see it, ably supported by some non-accounting professionals whose subject disciplines are found to interweave with that of the accountant. We hold the view that the accountant has a unique central and deeply embedded role in an organisation. This team-style delivery that you will see evident in this book is purposefully designed. Non-accounting professionals have many discerning and relevant skills and knowledge that help them see the world from a different contributory perspective to the accountant, and vice versa. Accounting professionals need to work with, discuss with and challenge themselves and their own knowledge though others.

A recent headline in the accounting periodical, *PQ Magazine* (2017, p. 1) claimed, 'Audit isn't sexy enough anymore'. It seems to us that the world of business is continually evolving, business is big news. The cover article in *PQ Magazine* discussed how fewer people are being drawn to a career in audit. The skill-set of potential recruits was questioned; 'Accountancy could be asked to take a back seat as firms look to recruit more data and risk analysts, and cyber security experts' (*PQ Magazine* 2017, p. 1). Skills and in particular, technology skills are likely to be an area of significant change in accountancy which we address in several chapters as we discuss the impacts of Big Data and other technologies such as blockchain. Data collection is also an important concept in performance measurement, and we consider when there is too much data: 'measuring the shadow of the shadow'. The skills-gap is also covered in a later chapter on self-leadership which discusses some of the softer skills which will be required in future professionals.

The word 'professional' is used frequently throughout this introductory chapter—this is by design. We believe that the profession—despite some occasional scandalous financial behaviour that is laid at the doorstep of the accounting profession—will thrive, albeit change. There is continued scrutiny of the accountability of business and accounting firms, particularly in the wake of the business collapses (for example following the recent collapse of Carillion (*The Guardian* 2018)). This trend to greater transparency will no doubt continue, with increased emphasis on ethics and humanity, in terms of being accountable to wider society. Whilst the profession may increasingly rely on technology for basic data capture and analysis, which should eliminate many errors intrinsic to human data input, it will still require the human touch to unlock the value contained within it.

This aspect of humanity as the impact of oneself on one's environment is also evident in Parker and Warren's (2017) work, where they refer to an 'undesirable accountant stereotype' held in the public perception of accountants within society. Their findings focused upon the perception of accountants' own professional identity in relation to their own career aspirations. Their study suggested that accountants align their professional duties with their own personal values, strengthening interpersonal communication as they develop, but that they actively attempt to improve the image of the accountant's impact upon their immediate and wider environment and community—this being done by being intertwined with their professional career development. In other words, their job did not take over their life, it was described as a 'subset' of it. Parker and Warren (2017) concluded that accountants 'attempt to recraft their role and portray an image that reflects an interactive, advisory, leadership identity to which they aspire and wish to project' (2017, p. 1917).

Hence this book presents a set of chapters that will help you, the accounting professional, to be able to be aspirational, to work towards a fuller knowledge of the interwoven aspects of your professional career. We have chosen pertinent themes and areas of current note that you will find that you need to be well versed upon.

1.2 Guide to the Structure of This Book

This book is arranged into two sections following this initial introduction.

Section One outlines in more detail over three chapters what we believe the most pressing challenges are. Sustainability, the Triple Bottom Line and Corporate Social Responsibility (CSR) are assessed in Chapter 2, where the wider impact of businesses and governments on society and the environment are discussed. Chapter 3 introduces the challenges of a circular economy—where we discuss the new model for our economic existence and the role of the accountant within that model. The last chapter in this section, Chapter 4 looks at the advent and progress of accounting technology. Here the proliferation of technology change is considered, Big Data, Cloud Computing, Artificial Intelligence and blockchain are explained and contextualised for the accountant.

Section Two, consisting of five further chapters, outlines accounting and business' responses to these external environment challenges. In Chapter 5 we cover 'fair' corporate tax strategies in the context of being perceived as a good corporate citizen. We look at how corporate reporting has developed beyond the numbers in Chapter 6 to include narrative that underpins the broader strategic focus of the company. Developments in auditing, along with what is expected of the audit function and the skills needed by future auditors are covered in Chapter 7. Chapter 8 recognises how firms need to adapt their performance management systems to account for their many diverse priorities, and finally Chapter 9 outlines how further skills development in accounting can help individuals to adapt to the ever-changing business environment, developing for example, 'self-leadership' skills.

Our concluding Chapter 10 brings many of these issues together as we summarise—looking at the way forward for the accounting profession beyond the numbers.

1.3 Who Have We Aimed This Book at?

This book differs from standard texts, in that chapters are standalone introductory pieces to provide useful precis of key topics and how they apply to the accounting professional in particular. It aims to deliver key readings on 'hot topics' that are not addressed in other texts which the accounting profession is already tackling or are likely to need to tackle in the future. Hence the book provides accounting students with a good grounding in a broad range of highly relevant non-technical accounting themes which will impact upon their careers. It looks at the bigger environment in which future accountants will be operating, involving considerations of strategic corporate governance issues and highlighting competences beyond the standard technical accounting skillsets.

The book is aimed at supporting a modular undergraduate university course on contemporary issues for accounting students (for programmes such as BA in Accounting & Finance or BA in Business Accounting). It will also be a valuable addition to the reading lists on a number of modules taught on postgraduate programmes, such as Master of Business Administration (MBA), MSc International Business, MSc Accounting & Finance.

Students studying for professional accounting qualifications may also be interested in this work as a general introduction to broader business issues of which the professional bodies increasingly demand an awareness.

Finally, the book will also provide useful teaching material for academics who may be running a 'Contemporary Issues' style module on any accounting or business course.

1.4 Introductions to the Chapters

There are several key themes which weave throughout many of the chapters of this book: future business, sustainable business, CSR, circular economy, accounting and business technology, tax strategy, corporate reporting, corporate environment, corporate accountability, audit and governance, performance management, change management skills, leadership and the professional accountant.

To structure these themes a little more lucidly, we have two sections, the first about the key external environmental challenges which are emerging, and the second which represents the responses of the accounting profession to some of these challenges.

1.4.1 Section One: External Environment Challenges

Our benchmark for our discussions concerning external environment challenges starts with Chapter 2, with a comprehensive and up-to-date background of Sustainability, the Triple Bottom Line and Corporate Social Responsibility by Elaine Conway. Defining and using a discussion of sustainability, Conway explains how economic growth is not sustainable with finite resources. Adaptation and transformation become key watchwords in this arena. A social disparity between rich and poor is observed and, along with global environmental issues, we find that a 'wicked problem' emerges (Mulligan 2018). Conway outlines the United Nations seventeen Sustainable Development Goals, and debates how businesses and individuals contribute to these through policy and personal commitment. Elkington's (1997) Triple Bottom Line concept is reprised. We learn about many recent examples from across the globe regarding the three pillars of sustainability, or 'P's' of People, Planet and Profits (Elkington's environmental, social and economic categories rephrased). The accountant's role in measuring these pillars, in terms of 'metrics' is presented, alongside a discussion regarding whom is morally responsible for risk and performance within these metrics. A final section allows Conway to remind us of the debate upon CSR. Conway states that societal perceptions of what business is expected to do has evolved (Lacey et al. 2015; Hemingway and Maclagan 2004), and aligns CSR to good corporate governance. Conway concludes by suggesting that organisations should focus on only a few activities, 'to maximise the likelihood that they are achieved', and that a 'wider skillset' than that of the traditional accountant is required; that they will need 'to engage with and assure a much broader set of metrics'. We learn more about these aspects from Thompson in Chapter 7, and regarding skillsets from Byrne and Lees in Chapter 9.

Chapter 3 introduces us to the concept of the circular economy, Simon Peter Nadeem, Jose Arturo Garza-Reyes and Denise Glanville neatly give us a broad overview of the circular economy. They set this in the global context of resource depletion, relating this to increasing levels of technology that contribute to the extraction, production and consumption of these resources, a debate about which many of us are becoming increasingly aware. Informing us of the latest elements of this debate, we find out exactly what the concept of the circular economy entails. Recycling, efficiencies and sustainable consumption are watchwords in this discussion—but we are introduced to many more facets. The authors regularly cite the Ellen MacArthur Foundation within the chapter, which holds as its mission to "accelerate the transition to a circular economy" (The Ellen MacArthur Foundation 2018) but also present frameworks proposed by Ken Webster (2015) and the Circle Economy organisation (Circle Economy 2016) within their discussion. We learn about three barriers/challenges to circular economy; the lack of a structured policy, technological advancements, and public participation (Geng and Doberstein 2008). The implications for accounting information systems and hence accountants are considered, with a review of the status of adoption across the world. Nadeem, Garza-Reyes and Glanville relate the extent of adoption of the circular economy with that of increased provision of information in companies' narrative reports, a theme we return to in Chapter 6. They cite the lack of experience of these new circular economy models as being the main challenge to implementation, even the resistance to change presented by accounting practices (which should perhaps be an enabler). The authors also cite many real-world examples of successful implementations; for example, Germany, China and Japan are cited as early adopters. The chapter ends by considering the interventions required for the implementation of the circular economy and organisational level requirements, including the need for engagement with the circular economy as part of longer term strategic objectives.

Liz Crookes and Elaine Conway present the last of our three chapters setting the scene upon the external environment in Section One. They refer to the effects of emerging technologies on the role of the accountant within Chapter 4. Thus, we are introduced to the realms of what future business will look like from the accountant's perspective. Big Data forms a pivotal part of this chapter, here the authors give us a comprehensive explanation of what Big Data is, explaining this in terms of the five V's; Volume, Velocity, Variety, Veracity and Value (Laney 2001; Shafer 2017; Marr 2016). Many examples of Big Data are evident around us, particularly in a business sense, for instance, when we go shopping Electronic Point of Sale Terminals capture data about us, and in logistics Radio Frequency Identification tags are used for tracking real-time data. These create immense quantities of data and this is outlined in this chapter. Accountants thus have a pivotal role in managing data, particularly managing financial data and identifying trends therein. The implications of Big Data usage are immense, Crookes and Conway discuss how it can even be used in medicine, within the security services and in public transport to name but a few applications. Their chapter also sheds light on the application of Big Data within accounting. They recommend that management accountants will have to be more skilled in working with larger datasets than they have previously. Other emerging technologies are also discussed in this chapter: Cloud Computing, Artificial Intelligence and Blockchain. We learn that even though cloud computing is undoubtedly beneficial in terms of lower operating costs and scalable operations, it also presents concerns too, for example data security, with more and more firms becoming more reliant on holding their business-critical data in third party depositories (Armbrust et al. 2010), and with new legislation concerning General Data Protection Regulation (EU Parliament 2016) evolving. Artificial Intelligence is explained, and current developments in each of its facets; process automation, cognitive insight and cognitive engagement are offered to update our knowledge. Crookes and Conway introduce the ethical concept of control within the discussion at this point. Blockchain is left to the end of the chapter and although last—is by no means least. We learn how blockchain is the technology that underpins cryptocurrencies and the authors suggest that it is 'potentially a fundamental game changer', referring to the potential for businesses on a global scale. Here the authors outline the benefits, the challenges and the implications upon the skillsets of future accountants and auditors, suggesting that they will increasingly be valued as a 'bridge' between the data specialists who manage the data and the business world who need to unlock the value contained within it (ICAEW 2017).

1.4.2 Section Two: Accounting Responses to External Environment Challenges

Juliet Hogsden considers the contemporary corporation tax environment. Within Chapter 5, she outlines how this environment is now much more complex due to many of the issues covered in the first section of the book. Corporation tax strategies must be managed carefully. Globalisation has been a huge influence upon corporate tax strategies as compliance requirements evolve, and companies seek to take 'opportunities' in this still developing arena. Directors and accountants must be mindful of the public scrutiny that this entails, and the author discusses how companies' management of their 'fair share' of tax payments can impact upon their reputation and their brand. Management of these opportunities is an all-important skill that accountants must master. Hogsden argues that companies need to proactively manage the stringent compliance and disclosure requirements. Drawing on concepts of ethics and technological advances, the author introduces us to many examples of international tax planning opportunities. We are reminded of the debate behind tax planning in terms of the law, about ethical and moral practice and what constitutes a 'fair share of tax' and the author provides us with examples of real case-studies, most notably that of Starbucks. The Fair Tax Mark is introduced, an accreditation which has been developed to encourage business to show responsible tax leadership and improve transparency (Fair Tax Mark 2018). Governments' perspectives are also analysed here and the activities of the OECD (2017) for example, the Common Reporting Standard regarding tackling tax avoidance is outlined. An argument is proffered upon the role of professionals; tax professionals should be supported in keeping up-to-date with tax legislation, and, as Hogsden argues, investment in reliable and rigorous accounting information systems and internal controls should be put in place to effectively manage the compliance risks that are described thoroughly within this chapter.

Chapter 6 'Corporate Reporting—Numbers to Narrative' authored by Parminder Johal provides an insight into the changing shape and scope of the corporate reporting function by focusing on the move towards the inclusion of narrative content in financial reports published by businesses. Johal describes narrative reporting as, 'the umbrella under which organisations can manage their communication of non-financial information', and this chapter initially provides us with a succinct precis of the historical reporting requirements of recent times. The corporate reporting debate we learn has extended from simple statutory requirements to the inclusion of much more: non-financial information, environmental reporting, CSR, sustainability and integrated reporting. A review of how these reporting requirements are working in practice is outlined, whereby the provision of guidance from professional bodies, committees, political lobbyists, boards and frameworks leading to the present balance between mandatory reporting requirements and voluntary, is analysed in a practical context. Furthermore, narrative reporting, Johal says, is a way of 'plugging the information needs gap', and it lends itself to the 'creation of greater transparency'. A final contemporary section considers the impact that recent events, for example the EU's Non-Financial Reporting Directive and Brexit, have had and will have, upon the corporate reporting function. Items of debate here include: how the EU directive requirement for disclosure lies with large companies, and how a narrative upon the impact of Brexit will be expected by shareholders and stakeholders alike, with future further narrative requirements probably needing to be balanced alongside reporting numbers.

David Thompson's aim in Chapter 7, is to outline the key challenges to audit. He argues for enhanced audit quality to deal with the key challenges such as innovation and other external factors covered earlier in Section One. Introducing us to recent developments in the industry, for example, ICAEW's Audit Quality Forum and the Audit Firm Governance Code, Thompson outlines where the industry is attempting to improve upon its quality procedures. The FRC too, with their updated ethical code for auditors is cited as further iterative development to protect quality and assurance within the profession. Linking these developments to ethical principles and professional scepticism, Thompson contends that good mentorship in audit firms could help with these quality issues. Moving more specifically to a discussion regarding skills requirements for auditors, here we find extensive links to other chapters in this book regarding the changing environment that auditors operate within. Modern technology has led to increased innovation within the auditing world, Artificial Intelligence, Computer Assisted Audit Techniques, embedded audit software, Big Data, Blockchain and RFID; many of the innovative concepts that we have met elsewhere in this book reappear here. And although perhaps a little daunting, the auditor of the future will need to acquire at least a working knowledge of each of these in their role. Narrative reporting too, although covered elsewhere in this book, leads to its own intrinsic skills needs.

As Thompson recognises, 'it may be necessary for the auditor to be capable of auditing not just the figures, but this extended narrative as well'. See Johal's Chapter 6 for further discussion regarding narrative reporting. Both Thompson and Johal observe the difficulties in dealing with subjective aspects of reporting and hence its credibility. Chapter 7 also links the work of the auditor to that required in pursuit of environmental audits (another external influence that we have touched upon in Section One). Again, we find that the role of the accountant or auditor is undergoing an evolution, requiring an enhanced skillset. Thompson says that auditors need to 'endeavour to evolve to stay relevant', to stay 'fit for purpose'; and advocates self-preservation in the field of audit.

Hilary Coyle asks us, 'Why Do We Need to Measure Performance?' in Chapter 8. Opening with a discussion that sets out some key seminal theories within the literature, Coyle debates the merits of individual target setting and performance measurements. Noting too, as many chapters have done before, the constantly changing business environment, Coyle explains how a well-designed performance measurement system can help the strategic objectives of the organisation. However, this can depend upon the quality of the data that is collected. Coyle offers a retrospective look at the development of the Balanced Scorecard technique used in performance measurement, showing us how it provides a link between the strategic objectives of the organisation and the targets and measures it believes necessary to successfully implement that strategy. Citing Bourne (2013), Coyle explains how the Balanced Scorecard has survived the test of time, but it has its detractors, which are also discussed. The debate we learn, now centres around the number of measurements that are made: are there too many? Which ones should be used? The organisational environment used as an exemplar to discuss the concepts introduced within this chapter is that of the UK local government sector. Literature is presented that brings us up-to-date with the public-sector view. How can we know when we are looking at good performance? Performance can depend upon which measures are chosen, and there are time issues involved with setting up a system of measurement. We have created a "performance measurement industry" (Arnaboldi et al. 2015, p. 2). The accountant must bear in mind the costs involved of a performance management system, ensuring that these do not outstrip the benefits gained. Coyle concludes by reminding us, the finance professionals, that 'there is no right or wrong way to measure performance and each organisation will be different'.

In Chapter 9, we are treated to a more specific discussion regarding the skillsets required for the accounting and finance professional touched upon in many chapters beforehand. Darren Byrne and David Lees invite us to go beyond the numbers yet again, and to learn about self-leadership and the skills that employers look for in future employees. Using the medium of the typical university undergraduate 'project-based' module as a vehicle for skills development, the authors explain how non-technical modules such as a business impact project or consultancy project ideally lend themselves to developing students' skillsets and hence careers in more ways than may be initially apparent. Communication skills, creativity and problem-solving skills are much in demand from employers, and these are practised within these project-based modules. Indeed, drawing upon work by Paszkiewicz and Gembka (2014), Byrne and Lees reiterate how qualifications could soon become dated, and that candidates who have developed the ability to exhibit soft competencies will become more employable. The case for these skills is made through a review of literature associated with accounting and finance, predominantly from an employer's perspective. Self-leadership is one such soft skill, and employers expect students to be 'work-ready' when they graduate. The use of projects whilst at university to support skills enhancement, for example, in terms of the development of authenticity, responsibility and the capacity to self-lead is discussed. Sometimes these skills are cited as more important than technical skills. Manz's model (2015) of the Self-Leadership High Road is used to illustrate this concept further. Byrne and Lees urge you to 'take ownership for managing your own growth', including emotional intelligence and other professional behavioural skills which remain relatively untapped within many academic accounting courses. The chapter ends by returning to the value of independent, but supported, study to foster development of these added skills for the benefit of students' professional careers.

Finally, Elaine Conway provides a neat, concise and thought-provoking concluding chapter. Chapter 10 seeks to look at the way forward for the accounting profession to look beyond the numbers.

We hope you enjoy this book. You can read it in whichever order you like, all the chapters are independent of each other—but linked by some common contemporary issues. It will hopefully provide you with all the introductory knowledge that you were looking for and will encourage you to follow this up in more depth as the issues evolve. Naturally, some of these issues will become dated, but we recognise that is the nature of change. We enjoy engaging with these developing issues and are enthused by the ever-evolving world and profession in which we work.

References

Armbrust, Michael, Ion Stoica, Matei Zaharia, Armando Fox, Rean Griffith, Anthony D. Joseph, Randy Katz, et al. 2010. "A View of Cloud Computing." *Communications of the ACM* 53 (4): 50. https://doi.org/10.1145/1721654.1721672.

Arnaboldi, Michela, Irvine Lapsley, and Ileana Steccolini. 2015. "Performance Management in the Public Sector: The Ultimate Challenge." *International Journal of Public Sector Management* 31 (1): 1–22. https://doi.org/10.1111/faam.12049.

Bourne, Mike. 2013. "What Is Balanced Scorecard." https://connect.som.cranfield.ac.uk/p7m07c9otnu/.

Circle Economy. 2016. "About the Circular Economy." http://circle-economy.com/circular-economy/.

Elkington, John. 1997. *Cannibals with Forks: The Triple Bottom Line of 21st Century Business.* Oxford: Capstone.

Ellen MacArthur Foundation (2018). "Mission Statement." Available at https://www.ellenmacarthurfoundation.org/. Accessed 18 Mar 2018.

EU Parliament. 2016. "General Data Protection Regulation (GDPR)." https://www.eugdpr.org/.

Fair Tax. 2018. "The Fair Tax Certification Scheme." Available at https://fairtaxmark.net/who-we-are/. Accessed 18 Mar 2018.

Geng, Yong, and Brent Doberstein. 2008. "Developing the Circular Economy in China: Challenges and Opportunities for Achieving 'Leapfrog Development.'" *International Journal of Sustainable Development & World Ecology* 15 (3): 231–239. https://doi.org/10.3843/susdev.15.3:6.

Hemingway, Christine A., and Patrick W. Maclagan. 2004. "Managers' Personal Values as Drivers of Corporate Social Responsibility." *Journal of Business Ethics* 50 (1): 33–44. http://search.ebscohost.com/login.aspx?direct=true&db=bth&AN=12991584&site=ehost-live.

ICAEW. 2017. "Blockchain and the Future of Accountancy." https://www.icaew.com/en/technical/information-technology/technology/blockchain/blockchain-and-the-accounting-perspective.

Lacey, Russell, Pamela Kennett-Hensel, and Chris Manolis. 2015. "Is Corporate Social Responsibility a Motivator or Hygiene Factor? Insights into Its Bivalent Nature." *Journal of the Academy of Marketing Science* 43 (3): 315–332. https://doi.org/10.1007/s11747-014-0390-9.

Laney, Doug. 2001. "META Delta." *Application Delivery Strategies* 949 (February): 4. https://doi.org/10.1016/j.infsof.2008.09.005.

Manz, Charles C. 2015. "Taking the Self-Leadership High Road: Smooth Surface or Potholes Ahead?" *Academy of Management Perspectives* 29: 132–151. https://doi.org/10.5465/amp.2013.0060.

Marr, Bernard. 2016. *Big Data in Practice*, 1st ed. Chichester, UK: Wiley.

Merriam-Webster. 2018. *The Merriam-Webster Dictionary*. Martinsburg, USA. https://www.merriam-webster.com/.

Mulligan, M. 2018. *Introduction to Sustainability*, 2nd ed. Oxford, UK: Earthscan—Routledge.

OECD. 2017. "OECD Work on Taxation 2016–17 Centre for Tax Policy and Administration." www.oecd.org/tax. Accessed 17 Aug 2017.

Parker, Lee D., Samantha Warren. 2017. "The Presentation of the Self and Professional Identity: Countering the Accountant's Stereotype." *Accounting, Auditing & Accountability Journal* 30 (8): 1895–1924. https://doi.org/10.1108/AAAJ-09-2016-2720.

Paszkiewicz, Aleksandra, and Sylwia Silska Gembka. 2014. "The Role of Soft Competencies in the Accountant's Work—Results of Empirical Research From Poland." Available at https://www.researchgate.net/profile/Sylwia_Silska_Gembka/publication/308695804_The_Role_of_Soft_Competencies_in_the_Accountant%27s_Work_-_Results_of_Empirical_Research_from_Poland/links/57eba9ef08ae5a3c9e6354ab/The-Role-of-Soft-Competencies-in-the-Accountants-Work-Results-of-Empirical-Research-from-Poland.pdf. Accessed 31 Jan 2018.

PQ Magazine. 2017. "Audit Isn't Sexy Enough Anymore." *PQ Magazine*, March 2017: 1.

Shafer, Tom. 2017. "The 42 V's of Big Data and Data Science." *Elder Research*. https://www.elderresearch.com/company/blog/author/tom-shafer.

The Guardian. 2018. "Carillion Collapse Prompts Fresh Scrutiny of UK Accounting Giants." Available at https://www.theguardian.com/business/2018/jan/30/carillion-collapse-prompts-fresh-scrutiny-of-uk-accounting-giants. Accessed 7 Mar 2018.

Webster, Ken. 2015. *The Circular Economy: A Wealth of Flows*. Isle of Wight, UK: Ellen MacArthur Foundation.

CHAPTER 2

Sustainability, the Triple Bottom Line and Corporate Social Responsibility

Elaine Conway

2.1 Introduction

The traditional economic business model is predicated on 'making money', in terms of a financial return on investment either through paying dividends from profits or through capital growth in share prices (Larrinaga-González et al. 2002). It is based on a largely single-use linear model, extracting raw materials, converting them into products, selling these products to a final consumer and then once the useful life of the product is over, scrapping the residual product as waste into the environment (Murray et al. 2017; Ellen Macarthur Foundation 2012). This economic model assumes that resources can be substituted for each other in monetary terms such that the depletion of one resource (e.g. reduced natural resources) is compensated for by another (e.g. increased profits). The overriding driver is to complete this process as effectively and efficiently as possible to extract maximum financial return to those who have invested money (equity or debt) into the process (Mulligan 2018). Equally, traditional business is focused on growth—the expectation of continual growth in sales, profits, cash, dividends and

E. Conway (✉)
Derby Business School, University of Derby, Derby, UK

E. Conway and D. Byrne (eds.), *Contemporary Issues in Accounting*,
https://doi.org/10.1007/978-3-319-91113-7_2

investment. Indeed, even the business literature which is used to train future managers supports this ethos; it encourages businesses to seek out ways to develop new markets, expand the product offer, sell more to each customer and to encourage repeat purchases.

However, these behaviours cannot be maintained indefinitely, since the availability of many of the world's natural resources is limited and hence eventually some raw materials will cease to be available or will be available only at a much higher price as they become scarcer. As third world economies continue to develop and their citizens increase their demands and expectations about living standards and consumption, this pressure on scarce resources will undoubtedly increase exponentially (Larrinaga-González et al. 2001). In that sense, sustainable growth can be considered something of an oxymoron: it is not possible for growth to continue indefinitely when some key resources are finite. Hence a much more considered approach to production and consumption globally in the future will be needed and this is the basic premise around sustainability (Daly 1991).

2.2 What Is 'Being Sustainable' or 'Sustainability'?

What is meant by being 'sustainable' or 'sustainability'? The standard dictionary definition of the word 'sustainable' in isolation is something which is 'capable of being sustained' or 'being a method of harvesting or using a resource so that the resource is not depleted or permanently damaged' (Merriam-Webster 2016). Hence the adjectival use of it with other words such as 'development', 'manufacturing' or 'agriculture' suggests that these actions are also capable of being sustained such that resources are not permanently depleted.

This was conceptually at least what the ex-prime minister of Norway, Gro Harlem Brundtland might well have had in mind when defining sustainable development as part of work done for the World Commission on Environment and Development (WCED). This definition was:

> Sustainable development is development that meets the needs of the present without compromising the ability of future generations to meet their own needs. (Brundtland and WCED 1987)

This definition has since become one of the most popular definitions of sustainable development used globally (White 2013). It has influenced governments and organisations worldwide to incorporate the twin concepts of human and environmental 'well-being' into their own policies (Kates et al. 2005). Indeed, the idea of current generations considering their impacts on future generations was also echoed in the UK government's view of sustainable development in 1994:

> Most societies want to achieve economic development to secure higher standards of living, now and for future generations. They also seek to protect and enhance their environment, now and for their children. Sustainable development tries to reconcile these two objectives. (Department of the Environment 1994)

And more recently in 2015, despite the impacts of the intervening global financial crisis in 2008/2009:

> [Sustainable development] means making the necessary decisions now to realise our vision of stimulating economic growth and tackling the deficit, maximising wellbeing and protecting our environment, without negatively impacting on the ability of future generations to do the same. (DEFRA 2015)

Even beyond the purely national context, it is important to consider the wider role of sustainability to provide an improvement in living standards for the whole of the earth's population, yet remaining within the capacity of the earth to sustain those improvements (IUCN et al. 1991).

Whilst there are criticisms that even 'development' as well as 'growth' cannot be infinitely sustainable (Costanza and Patten 1995; White 2013), other authors have noted that what is considered to be sustainable can change over time as new practices and organisations evolve to take advantage of new opportunities and technologies whilst old ones decline or are superseded. This evolution has occurred throughout both the natural world as new species have evolved, and the human-derived world as ailing industries are taken over by new ways of working or technologies (Voinov and Farley 2007). Hence by allowing processes and practices to change and evolve rather than considering something to stay the same, sustainability can be defined as:

> transforming our ways of living to maximize the chances that environmental and social conditions will indefinitely support human security, well-being and health. (McMichael et al. 2003)

This idea of adaptation and transformation will undoubtedly be key to long-term development, rather than unlimited economic growth. The world's population is expected to rise from a mid-2017 level of 7.6 billion to 11.2 billion by 2100 (World Bank 2015); much of this growth will come from relatively underdeveloped countries in Africa, with Asia, Latin America, the Caribbean, Northern America and Oceania seeing more modest growth and Europe actually expecting to see a fall in population (United Nations Department of Economic and Social Affairs 2017). With this burgeoning population and finite natural resources, governments and businesses are recognising that 'business as usual' will not work in the future (Gray 2002). Not only will natural resources be depleted, but pollutants released to the atmosphere and other waste from the current traditional linear business model are creating environmental problems for humans and other species as well (Boulding 1966; Ellen Macarthur Foundation 2012). Whilst there is much debate about the reality (or not) of global warming, it is nonetheless clear to the majority of people that unless there is a change in approach, the current business model which takes little heed of the overall impact of the organisation and its products on the long-term sustainability of the planet, is only adding to the depletion of the earth's resources.

Of equal concern is the great social disparity between rich and poor within the population of the world. Although this has always existed and will always exist in some form or other, it has widened considerably in recent years (OECD 2015). Unchecked, this can lead to untapped human potential, a continued fall in social mobility and exploitation of poorer individuals whose quality of life is often below subsistence level (OECD 2015).

This combination of social disparity and environmental issues on a global scale has created what can be regarded as a 'wicked problem' (Mulligan 2018). Such a problem may be regarded as intractable since it defies a simple known solution but requires a more holistic and fundamental rethink of the issues or root causes of the issue (Rittel and Webber 1973). This necessitates a different approach and increasingly, there is recognition that not only governments but business has a wider responsibility to its broader environment throughout its supply chain, and to those invested in the supply chain such as employees, customers, suppliers and the wider community and environment. This is where the debates about sustainability, sustainable business and Corporate Social Responsibility (CSR) have emerged. There are now increasing discussions held globally around the responsibilities of humans to their fellow humans which do seek to address the fundamental issues of this 'wicked problem' of limited resources, environmental problems and inequitable societal standards.

2.3 Policy and Sustainability

In response to this multiplicity of concerns globally, the United Nations has developed seventeen Sustainable Development Goals (SDGs), which seek to address these major issues and help national governments and other organisations to consider their impacts on them (UN 2015a). Individual countries signed up to these goals on September 25th, 2015 with the aim of achieving specific targets in each area by 2030, which are depicted in Fig. 2.1.

Behind each of the seventeen goals are a further 169 more detailed targets, designed to support governments and society make the changes necessary to achieve the goals. The seventeen goals are:

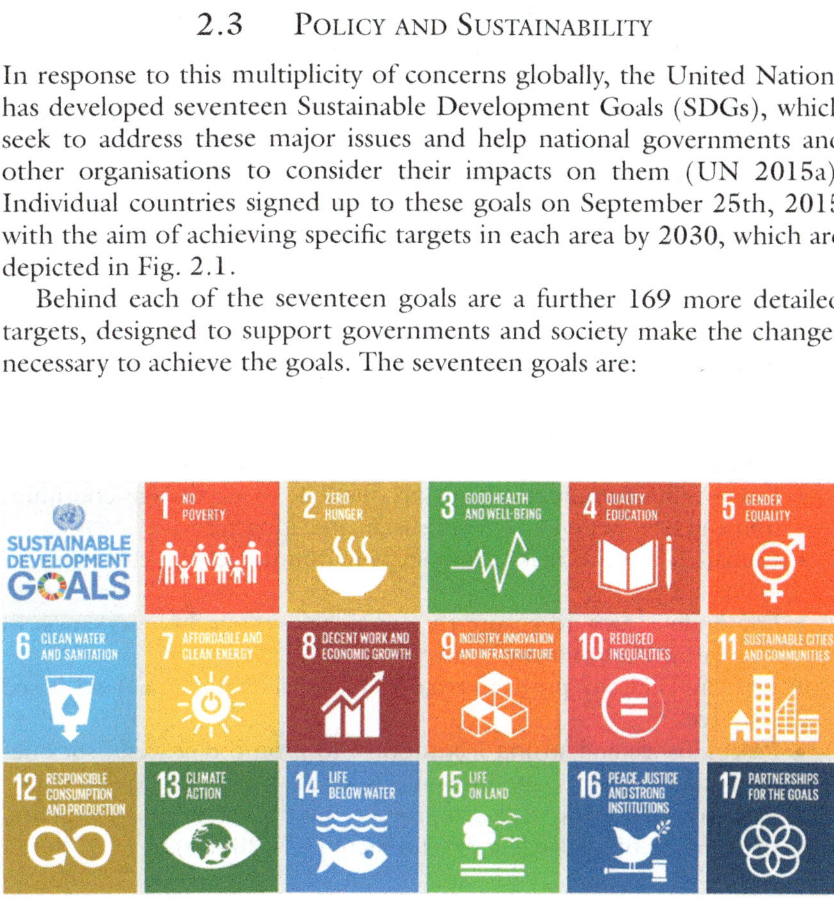

Fig. 2.1 United Nations Sustainable Development Goals (*Source* UN 2015b with kind permission)

- No poverty: to eradicate poverty in all forms globally;
- Zero hunger: to ensure adequate food and nutrition for all and encourage sustainable agriculture;
- Good health and well-being: to ensure that all people, irrespective of age, can lead healthy lives;
- Quality education: to make sure that all people have access to inclusive and equitable learning opportunities throughout their lives;
- Gender equality: to achieve equality for both genders;
- Clean water and sanitation: to ensure clean water and adequate sanitation is available to all;
- Affordable and clean energy: to ensure that all people have access to affordable and sustainable energy;
- Decent work and economic growth: to ensure that all people have the opportunity to benefit from sustainable economic growth through productive and decent work;
- Industry, innovation and infrastructure: to establish suitable infrastructure, promote innovation and sustainable development of economies;
- Reduced inequalities: to reduce inequality between people both within and between countries;
- Sustainable cities and communities: to make all human settlements (whether cities, towns or villages) safe and sustainable;
- Responsible consumption and production: to encourage consumption and production which are sustainable long term;
- Climate action: to make rapid steps to counteract the effects of climate change;
- Life under water: to ensure the sustainable use and conservation of the marine environment;
- Life on land: to protect, restore and sustainably use land-based resources;
- Peace, justice and strong institutions: to promote peaceful societies with effective justice and institutions for all;
- Partnerships for the goals: to promote global partnerships to assure the delivery of sustainable development (UN 2015b).

Since their launch, these SDGs have been incorporated into national policy around the world, and clearly whilst governments have the power to drive the most change, the engagement of business and wider society is critical to the goals' successful achievement (Carraro et al. 2012).

On an individual human or individual business level, having any kind of impact on some of the goals may seem daunting. Whilst ideally everyone should strive to help achieve all seventeen goals, many start their engagement with the SDGs by selecting those which are of closest fit with the individual's interests or the firm's business strategy. As a result, 83% of UK businesses and 62% of global firms are now engaged with the SDGs in their corporate reporting to some degree, although many are not engaged with every goal or do not link their activities across the goals to gain maximum leverage from their activities (PWC 2018).

2.4 Corporate Engagement with Sustainability

Whilst many large organisations are now actively engaged with the SDGs, other organisations choose to address their environmental or social activities in other ways. One such approach is known as the Triple Bottom Line (TBL), a concept which considers a business to be sustainable if it takes account of the three 'pillars' of sustainability, which are environmental, social and economic (Elkington 1997, 2001). Other firms use the term 'CSR' to define their activities and include separate sections in their annual corporate reports or on their websites to explain what issues they are addressing beyond their day-to-day business activities. Both of these approaches can map to the SDGs even if organisations do not explicitly report against them. The following sections will explain these two key concepts of TBL and CSR.

2.4.1 The Triple Bottom Line

John Elkington's (1997) TBL concept is comprised of three elements to underpin a sustainable business: environmental, social and economic sustainability, often also referred to as the three 'Ps' of People, Planet and Profits (Slaper and Hall 2011). Many of these elements relate to the SDGs mentioned earlier, but they are often the first step organisations take as a focus beyond their purely business-related activities. A discussion of each of the three pillars now follows.

2.4.1.1 Environmental Sustainability

As developing economies such as many in sub-Saharan Africa and some parts of Asia continue to develop and increase population, their desires to 'consume' will also continue to grow exponentially. Whilst it is socially desirable to encourage a better standard of living across the globe, the impact of this is likely to be unsustainable, particularly when the current first world economies also continue to expect greater consumerism and rise in economic 'wealth' and prosperity. The impacts of this unchecked growth on the environment are numerous from both an input (for example, supply of raw materials) and output (for example, emissions) standpoint.

From an input standpoint, an understanding about the long-term access to key natural resources is of paramount importance. Not all resources can be regarded in the same way. Whilst no individual living thing can be sustained indefinitely, the species and ecosystems to which each individual belongs can be. It is this wider remit to which sustainability relates. Living resources (such as plants and animals) can be 'harvested' as long as they are not depleted beyond their ability to reproduce. Some resources such as water and energy (for example, solar energy) can be used but they cannot be completely destroyed as they may change in form, be recycled into the ecosystem or have a long enough lifecycle that their supply is not of immediate concern (for example, the sun). However, some of these resources like water are challenging due to the misalignment of where the demand and supply of freshwater and sanitation may manifest themselves (Blowfield 2013). Other resources (such as fossil fuels) are not sustainable since they can only be depleted and cannot be replenished within a reasonable lifecycle. Whilst they may be used, their use should be regarded as a means to generate more sustainable outputs in the long term.

From an output standpoint, the pollutants and waste released as part of the current economic model have impacts on the environment. Greenhouse gas (GHG) emissions (which comprise carbon dioxide (CO_2), methane (CH_4), nitrous oxide (N_2O), hydrofluorocarbons (HFCs), perfluorocarbons (PFCs) and sulphur hexafluoride (SF_6) (DEFRA 2013)) have been steadily increasing as economic output has risen, from 27,660,218 kilotonnes (kt) of carbon dioxide equivalent (CO_2E) in 1970 to 53,526,302 kt CO_2E in 2012 (Janssens-Maenhout et al. 2017). These GHGs prevent the long-wave infrared radiation from escaping from the earth's atmosphere whilst allowing the short-wave radiation from the sun to enter: by allowing GHGs to build up in the environment, the temperature of the earth's surface rises. This can impact on habitats and species causing irreversible damage (US EIA 2017) and can affect the ability of the earth to continue to absorb excessive levels of CO_2.

Hence environmental sustainability is the aim to keep human activities within the capabilities of the earth to continue to sustain human life. Businesses should review their dependence on different natural resources from an input point of view, but also their impacts of the outputs that their business processes make on the environment. Businesses start by doing this by measuring their inputs (tonnes of raw materials, electricity and water consumed, for example) and their outputs (such as the GHGs). Indeed, it is now mandatory for listed companies in the UK to report on their GHG emissions in their annual report following the Climate Change Act 2008 (DEFRA 2013). Once a base line has been set for these inputs and outputs, many firms then start to set targets to reduce them; often driven by the need to cut costs, but this can also have a beneficial effect on the environment and reduce risk for the firm in avoiding fines for pollution or reducing dependency on key natural resources.

There are a myriad of methods to measure the impact of a business on the environment (Conway 2017), such as calculating the organisation's carbon footprint (where all activities are measured for their impact on carbon emissions) or via standards such as those issued by the Global Reporting Initiative (GRI 2014) or British Standards Institute (BSI 2018). It is usually in the measurement, tracking and analysis of these various metrics that accountants become involved. As this is a growing area of concern, it is therefore important that accountants become increasingly involved in managing the risks around environmental sustainability: they should take an interest in managing the dependence of the firm on certain resources whilst ensuring that the business reduces its impact on the environment, both to avoid fines and reduce costs but also to improve living conditions.

2.4.1.2 Social Sustainability

As globalisation has expanded the extent of the supply chain for many organisations, it has raised the issue of moral dilemmas where they are employing directly or indirectly (through suppliers) people to make their products, often at very low wages. The dilemma may be that people in poorer countries might not otherwise have a job without the work they do for the multinational corporation, and therefore it is good that these jobs are provided. However, there is often a perceived 'fine line' between employing people cheaply (which is what reduces the cost of the goods and is the main driver for multinational companies to employ these people) and exploitation, where working conditions are poor, such as inadequate pay, unsafe buildings or work stations, the availability of adequate sanitation, healthcare and even breaks during the working day (Jayasuriya 2008). If the conditions are 'legal' in the country where the workers are employed and the workers would be worse off without the multinational jobs, then is the multinational exploiting the workers? This is a popular debate across many supply chains and has provoked a number of social media campaigns where individuals have called on consumers to boycott certain companies or their products and services. For example, a boycott of the company Primark was incited on social media in 2013 after a factory building in Bangladesh collapsed, killing more than 300 people who were employed making clothing for the company. It was apparently known that the conditions in the building were poor prior to the incident, but no action was taken by any of the organisations who purchased clothing from the factory (The Huffington Post 2013).

This exploitation of employees is not limited to multinational companies operating overseas supply chains. There have been examples of exploitation of workers in Western countries, such as employing staff on zero hours contracts or expecting workers to work without adequate breaks (Osborne 2016; Farrell 2016). This can often arise when a company is overly focussed on profits and the need to reduce costs throughout their production/service chain. It may also be when a firm has grown extremely large and has effectively squeezed out competing smaller firms by being able to wield their buying power and influence on the market by reducing prices. These smaller firms may then be forced to exit the market, leaving the dominant firm as a monopoly (either in a specific area) or an oligopoly, where only a few large firms are competing (Smithers 2007). This abuse of market power can lead to a fall in innovation and quality as the firm has little or no competition and potentially poorer conditions for employees and suppliers who have to accept poorer rates (Williams 2015). This shifts costs and risks onto others which can have an adverse effect on society (Cannon 2012).

On an internal business level, social sustainability expectations require that all employees are treated fairly and safely, even if not at the extreme level of exploitation. Organisations should therefore ensure that they have policies (and use them) to promote equality, diversity, safe working practices and wider engagement with the communities they serve (Gimenez et al. 2012).

It is incumbent on accountants to manage risk and performance in their businesses, and whilst there has to be concern for the economic sustainability of the firm (see next section), it is equally important that profits are generated in a socially sustainable way. It is no longer acceptable to 'turn a blind eye' to socially detrimental practices from a legal, reputational or financial point of view (for example because of the risks of being sued, losing business or being fined), but more importantly, from a moral standpoint.

2.4.1.3 Economic Sustainability

Economic sustainability is the ability of the organisation to continue to exist on a strong financial footing, or for governments to continue to provide the means to run their country efficiently and effectively. Of the three pillars, it is the most readily understood and measured (Gimenez et al. 2012), since there are a plethora of established metrics for tracking the performance of an organisation, whether profit-making or not, such as return on assets, return on capital employed, cash flow and a whole host of profitability, efficiency and investor ratios. Although 'making profits' might be regarded by some as unethical (Liebowitz 2003), without financial rewards such as dividends and capital growth, people with surplus money (investors) would not invest in businesses, allowing them to provide the goods and services which people need. Without continued rewards given to investors, funds could be withdrawn from businesses, stifling their ability to grow and innovate.

Hence making profits is not intrinsically 'bad'; however, it is often the relentless, single-minded pursuit of profit which can distort behaviour and create negative impacts on the environment and society. Whilst financial performance tracking and target-setting are well-established financial management techniques in all businesses, continually rising profits and economic growth in firms can be unsustainable if they rely on practices which undermine the other two pillars of sustainable business (Elkington 1997). Therefore, whilst it is clearly the responsibility of the accountant to report on the financial performance of the organisation and to continue to set targets for its improvement, they should be mindful of the risks of their business model in the long run.

Many financial metrics are quite short term in nature, and indeed both managers and investors tend to be very focussed on short-term performance (the next bonus, pay rise, promotion or dividend) rather than taking the longer term view (Slawinski et al. 2017); after all, some actions, like tackling emissions can be slow to payback financially and therefore can be seen as a drain on resources in the short term. Equally, low pay for employees increases profits, again at least in the short term: increased staff turnover and poor morale can however undermine those profits in the longer term if employees are not reasonably rewarded for their efforts. Despite their inherent focus on short-term profits, investors are also wary of risk and uncertainty; they are more likely to reward firms by investing in those that manage their risks effectively in order to protect shareholder dividend payments and share price growth, rather than those who do not (Rodriguez-Fernandez 2016; Rakotomavo 2012). Hence, active management of business risks stemming from the wider environment or social issues is a key part of the accountant's remit in both measuring performance (choosing an appropriate mix of metrics to measure) and in setting targets to ensure the longevity of the firm economically.

2.4.2 Corporate Social Responsibility

CSR is also very closely allied with the Triple Bottom Line approach, since it likewise focuses on the environmental and social aspects of business, however it also tends to address the concept of governance as well. Many businesses, particularly those listed on stock exchanges, now report on their CSR activities either on their websites or in their annual reports, so it is not uncommon to see an environmental report, a social responsibility report, a governance report or a generic CSR report informing the external stakeholders of the firm about the activities which the organisation is undertaking in order to be responsible beyond its day-to-day business.

Like sustainability, CSR has a plethora of definitions; some texts even refer to it as Corporate Social Performance (CSP) (Wood 2010; Waddock and Graves 1997) to emphasise the performance (i.e. 'actively doing something and recording it'), rather than the 'responsibility' aspect of an organisation's activities (which may be more 'intent' than actual action). This latter aspect of 'intent rather than action' is also referred to as 'greenwashing' (Lyon and Maxwell 2011; Wu and Shen 2013), where firms disclose some activities which are easy to achieve and look appealing, but in reality mask inactivity in other areas or worse, are exaggerated depictions of their actual activities.

The most common definitions of CSR include McWilliams and Siegel's (2000) which depicts CSR as:

> actions that appear to further some social good, beyond the interests of the firm and that which is required by law. This... means going beyond obeying the law. Thus, a company that avoids discriminating against women and minorities is not engaging in a socially responsible act; it is merely abiding by the law. (p. 604)

Waddock's (2004) definition also includes the concept of environment in her depiction of CSP as being:

> the broad array of strategies and operating practices that a company develops in its efforts to deal with and create relationships with its numerous stakeholders and the natural environment. (p. 8)

A further consideration of 'being a good corporate citizen' is encompassed in Carroll's (1979) pyramid of CSR which stressed that an organisation has

> not only economic and legal obligations, but ethical and discretionary (philanthropic) responsibilities as well. (Carroll 1991, 1979, p. 40)

So why should businesses get involved in CSR? After all, they are responsible to their shareholders and capital providers to provide adequate returns. This is the classical position adopted by Friedman (1970) who stated that only people, not organisations have a 'social responsibility' and that if corporate managers diverted shareholders' funds away from the core business of making money, that they were acting beyond the shareholders' desires, or no longer 'serving the interests of the principle' (Friedman 1970, p. 3) in the agent (manager)—principle (shareholder) relationship. Friedman (1970) stated that anything beyond a focus on returning profits to shareholders was outside of the responsibility of management and even a breach of the trust of those who have entrusted their money to the company. The logic behind Friedman's argument was that if a firm focuses on making profits, then it is using the capital provided to it in the most efficient way and is employing people and assets effectively and efficiently, which is all that business could be expected to do within the rule of law in a given country.

However, what this classical approach did not consider was the changing perception of business and its role. For example, whilst it may have been financially efficient and socially acceptable to use child labour in mills in the Victorian era, it is not deemed morally acceptable now (although there is no suggestion that Friedman was advocating this behaviour). Societal perceptions of what business is expected to do have evolved (Lacey et al. 2015; Hemingway and Maclagan 2004). Whilst there is still recognition that making money is the role of most organisations (though clearly not true for public sector organisations or charities, although they still need to manage their finite resources), it is no longer deemed acceptable for firms to utilise child labour, either in their country of origin or elsewhere in their supply chain wherever in the world that may be. This is true of other business practices that were once deemed societally 'acceptable', including regarding labour as merely a 'factor of production' in line with classical economists such as Adam Smith, Thomas Malthus and John Stuart Mill, rather than seeing an employee in a business today as a contributory participant (Parks 1995).

Considering the broader impacts of business on the people within it and affected by it is the underlying principle to stakeholder theory. Commonly attributed to Freeman (1984), stakeholder theory is 'about value creation and trade and how to manage a business effectively' (Freeman et al. 2010, p. 9). This is achieved by considering the multiplicity of stakeholders (individuals or groups) who are affected in some way by the activities of a business and attempting to tend to their needs as far as is practical. It is acknowledged that for any given business, it is impossible to address every stakeholder's needs, since the capacity (both financial and human) of the organisation to do so is finite. However, the idea is that some consideration is made of the impacts of the business on other stakeholders beyond merely the capital providers (for example, loan providers and shareholders); which is the classical view (Friedman 1970) as discussed previously.

As such, stakeholder theory is the underpinning concept of CSR, that by 'doing good', businesses will also perform well due to a reduction in costs and business risk (of litigation or fines for poor practices), improved employee relationships and motivations, and legitimacy (or the support to exist) from the wider community (Chernev and Blair 2015; Garay and Font 2012). CSR should be embedded throughout the organisation and form part of corporate policy-making. Business decisions should consider all three aspects (environmental, social and governance) of CSR, in order to ensure sustainability and longevity not only to the business but society too. That is not to say that this is easy; there are undoubtedly trade-offs which firms need to make with the finite resources at their disposal. Equally, one cannot lose sight of the fact that most organisations have shareholders who require returns on their invested capital and can withdraw their support should they feel that organisations are no longer delivering what they expect.

Hence the third aspect that CSR activities encompasses, that of corporate governance, serves to reassure shareholders of the good management activities of the organisation. Due to the often poor reputation business has with regards to unethical business practices which can lead to large business collapses or scandals, such as Enron, Worldcom and Parmalat (Bayou et al. 2011), corporate governance practices have been developed across the world (such as the UK Corporate Governance Code (Financial Reporting Council 2012). The purpose of these practices is to ensure that companies are well managed from the board downwards and that there are adequate policies and procedures in place to foster an environment of good management. To this end, organisations now routinely publish reports on their governance and board processes to provide a level of reassurance to the investment community.

From an accountant's point of view, engagement with CSR, like that of the Triple Bottom Line or sustainability in general, should be a normal business activity. Crossing all departments and levels in an organisation as all these concepts do, accountants are well-placed to be able to influence and design systems of performance management and policy-setting in order to encompass the wide-ranging requirements to report on the myriad of activities taking place.

2.5 Conclusion: Assessing Sustainability and Social Responsibility: The Role of the Accountant?

The business world is very data or evidence-driven (Davenport and Bean 2018). Given the vast range of activities that a firm could undertake and the finite nature of the resources available to it, it is necessary for organisations to focus on only a few activities at any one time, to maximise the likelihood that they are achieved. What the organisation chooses to focus on is usually determined with reference to the overall aims and objectives of the firm through its strategy. This strategy process may be driven by a myriad of motivations: increasing profit, maintaining competitiveness or reducing risk. Whilst arguably historically much was driven by increased profitability or maintenance of dividend payments, increased focus on business risk and changing perceptions of the role of organisation has highlighted the reliance of firms on their environment for basic raw materials, skilled workforce or legitimacy within the community. Indeed, many businesses are already actively engaging in sustainability, whether through pressure external to the firm or internally-driven by management perceiving it as an opportunity as well as a challenge (Blowfield 2013; Blowfield and Murray 2011).

This change in perspective to a multi-stakeholder accountability model (Harrison and Freeman 1999) has led to a plethora of data and metrics to measure corporate sustainability and social responsibility and to demonstrate the impact of the business outside its economic performance. Whilst many of these metrics are focused on environmental impacts, there are some associated with social impacts also included in the 17 UN Sustainable Development goals (UN 2015b), which should form the basis for government and corporate policy worldwide. Whilst organisations may not be explicitly working towards these development goals, inevitably many firms will choose (or be mandated) to select targets to improve environmental and social performance as well as economic. This means that accountants, including auditors, will need to engage with and assure a much broader set of metrics (both financial and non-financial) in order to demonstrate progress being made. This will require a wider skillset than that of the traditional accountant and will need to consider the governance and ethical compass of the organisation (Hemingway and Maclagan 2004; Liebowitz 2003) in the setting of strategy, the prioritisation of targets and the development of measurement systems to support the multivariate nature of the modern business landscape.

References

Bayou, Mohamed E., Alan Reinstein, and Paul F. Williams. 2011. "To Tell the Truth: A Discussion of Issues Concerning Truth and Ethics in Accounting." *Accounting, Organizations and Society* 36 (2): 109–124. https://doi.org/10.1016/j.aos.2011.02.001.

Blowfield, Michael. 2013. *Business and Sustainability*. Oxford, UK: Oxford University Press.

Blowfield, Michael, and Alan Murray. 2011. *Corporate Responsibility*, 3rd ed. Oxford, UK: Oxford University Press.

Boulding, K.E. 1966. "The Economics of Coming Spaceship Earth." In *Environmental Quality in a Growing Economy*, edited by H. Jarret. Baltimore: John Hopkins University Press.

Brundtland, Gro Harlem, and WCED. 1987. *Our Common Future*. Oxford: Oxford University Press.

BSI. 2018. "ISO 14001—Environmental Management—EMS|BSI Group." https://www.bsigroup.com/en-GB/iso-14001-environmental-management/.

Cannon, T. 2012. *Corporate Responsibility*, vol. 2. Harlow: Pearson.

Carraro, Carlo, Alice Favero, and Emanuele Massetti. 2012. "Investments and Public Finance in a Green, Low Carbon, Economy." *Green Perspectives* 34: S15–28. https://doi.org/10.1016/j.eneco.2012.08.036.

Carroll, Archie B. 1979. "A Three-Dimensional Conceptual Model of Corporate Performance." *Academy of Management Review* 4 (4): 497–505. https://doi.org/10.5465/AMR.1979.4498296.

Carroll, Archie B. 1991. "The Pyramid of Corporate Social Responsibility: Toward the Moral Management of Organizational Stakeholders." *Business Horizons* 34 (4): 39–48. http://search.ebscohost.com/login.aspx?direct=true&db=bth&AN=9707074820&site=ehost-live.

Chernev, Alexander, and Sean Blair. 2015. "Doing Well by Doing Good: The Benevolent Halo of Corporate Social Responsibility." *Journal of Consumer Research* 41 (6): 1412–1425. https://doi.org/10.1086/680089.

Conway, Elaine. 2017. "Measuring Carbon: An Organisational Management Perspective." In *The Low Carbon Economy: Understanding and Supporting a Sustainable Transition*, edited by P. Baranova, E. Conway, N. Lynch, and F. Paterson. London: Palgrave Macmillan.

Costanza, R., and B.C. Patten. 1995. "Defining and Predicting Sustainability." *Ecological Economics* 15: 193–196.

Daly, Herman E. 1991. *Steady-State Economics*, 2nd ed. Washington, DC: Island Press.

Davenport, Thomas H., and Randy Bean. 2018. "Big Companies Are Embracing Analytics, But Most Still Don't Have a Data-Driven Culture." *Harvard Business Review*. https://hbr.org/2018/02/big-companies-are-embracing-analytics-but-most-still-dont-have-a-data-driven-culture.

DEFRA. 2013. *Environmental Reporting Guidelines: Including Mandatory Greenhouse Gas Emissions Reporting Guidance*. London: Department for Environment Food & Rural Affairs.

DEFRA. 2015. *Government Definitions of Sustainability*. London: Department for Environment Food & Rural Affairs.

Department of the Environment, UK Government. 1994. *Sustainable Development: The UK Strategy (Command Paper)*. London: HMSO.

Elkington, John. 1997. *Cannibals with Forks: The Triple Bottom Line of 21st Century Business*. Oxford: Capstone.

Elkington, John. 2001. "Enter the Triple Bottom Line." *The Triple Bottom Line: Does It All Add Up?* (1986): 1–16. https://doi.org/10.1021/nl034968f.

Ellen Macarthur Foundation. 2012. "Efficiency vs Effectiveness in the Circular Economy." https://www.ellenmacarthurfoundation.org/circular-economy/interactive-diagram/efficiency-vs-effectiveness.

Farrell, Sean. 2016. "MPs Launch Inquiry into UK Working Conditions Amid Exploitation Fears|Business|The Guardian." *The Guardian*. https://www.theguardian.com/business/2016/oct/26/mps-inquiry-uk-working-conditions-pay-exploitation-gig-economy.

Financial Reporting Council. 2012. "The UK Corporate Governance Code." *Financial Services Authority*, September.

Freeman, R. Edward, Jeffrey S. Harrison, Andrew C. Wicks, Bidhan L. Parmar, and Simone de Colle. 2010. *Stakeholder Theory: The State of the Art*, 1st ed. New York: Cambridge University Press.

Freeman, R. Edward. 1984. *Strategic Management: A Strategic Approach*. Boston: Pitman.

Friedman, Milton. 1970. "The Social Responsibility of Business Is to Increase Its Profits." *New York Times Magazine*, September 13.

Garay, Luis, and Xavier Font. 2012. "Doing Good to Do Well? Corporate Social Responsibility Reasons, Practices and Impacts in Small and Medium Accommodation Enterprises." *International Journal of Hospitality Management* 31 (2): 329–337. http://dx.doi.org/10.1016/j.ijhm.2011.04.013.

Gimenez, Cristina, Vicenta Sierra, and Juan Rodon. 2012. "Sustainable Operations: Their Impact on the Triple Bottom Line." *International Journal of Production Economics* 140 (1): 149–159. https://doi.org/10.1016/j.ijpe.2012.01.035.

Gray, Rob. 2002. "Of Messiness, Systems and Sustainability: Towards a More Social and Environmental Finance and Accounting." *British Accounting Review* 34 (4): 357–386.

GRI. 2014. "G4 Sustainability Reporting Guidelines". https://www.globalreporting.org/standards/g4/Pages/default.aspx.

Harrison, Jeffrey S., and R.E. Freeman. 1999. "Stakeholders, Social Responsibility, and Performance: Empirical Evidence and Theoretical Perspectives." *Academy of Management Journal* 42 (5): 479–485. https://doi.org/10.2307/256971.

Hemingway, Christine A, and Patrick W. Maclagan. 2004. "Managers' Personal Values as Drivers of Corporate Social Responsibility." *Journal of Business Ethics* 50 (1): 33–44. http://search.ebscohost.com/login.aspx?direct=true&db=bth&AN=12991584&site=ehost-live.

IUCN, UNEP, and WWF. 1991. *Caring for the Earth: A Strategy for Sustainable Living*. Switzerland: IUCN—The World Conservation Union, UNEP—United Nations Environment Programme, WWF—World Wide Fund for Nature.

Janssens-Maenhout, G., M. Crippa, D. Guizzardi, M. Muntean, E. Schaaf, F. Dentener, P. Bergmaschi, et al. 2017. "Global Atlas of the Three Major Greenhouse Gases Emissions for the Period 1970–2012." *Earth System Science Data*. https://doi.org/10.2904/JRC_DATASET_EDGAR.

Jayasuriya, Ruwan. 2008. "World Bank Employment Policy Primer." *The Effects of Globalization on Working Conditions in Developing Countries: An Analysis Framework and Country Study Results* 9: 1–6.

Kates, R.W., T.M. Parris, and A.A. Leiserowitz. 2005. "What Is Sustainable Development? Goals, Indicators, Values and Practice." *Science and Policy for Sustainable Development* 47 (3): 8–21.

Lacey, Russell, Pamela Kennett-Hensel, and Chris Manolis. 2015. "Is Corporate Social Responsibility a Motivator or Hygiene Factor? Insights into Its Bivalent Nature." *Journal of the Academy of Marketing Science* 43 (3): 315–332. https://doi.org/10.1007/s11747-014-0390-9.

Larrinaga-González, Carlos, Francisco Carrasco-Fenech, Francisco Javier, Caro-González Carmen, Correa-Ruíz José, María Páez-Sandubete, and María Páez. 2001. "The Role of Environmental Accounting in Organizational Change—An Exploration of Spanish Companies." *Accounting, Auditing & Accountability Journal* 14 (2): 213–239. http://dx.doi.org/10.1108/09513570110389323.

Larrinaga-González, Carlos, Francisco Carrasco, Carmen Correa, Fernando Llena, and José Moneva. 2002. "Accountability and Accounting Regulation: The Case of the Spanish Environmental Disclosure Standard." *European Accounting Review* 11 (4): 723–740. https://doi.org/10.1080/0963818022000001000.

Liebowitz, Bernard. 2003. "What's Wrong with Being 'Borderline Ethical'? Everyone Would Agree That Lying, Cheating, Stealing, or Creating Dangerous Working Conditions Just to Increase Profits Are Unethical Business Practices." *Healthcare Financial Management*, September. Academic OneFile. Accessed 13 Mar 2018.

Lyon, Thomas P., and John W. Maxwell. 2011. "Greenwash: Corporate Environmental Disclosure under Threat of Audit." *Journal of Economics and Management Strategy* 20 (1): 3–41. https://doi.org/10.1111/j.1530-9134.2010.00282.x.

McMichael, A.J., C.D. Butler, and C. Folke. 2003. "New Visions for Addressing Sustainability." *Science* 302 (5652): 1919–1920.

McWilliams, Abagail, and Donald Siegel. 2000. "Corporate Social Responsibility and Financial Performance: Correlation or Misspecification?" *Strategic Management Journal* 21: 603–609.

Merriam-Webster. 2016. *The Merriam-Webster Dictionary*. Martinsburg, USA. https://www.merriam-webster.com/.

Mulligan, M. 2018. *Introduction to Sustainability*, 2nd ed. Oxford: Earthscan—Routledge.

Murray, Alan, Keith Skene, and Kathryn Haynes. 2017. "The Circular Economy: An Interdisciplinary Exploration of the Concept and Application in a Global Context." *Journal of Business Ethics* 140 (3): 369–380. https://doi.org/10.1007/s10551-015-2693-2.

OECD. 2015. "In It Together: Why Less Inequality Benefits All." https://doi.org/10.1787/9789264235120-en.

Osborne, Hilary. 2016. "Amazon Accused of 'Intolerable Conditions' at Scottish Warehouse|Technology|The Guardian." *The Guardian*. https://www.theguardian.com/technology/2016/dec/11/amazon-accused-of-intolerable-conditions-at-scottish-warehouse.

Parks, Susan. 1995. "Improving Workplace Performance: Historical and Theoretical Contexts." *Monthly Labor Review* 118: 18–28. http://heinonline.org/HOL/LandingPage?handle=hein.journals/month118%26div=56%26id=%26page=.

PWC. 2018. "Is Business Grasping the Full Potential of SDGs?—PwC's SDG Reporting Challenge." https://www.pwc.co.uk/press-room/press-releases/Is-business-grasping-the-full-potential-of-SDGs.html.

Rakotomavo, Michel T.J. 2012. "Corporate Investment in Social Responsibility versus Dividends?" *Social Responsibility Journal* 8 (2): 199–207. https://doi.org/10.1108/17471111211234833.

Rittel, Horst, and Melvin Webber. 1973. "Dilemmas in a General Theory of Planning." *Policy Studies* 4: 155–169.

Rodriguez-Fernandez, Mercedes. 2016. "Social Responsibility and Financial Performance: The Role of Good Corporate Governance." *BRQ Business Research Quarterly* 19 (2): 137–151. https://doi.org/10.1016/j.brq.2015.08.001.

Slaper, Timothy F., and Tanya J. Hall. 2011. "The Triple Bottom Line: What Is It and How Does It Work?" *Indiana Business Review* 86 (1): 4–8.

Slawinski, Natalie, Jonatan Pinkse, Timo Busch, and Subhabrata Bobby Banerjeed. 2017. "The Role of Short-Termism and Uncertainty in Organisational Inaction on Climate Change: Multilevel Framework." https://doi.org/10.1177/0007650315576136.

Smithers, Rebecca. 2007. "Forget Tesco: The Bigger Threat to Small Shops May Be Waitrose|UK News|The Guardian." *The Guardian*. https://www.theguardian.com/uk/2007/jul/03/shopping.business.

The Huffington Post. 2013. "Primark Targeted By Protesters After Bangladesh Building Collapse." http://www.huffingtonpost.co.uk/2013/04/27/primark_protesters-bangladesh-building-collapse-_n_3169781.html.

UN. 2015a. "SDGs … Sustainable Development Knowledge Platform." https://sustainabledevelopment.un.org/sdgs.

UN. 2015b. "United Nations Sustainable Development Goals." *United Nations Sustainable Development Goals*. Available at http://www.un.org/sustainabledevelopment/sustainable-development-goals/.

United Nations Department of Economic and Social Affairs, Population Division. 2017. "World Population Prospects the 2017 Revision Key Findings and Advance Tables." *World Population Prospects the 2017*, 1–46. https://doi.org/10.1017/CBO9781107415324.004.

US EIA. 2017. "What Are Greenhouse Gases and How Do They Affect the Climate?—FAQ—U.S. Energy Information Administration (EIA)." *US Energy Information Administration*. https://www.eia.gov/tools/faqs/faq.php?id=81&t=11.

Voinov, A., and J. Farley. 2007. "Reconciling Sustainability, Systems Theory and Discounting." *Ecological Economics* 63 (1): 104–113.

Waddock, Sandra. 2004. "Parallel Universes: Companies, Academics, and the Progress of Corporate Citizenship." *Business and Society Review* 109 (1): 5–42.

Waddock, Sandra A., and Samuel B. Graves. 1997. "The Corporate Social Performance- Financial Performance Link." *Strategic Management Journal* 18 (4): 303–319. http://search.ebscohost.com/login.aspx?direct=true&db=bth&AN=12493386&site=ehost-live.

White, Mark A. 2013. "Sustainability: I Know It When I See It." *Ecological Economics* 86: 213–217. https://doi.org/10.1016/j.ecolecon.2012.12.020.

Williams, Chris. 2015. "Tesco Faces Fresh Accusations of 'Bullying' Suppliers over Price Cuts—Telegraph." *The Telegraph*. https://www.telegraph.co.uk/finance/newsbysector/retailandconsumer/11399558/Tesco-faces-fresh-accusations-of-bullying-suppliers-over-price-cuts.html.

Wood, Donna J. 2010. "Measuring Corporate Social Performance: A Review." *International Journal of Management Reviews* 12 (1): 50–84. https://doi.org/10.1111/j.1468-2370.2009.00274.x.

World Bank. 2015. "The Future of the World's Population in 4 Charts|The Data Blog." *The Future of the World's Population in 4 Charts*. https://blogs.worldbank.org/opendata/future-world-s-population-4-charts.

Wu, Meng-Wen, and Chung-Hua Shen. 2013. "Corporate Social Responsibility in the Banking Industry: Motives and Financial Performance." *Journal of Banking & Finance* 37 (9): 3529–3547. https://doi.org/10.1016/j.jbankfin.2013.04.023.

CHAPTER 3

The Challenges of the Circular Economy

Simon Peter Nadeem, Jose Arturo Garza-Reyes and Denise Glanville

3.1 Introduction

Economic growth and development are an aspiration/ambition for almost every individual, organisation, industry and nation. The pursuit of economic well-being and development itself is not without merit, but the way in which it has been, and is, being managed has raised serious concerns to both practitioners and researchers. The extent of the negative impact is not just limited to the planet and current human population, but also impacts future generations (Nadeem et al. 2017). Technology has helped soaring production levels and has impacted the behaviour of consumers, resulting in higher consumption, with shorter life cycle of products, globally. This attitude towards production and consumption has reached an alarming level of resource depletion.

Excessive extraction of resources as well as pollutant emissions has contributed to an '*ecological credit crunch*', as the current resource usage ratio is approximately 30% higher than the earth can replenish each year (Jowit 2008). Technological advancement has helped to fast-track the processes of extraction, production and consumption. The problem does

S. P. Nadeem (✉) · J. A. Garza-Reyes · D. Glanville
Derby Business School, University of Derby, Derby, UK

E. Conway and D. Byrne (eds.), *Contemporary Issues in Accounting*,
https://doi.org/10.1007/978-3-319-91113-7_3

not lie in technological development but the way in which it is utilised and managed. Scholars have highlighted that the current economic system has developed with no concern for the environment or little interest in recycling (Su et al. 2013). Jowit (2008) further highlights that if the current pattern of resource utilisation continues at this pace, there would be a need for a second planet to sustain life.

Scholars have raised their concerns over the last five decades, in particular, when Boulding (1966) pointed to the resource depletion and damage to the environment. Initiatives such as Green, Ecological, Environment Friendly, Sustainability, Lean, Recycling, etc. have significantly contributed to the conservation of resources, but in most of the cases in a reactive way. The current global economy can arguably be seen as not much more than a race for the remaining resources (Webster 2015). The challenge of rapid depletion of resources demands different game rules (Webster 2015); a pro-active approach which seems to have emerged is the concept of the circular economy, where the main idea is that there is no waste created but that the whole system is designed for waste to be re-utilised in one form or another, for example re-cycled, up-cycled, down-cycled, or used as raw material for other production (Ellen MacArthur Foundation 2015a).

3.2 Origins of the Circular Economy

While the concept of the circular economy emerged about five decades ago and has received popularity recently, it is believed that its roots cannot be traced back to any specific point in time (Webster 2015). The core underlying drivers for the rise of the concept of circular economy are scarcity of resources, increased extraction, rising resource prices, climate change, and changing attitudes towards the issue (Gregson et al. 2015; Boulding 1966). The concept can also be linked back in history to the strategies adapted by Henry Ford, envisaged through his credo: '*You must get the most out of the power, out of the material, and out of the time*' (Braungart and McDonough 2002). Later on, similar efforts have been made elsewhere with further expansion of theoretical frameworks and strategic initiatives such as Just in Time (JIT) (Liker 2004), Green Production and Logistics (McKinnon et al. 2015) and Lean (Goldsby and Martichenko 2005). As much as all these approaches are praiseworthy, and no doubt, have and are making their significant contribution to the industrial and business world globally, all of these approaches have mainly focused on the optimisation and careful use of resources in the linear approach, which is *Take–Make–Dispose* (Ellen MacArthur Foundation 2015b), also known as '*Cradle to Grave*' (Braungart and McDonough 2002). The linear model of production: *Take–Make–Dispose*, heavily relies on large quantities of easily accessible resources and energy, which is unrealistic in a world of scarce resources (Webster 2015). Lacy and Rutqvist (2015) pointed out that the economic growth model over the last 250 years is living on borrowed time.

The circular economy concept is believed to have emerged from Ecological and Environmental Economics (Ghisellini et al. 2016) and Eco-Industrial Development (EID), which suggests that both a healthy economy and a healthy environment can coexist (Geng and Doberstein 2008). Regardless of different approaches, it would be right to say that the emergence of the concept of the circular economy is not by choice but by necessity as the earlier business models have mainly focused on economic well-being, this has created an alarming scenario, compelling the rethink regarding sustainability.

3.3 What Is the Circular Economy?

The circular economy (CE) concept differs from Green and/or Recycling and offers a proactive contrasting approach to the current linear system of *Take–Make–Dispose* (Ellen MacArthur Foundation 2015a) (see Fig. 3.1) and introduces the idea of '***roundput***' instead of '***throughput***'; where the resources are used but not used up (Webster 2015).

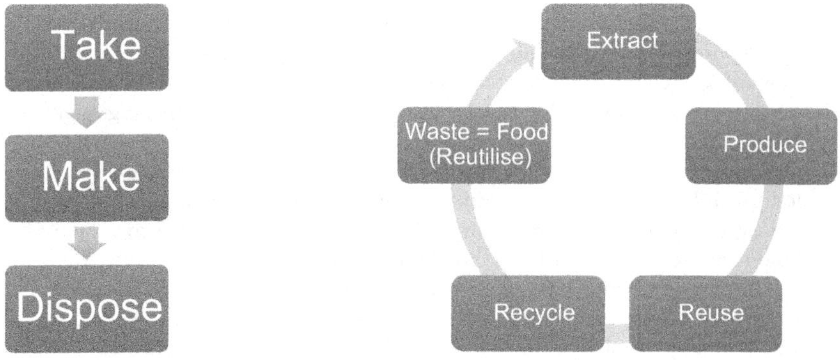

Fig. 3.1 Linear versus circular model

The differentiating feature of circular economy is that it tackles the problem at its roots and manages it at the design stage, instead of a reactive approach at the end of the life cycle of any product. It keeps the resources in loop, for which the design stage already plans for the product/resource coming back into loop after the produced designed life cycle is completed.

3.4 Definitions of Circular Economy

Circular economy is not just another name for recycling. Although recycling is one of the key elements, the concept envelopes a wider perspective and delivers a broader approach, dealing with resource recovery (Gregson et al. 2015; Singh and Ordoñez 2016; Li et al. 2013), resource efficiency and effectiveness (Schulte 2013; Hu et al. 2011), sustainable consumption and production, systems of provision, industrial symbiosis, urban metabolism, zero waste, eco-design, materials criticality, design for recycling, up-cycling/down-cycling and cascade models, remanufacturing, waste prevention and minimisation (Velis 2015). In order to understand the breadth and scope of circular economy, the following definitions have been selected to provide foundational understanding of the concept.

> A circular economy is one that is waste-free and resilient by design. It is a new economic model that is ambitious as well as practical. Designing the economy in a way that is restorative of ecosystems, ambitious with its innovation, and impactful for society, is a bold challenge but one that is achievable when guided by the principles of the circular economy. (Circle Economy 2016)
>
> In a circular economy, profits, jobs and growth come not from extracting, moving, shaping, selling and dumping ever more resources, but from the work done and value created by handling resources with sufficient care that ecosystems and total natural resources actually expand, making it possible to meet human needs everywhere. (Greyson 2015)
>
> The circular economy is one that is restorative and regenerative by design and aims to keep products, components, and materials at their highest utility and value at all times, distinguishing between technical and biological cycles. (Ellen MacArthur Foundation 2015a, p. 19)
>
> The circular economy refers to an industrial economy that is restorative by intention; aims to rely on renewable energy; minimises, tracks, and hopefully eliminates the use of toxic chemicals; and eradicates waste through careful design. (Webster 2015, p. 52)

In order to design and direct the economic system to be considerate of resource utilisation and be contributing back to the system on which we depend, the following characteristics and architectural frameworks have been developed by scholars.

3.5 Characteristics/Architectural Frameworks for Circular Economy

One essential characteristic of CE is that '*the boundaries of circular economy are not defined, nor are they ever likely to be*' (Webster 2015). This is likely to be true as with growing technological advancement new avenues are emerging for the utilisation and management of resources, and as the circular loop can be reiterative without any limit, the boundaries for circular economy are hard to be drawn. These frameworks overlap on most aspects but do have some distinguishing elements.

All three frameworks discussed here (those proposed by Ken Webster, the Ellen MacArthur Foundation and the Netherlands-based Circle Economy organisation) as well as the concept of circular economy hinge on two main goals/strategies; max-min policy of waste and max-max policy of utility; where maximum effort is made to minimise/eliminate waste and maximum effort is made to maximise the utility of a resource (Nadeem et al. 2017). To do so, Webster (2015) suggests designing out any possibility of waste creation that can be prevented by redesigning

Fig. 3.2 Framework of circular economy

the system to be resilient; and to make maximum effort to utilise energy from renewable resources (see Fig. 3.2). He further encourages businesses to engage in systems thinking in pursuit of a broader picture of the economy. He regards industry as a key player and contributor to others by thinking in cascades where materials flow is maintained to the maximum utility and is managed appropriately towards the end of its life. The framework by Webster (2015) is foundational to the other two as they have the five aspects of Webster's proposition.

The Ellen MacArthur Foundation developed the ReSOLVE framework, as six action areas for businesses and countries wanting to move towards the circular economy (Ellen MacArthur Foundation 2015a). These action areas are described below:

- **Re**generate: Moving to renewable energy and utilising renewable resources to establishing good ecosystems by returning biological resources to biosphere.
- **S**hare: Promoting sharing economy where consumers as well as businesses can share their assets such as vehicles, buildings, equipment, appliances, etc. Another important factor is to reuse products by buying and selling in second-hand markets.
- **O**ptimise: Maximise the utilisation of the resources to be employed by designing the system for effective and efficient management through the adoption and use of technology to enhance the performance and to design out waste.
- **L**oop: Circular usage of raw material is extremely important for circular economy and it can be achieved by extending the life cycle of materials in closed loop.
- **V**irtualise: Utilising technology to help dematerialise, such as moving from paper based books to online and e-books, online shopping for effective utilisation of space, virtual offices.
- **E**xchange: Replacing old technology with new such as solar energy utilisation and 3D printing.

The Ellen MacArthur Foundation framework and action step model closely mirror the framework described by Ken Webster discussed earlier. The difference between the two is that Webster provides the foundational principle necessary for the existence of the circular economy concept and the Ellen McArthur Foundation provides the methodology through which circular economy can be realised and optimised. For instance, the elements of sharing and virtualisation are not directly highlighted in Webster's framework but are at the core of Webster's '*thinking in systems*' element.

The Circle Economy, a Dutch organisation identifies 6 principles, shown in Fig. 3.3, to change the system (Circle Economy 2016):

1. **Materials** are to be cycled infinitely
2. All **Energy** is derived from renewable or otherwise sustainable sources
3. Human activities support **ecosystems** and the rebuilding of natural capital
4. Resources are used to generate **value** both in terms of financial and other forms
5. Human activities support human **health** and happiness
6. Human activities support a healthy and cohesive **society** and culture.

The above mentioned 6 principles and Ellen MacArthur's ReSOLVE framework are quite similar as they both represent the same values at their core, except that the Circle Economy model has an added feature of human activities supporting the ecosystem and health aspects. These are not directly highlighted in the Ellen MacArthur framework.

The ReSOLVE framework envelopes all the five aspects of Webster's framework and further focuses on establishing a good ecosystem with an additional aspect of 'Share'—where people share their resources for

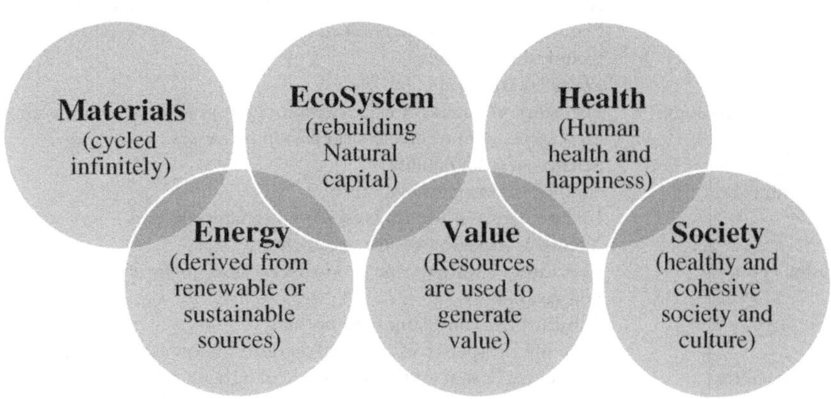

Fig. 3.3 Six principles to change system

maximum utility and promote reusage. The framework suggests to keep resources in a closed loop circle to extract maximum utility, and to use technology as an enabler to virtualise such as using e-books instead of paper books, using efficient technology such as solar panels, 3D printing, etc. The framework by Circle Economy (Circle Economy 2016) further extends to a health and society aspect, which is an end result of the circular economy; however, it is important to underpin it distinctly in order for the system to always be aware of the boundaries and goals.

3.6 Schools of Thought on the Circular Economy

Ken Webster (2015) is one of the leading scholars to have developed the concept of circular economy. He gathers various schools of thought that have shaped circular economy to its present state (see Table 3.1).

Table 3.1 Schools of thought and their core concepts

School of thought	*Key idea(s)*
Regenerative design	Regenerative design that could be applied to all systems
Performance economy	Closed loop approach: Product life extension Long life goods Reconditioning activities Waste prevention Functional service economy—sell services rather than products
Cradle to cradle	All material is nutrient of two categories: technical and biological Nature's biological metabolism as model for developing technical metabolism Waste equals food
Industrial ecology	Focusing on connections between operators within the industrial ecosystem—aim to create closed loop processes Science of sustainability
Biomimicry	Innovation inspired by nature Imitate nature's best ideas to solve human problems Nature as model, measure and mentor
Blue economy	Cascading—waste of one product becomes the input to create a new cash flow Substituting something with nothing Creating prosperity with what you didn't know you already had
Permaculture	Conscious design and maintenance of agriculturally productive ecosystem, which have diversity, stability and resilience of natural ecosystem

These developments over last few decades have laid the foundation stones for the development of the circular economy. The pursuit of economic growth itself is not harmful as long as all stakeholders are considered. The schools of thought (summarised in Table 3.1) are efforts to make the participants aware of alternative arrangements to achieve economic objectives with increased resilience and added value. They further broaden the vision that value creation is not just limited to product and economic benefit of the business itself, but it is broader and envelopes all the players: direct ones (business and customer involved), indirect players (tier 2 suppliers) and indirectly related players (environment, society, planet and future generations).

Like any other conceptual redesign, circular economy is also faced with enablers and barriers to its implementation. These are discussed further in the next section.

3.7 Enablers/Barriers

To a great extent, any challenges or barriers may become enablers or drivers, provided that they are addressed and managed in the right way. Three major barriers or challenges to the adoption of the circular economy identified by scholars are policy, technology, and public participation (Geng and Doberstein 2008) (Fig. 3.4).

Lack of a structured policy can lead to slow or no adoption of circular economy both at industrial and consumer level. Many countries

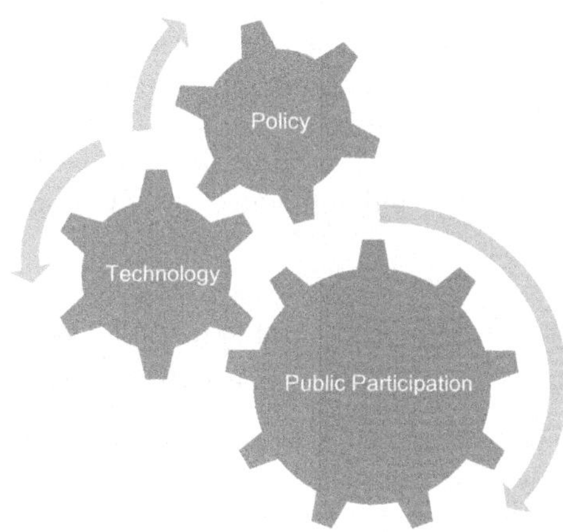

Fig. 3.4 Barriers/enablers of circular economy

(e.g. Netherlands, EU, etc.) as well as institutions (e.g. Ellen McArthur Foundation, UK; Circle Economy, Netherlands; WRAP, UK; etc.) have developed and are further developing policies to enact circular economy's principles at macro-, meso- and micro-level. Collaborative effort by governmental institutions and the private sector is a key requirement to take forward policy development and its outcomes.

Technological advancement is at an ever increasing pace. The rise of fuel efficient and electric vehicles, 3D printing, and virtualisation are some of the highlights that we see, and more are being developed every day. The current issue is that mass adoption of these developments is still a challenge both because of cost and awareness.

The third and most important enabler is public participation, without which both policy and technology cannot function to their full capacity. A current challenge at consumer level is the acceptance of goods produced using reclaimed material instead of virgin raw material. The general perception that a recycled/refurbished or a product produced by reclaimed material lacks the durability and performance of a completely new product is one of the key issues impeding the mass adoption of circular economy. Since demand drives supply, if consumer awareness and understanding is enhanced considerably, this will propel industries to adopt circular economy's principles in their regular operations.

It is crucially important for these three enablers (policy, technology and public participation) to be coordinated to support the rapid adoption of circular economy at all levels. Policy-making institutions need to play a crucial role by developing policies that promote circular economy. This then gives the push for industries/economies to adopt and contextualise the concept of circular economy into their practices and to drive demand for technological development to support it. This in turn, would inform the public of the need for CE and could help to change their perception about the durability of reworked products; resulting in increased public demand and adoption of CE principles.

3.8 CE Implementation and Implications for the Accounting Profession

The concept of a world moving from linear to circular is gaining considerable momentum, with the barriers to change as discussed previously, gradually being eroded. Many countries have developed or are in the process of establishing national policies to adopt circular economy principles. Among these, the early adopters were: Germany in 1996 by enacting a law for closed cycle waste management and environmentally compatible waste disposal (Su et al. 2013); in China, having acknowledged that economic growth has caused great damage to the environment, the government has embedded circular economy concepts in national policy since 2002 (Geng et al. 2012; Singh and Ordoñez 2016; Murray et al. 2017). The state has invested heavily in circular economy pilot projects in particular industries, municipalities and regional developments (World Economic Forum 2014); in Japan, the circular economy has progressed significantly, with substantial legislation since 2000, including a legal framework to move towards a recycling-based society (Ministry of Economy 2004; Su et al. 2013) including legislation on automobile end of life treatment in 2002 (World Economic Forum 2014).

In Europe, for example, from a policy perspective, the circular economy package adopted by the European Commission in December 2015 has provided support, legislative proposals and an Action Plan aimed to enable the circular economy throughout the value chain, by using targeted European Union (EU) funding to drive and assist policy initiatives related to research and technological development (European Commission 2017). More specifically, Denmark has initiatives such as banning the construction of incineration plants with the goal that by 2022 they will be recycling 50% of household waste (The Danish Government 2013); Scotland has a waste reduction goal of 25% by 2025; Sweden aims to increase recycling of paper-based packaging material from current levels of 65% to 85% by 2020 (Zero Waste Scotland 2016); and Poland in 2013 adopted the Act on Waste (European Commission 2015).

Clearly there is quite widespread realisation for the need of circular economy which is leading governments to rethink their future strategies. With such a move towards circular economy, its application is heavily dependent on all sectors of the economy to rethink and re-align their strategies and processes.

Throughout all levels of implementation—from policy making to information systems design and implementation—accountants have an important role to play in both driving and supporting the move away from the linear to the circular model. This may be via policies within a professional accountancy body, via regulatory change or governmental intervention, or by adoption within the public, private or charitable sectors. Accountants need to engage with the concept of the circular economy and consider the implications for accounting information systems.

3.9 Social and Environmental Accounting and CE

In recent years, substantial improvements have been made relating to methods of accounting for social and environmental activities within organisations. Published annual accounts include information relating to these aspects within their narrative reports. Although considerable progress has been made in the areas of integrated reporting and sustainability, with a substantial body of academic work on Social and Environmental Accounting (SEA) available, the majority of this research is focused on the waste output related to the production process within various industries. These output waste flows require innovative methods of measurement. Examples of metrics developed relate to greenhouse gas emissions, carbon dioxide equivalents and energy usage. Manufacturing organisations are increasingly realising that it is the inputs to the process, the raw materials used in production, which require relevant indicators and attention-directing metrics. This is gaining importance as natural resource scarcity and depletion becomes more pressing. Organisations need to review the sourcing and usage of their raw material inputs and to focus increasingly on recycling materials back into the manufacturing system. The use of regulatory 'sticks' encourages this review of operations by the introduction of waste legislation, extended producer responsibility and take-back systems (Ellen MacArthur Foundation 2015a). For example, the Waste Electrical and Electronic Equipment Regulations 2013 (UK Government 2013) include mandatory requirements relating to the 'take-back' of used consumer goods. There are also efforts to reduce the use of plastics and non-recyclable packaging in the retail sector; in 2015 a five pence levy on single-use plastic bags in large retailers was introduced. This led to an 80% reduction in the number of bags issued by retailers in 2016 (DEFRA 2017). The 'carrots' for businesses relate to the potential growth in market share, new markets, consumer approval and public relations. Examples of these include the development of recyclable coffee cups and packaging or innovative ways to make use of waste.

Policy-making institutions are crucial for the development of practical standards and advice. Whilst the International Accounting Standards Board (IASB) and the Financial Accounting Standards Board (FASB) in the USA have issued various new financial accounting standards over recent years, none have addressed the changing perspectives regarding business models. This is understandable in that considerable time is required for these institutions to gain approval for new standards. However, this is an area which does require more immediate attention as new business models, such as the circular economy, gain acknowledgement by all stakeholders.

Despite the increase in the use of social and environmental metrics in sustainability and improving Corporate Social Responsibility (CSR) reports over recent years, the concern is that it is otherwise 'business as usual' (Gray et al. 2002; Gray 2006) with no real long term planning and restructuring within businesses to address the major issues relating to finite natural resources and an increasing global population. Gray et al. (2002) argue that accountants, with their narrow focus on financial reporting standards and the emphasis on consistent financial evaluation, find the concept of sustainability and systems thinking challenging. The data used in providing relevant information pertaining to natural capital, social and environmental impacts, in addition to the increasingly complicated and novel businesses models and systems available are complex to understand. CSR reporting is a step in the right direction but continual innovation and improvements are required in relation to addressing the reporting of non-financial aspects in order to take into consideration the broader and complex relationship and dependency business have with the environment (Larrinaga-González et al. 2001).

3.10 Interventions Required for CE Implementation

The three levels of implementation initially adopted in China and other countries remain concentrated on the macro- and meso-levels regarding published CE indicators (Geng et al. 2012). This leaves the micro-level (e.g. organisations at corporate level) without generally accepted or agreed performance indicators. As it is business that often drives change in order to meet challenges and improve performance, it is crucial that this micro-level information as it is developed, is freely communicated to enablers such as accountants within industry in order to speed up adoption. There needs to be open discussion and sharing of knowledge, points clearly made within the EMF 'Toolkit for policy makers' (Ellen MacArthur Foundation 2015a). There are six policy intervention types discussed in this report. Those relating in particular to accountants and accounting information include:

1. Education—there is a requirement for the circular economy and systems thinking awareness and training to be included within accounting and finance degrees and professional examinations and continued professional development.
2. Collaboration platforms—these are already active across industries and value-chains, providing open-source developments and best practice tools to support CE adoption. Accountants need to engage with collaboration platforms, particularly when developing systems with value-chain partners, professional bodies and across business sectors in order to improve information and performance indicators.
3. Business support schemes—through collaboration and openness, technical support and best practice advice need to be freely available to both business and the public sector.
4. Regulatory frameworks—in particular in order to address accounting for natural capital and resource within reporting and financial regulations.
5. Fiscal frameworks—taxation issues with regard to acceptable methodologies to reduce the tax burden for circular products and services. This may include, for example, increasing the tax burden on resources used and reducing taxation on labour. As finite resources dwindle and society more generally recognises the severity of the problem, perceptions on environmental taxation will change (Larrinaga-González et al. 2001; Gray et al. 2002).
6. Public procurement and infrastructure—this includes criteria based on life-cycle costing and recyclability; areas where accountants can support an organisation to bid for and comply with specific procurement requirements.

These policy intervention examples cover both internal and external accounting information, within both financial and management accounting.

3.11 Organisational Level Requirements

Ideally, the spotlight should be focused on internal management accounting information systems—whereby policy and decision makers within the business are provided with useful financial information to aid decision-making. Accountants within individual organisations will be able to assist on a practical basis, providing meaningful information in order to accelerate the transition to a circular economy model. The accountant's role in this transition will be important at all levels of management, but particularly at the strategic level. Indeed management accountants are ideally positioned to ensure that these issues are raised at board level and the finance function should be able to provide information including both financial and non-financial indicators to assist in the decision-making process.

As a progression from sustainability and environmental accounting, for CE to be regarded as important at senior board level within an organisation, the trigger(s) will need to come from:

1. The board—perhaps from a personal interest about the CE model at board level, particularly by the CEO, to promote policy change within the organisation.
2. Stakeholder interest or pressure—for example, from shareholder groups, customer demand or competitor initiatives.
3. Supply chain shortages—the threat of shortages which could lead to loss of production and increases in material costs. This would be particularly important if there is a lack of substitute materials.
4. Government guidelines and/or legislation—the implementation of specific reporting requirements or taxation on waste may highlight that action is required.

There is a need for commitment at the most senior level within any organisation to encompass CE ideals into the business strategy, with emphasis on ensuring a goal-congruent organisation understanding and motivated by relevant key performance indicators (KPIs). Accountants within organisations should be involved in developing appropriate performance indicators and practical costing techniques to assist with focusing and measuring the success of internal process changes (Geng et al. 2012). By the very nature of operating variations throughout different industries and sectors, these would need to be suitable and flexible enough for individual business level adaptation. However, accountants do need clearer instruction and development on suitable techniques.

In order to address the current lack of CE micro-level guidance, the British Standards Institute (BSI) has published an advisory standard—BS8001:2017. This contains practical guidance for the implementation of CE principles at organisational level, regardless of the size or sector of a business. This is a necessary step to enable companies to take CE principles forward (BSI 2017). Close links are now required with the accounting professional bodies and practitioners to develop accounting methods and measurement tools that are relevant to CE business models (Pauliuk 2018). There is a danger that a proliferation of different indicators will be used to convey an organisation's CE credentials. Potentially this could lead to 'cherry-picking' indicators that show an organisation in the best light without truly fulfilling broader CE goals (Pauliuk 2018).

Emphasising the longer term strategic objectives of the organisation rather than short-term objectives is a perennial business issue. One area where much innovation is required relates to staff and director incentives and rewards. The short-termism within the linear business model and current rewards strategies within organisations is creating broad and complex issues. These range from lack of goal congruence and/or motivation all the way to fraudulent manipulation in order to meet performance targets. Appropriate non-financial KPIs and strategic goals related to sustainability, including circular economy buy-in, should be linked to the organisational rewards structure. Here again there is a requirement to ensure accurate and relevant measures and monitoring systems are designed and developed to encourage management and staff engagement and motivation, whilst avoiding any sub-optimal behaviour or unintended consequences from poorly designed measures and rewards systems.

3.12 CE and the Consumer

Passing on the full costs of a CE to the customer is a different matter. Without regulation, transition may be slow and depend more on customer understanding and competitor agreement. Often it is the pricing strategy—in particular low pricing—that motivates purchase. In Japan, a law passed in 2002 mandated that all purchasers of new motor vehicles are required to pay a recycling cost at point of sale. Dealers and service providers collect the vehicle and recycle accordingly. CE principles are also embedded within the Japanese culture and education system (World Economic Forum 2014). The Ellen MacArthur Foundation does envisage that government regulation will be required in order to encourage long-term systems thinking and underwriting some of the risks relating to new business models (Ellen MacArthur Foundation 2015a).

Leasing of products as an alternative to purchase (e.g. washing machines) will require correct financial treatment and accurate prudent profit measurement related to service or lease contracts and different, but potentially more profitable, business models. Issues around product pricing differentiation between new and reconditioned products, complicated pricing and control structures including service, return and reuse need to be considered. Using the washing machine to illustrate, the sales price under a linear manufacturing model would be set with reference to the cost of manufacture and competitor pricing. The cost of scrap value or disposal costs have little consideration. Moving to a CE model, the equipment would potentially be leased or based on pay-per-use. The machine would be taken back by the manufacturer and reconditioned and re-sold, leased or rented to consumers (Ellen MacArthur Foundation 2012). Consumer acceptance of reconditioned equipment and the concept of rental or leasing, rather than ownership, will require careful marketing, promotion and education in order to succeed.

3.13 CE and the Accountant

Product costing and revenue decisions, including warranty, servicing and financing costs leads to substantial complication relating to revenue recognition, inventory and leasing valuation and financing streams. Detailed guidance is required from the various accounting standard setting bodies. Advances in technology and the potential within blockchain technology (Andersen 2016; Ellen MacArthur Foundation 2016a) will need to be investigated: open source and collaborative platforms can assist in adoption and systems redesign.

An important aspect in profit forecasting is the security of materials supply. This risk could be reduced with more recycled inputs, however, the cost emphasis will move to higher labour and new business service costs and reduced material product cost elements. According to the Ellen MacArthur Foundation (2015a) using reverse-cycling, for example in mobile phone design, developing simpler methods of taking an old phone apart to harvest and reuse the materials within it, together with offering incentives for the end user to return redundant phones, should lead to substantially reduced costs of remanufacture.

This does not prevent individual organisations working on the building blocks required to move to more circular business models, with collaboration and project management across the business and supply chain generally. Cross-sector and cross-supply chain teams need to be committed to honest and transparent information gathering in order to define methods, statistics and incentives for all stakeholders. Team working and collaboration is key and accountants should take a lead in this respect. The accountant can be part of the broader conversation on defining measurement methods for environmental and social impacts not only within one organisation but in conjunction with suppliers and the entire value chain. The application of management accounting tools and techniques, such as scenario planning, full or material flow cost accounting, and life-cycle costing all help integrate sustainability matters into decision-making (CIMA 2013).

Within a circular economy environment there is an urgent requirement to provide information that is a reflection of 'real costs' (Webster 2015). Full-costing, including provision for natural capital such as land, water and energy is required. By including these 'real costs', even as a notional cost, within the management accounting information systems, organisations would be encouraged towards the transition to more circular methods.

Indeed, costing and pricing will require careful cost systems design to ensure reuse or remanufacturing, leasing and service costs are all correctly coded and applied in order to integrate with and develop the current management accounting information systems. Within management accounting, unique internal solutions will be required for each business. The underlying requirement will be to ensure the accuracy in collection and assurance of such data (CIMA 2013).

Consistent approaches to measurement and quantification of sustainability information for internal cost information, including the use of notional costs, are required. This will involve detailed data gathering, with clear analysis and measurement methods. The accounting function can also engage with impact assessment, using scenario planning and forecasting techniques. Internally, from a management accounting perspective, advancement in areas such as material flow accounting and analysis (Gray et al. 2002; Larrinaga-González et al. 2001; Bringezu et al. 2003; Bebbington et al. 2007) has provided enhancements to the data available to assess impact and aid decision-making.

Research and collaboration needs to continue in order to really get to grips with the substantial issues around moving away from linear business models, including accounting for natural capital and also the fiduciary duty of managers and shareholders (Ellen MacArthur Foundation 2015a). The finance industry should also work towards supporting and enabling companies to move towards CE. The challenge here is the lack of experience with such models. There will need to be changes in many aspects of traditional financing, for example, moves towards financing whole supply chains rather than individual companies, the perceived residual value of assets and the evaluation of risk (Ellen MacArthur Foundation 2016b).

3.14 Business Initiatives—An Example of CE in Practice

One example of a company that has changed its way of doing business in order to address these long-term challenges is Unilever, a global FMCG (fast-moving consumer goods) company with close ties to the Ellen MacArthur Foundation CE100 programme. This is an important collaborative platform building knowledge and opportunity with a growing number of like-minded organisations (Ellen MacArthur Foundation 2018).

Through their 'sustainable living' strategic aim Unilever are addressing a multitude of sustainability and ethical issues, including a focus on circular economy and piloting circular economy practices with the EMF and other FMCG organisations (Unilever 2018). The company has pledged to recycle 100% of plastics packaging produced by 2025. Development of staff includes training e-modules on the circular economy which aim to embed circular thinking throughout project development. It is interesting to note that there is a myriad of metrics used to monitor improvement in every aspect of their sustainable living report. These metrics are, however, independently assured by an external accounting firm. This is important as accuracy in reporting these non-financial measurements is necessary to ensure confidence from stakeholders. As part of management remuneration, Unilever also includes performance in the 'sustainable living plan' (USLP) by monitoring movement in a 'sustainability progress index' as an element in management and executive incentive schemes (Unilever 2017). As noted previously, in order to offer some assurance to stakeholders, Unilever have engaged an independent accounting firm to provide partial assurance on the sustainability metrics used. However, the point is made by the company that there are no industry standards or recognised practices for evaluating and measuring many performance indicators used (Unilever 2016).

3.15 Conclusion

Over recent years, the interest in the circular economy has grown, with greater recognition that the current linear model of production and consumption cannot support a growing population and increasing 'single-use' consumption in the face of rapidly depleting resources. The idea behind the circular economy is that nothing is wasted but becomes 'food' or input for another product or process indefinitely. Given this rising popularity, many organisations are adopting circular economy models. At a macro-level, there is also increasing acceptance of the need to approach the economic model differently.

As Webster (2013) cited from the words of Buckminster Fuller:

> You never change things by fighting against the existing reality. To change something, build a new model that makes the old model obsolete. (p. 544)

A completely different way of thinking and redesign of economic system is needed to realise the scope of circular economy to be able to fully benefit from the opportunities it may bring.

This chapter provides a broad overview of circular economy and its foundational characteristics and discusses its implications for accounting information. Multi-disciplinary collaboration at all levels—macro, meso and micro—and education are fundamental to success in this transition. Developments on practical standards and measurement tools relevant to CE principles are required to support transition. The accounting profession needs to ensure that they are an integral element, enablers rather than inhibitors, in progressing the move away from the linear and towards the circular economy.

References

Andersen, Nicolai. 2016. "Blockchain Technology a Game-Changer in Accounting?" https://www2.deloitte.com/content/dam/Deloitte/de/Documents/Innovation/Blockchain_Agame-changerinaccounting.pdf.

Bebbington, Jan, Judy Brown, and Bob Frame. 2007. "Accounting Technologies and Sustainability Assessment Models." *Ecological Economics* 61 (2–3): 224–236. https://doi.org/10.1016/j.ecolecon.2006.10.021.

Boulding, Kenneth E. 1966. "The Economics of the Coming Spaceship Earth." *Environmental Quality Issues in a Growing Economy*, 1–8. https://doi.org/10.4324/9781315064147.

Braungart, Michael, and William McDonough. 2002. *Cradle to Cradle*. New York: North Point Press.

Bringezu, Stefan, Helmut Schütz, and Stephan Moll. 2003. "Rationale for and Interpretation of Economy-Wide Materials Flow Analysis and Derived Indicators." *Journal of Industrial Ecology* 7 (2): 43–64. https://doi.org/10.1162/108819803322564343.

BSI. 2017. "Framework for Implementing the Principles of the Circular Economy in Organizations Guide." https://shop.bsigroup.com/ProductDetail/?pid=000000000030334443&_ga=2.49452838.1097910212.1496676287-782512447.1399452123.

CIMA. 2013. "Accounting for Natural Capital: The Elephant in the Boardroom." London. https://www.cimaglobal.com/Documents/Thought_leadership_docs/SustainabilityandClimateChange/CIMA-accounting-for-natural-capital.pdf.

Circle Economy. 2016. "About the Circular Economy." http://circle-economy.com/circular-economy/.

DEFRA. 2017. "Single-Use Plastic Carrier Bags Charge: Data in England for 2016 to 2017." https://www.gov.uk/government/publications/carrier-bag-charge-summary-of-data-in-england/single-use-plastic-carrier-bags-charge-data-in-england-for-2016-to-2017.

Ellen MacArthur Foundation. 2012. "In-Depth—Washing Machines." https://www.ellenmacarthurfoundation.org/circular-economy/interactive-diagram/in-depth-washing-machines.

Ellen MacArthur Foundation. 2015a. *Delivering the Circular Economy—A Toolkit for Policymakers*. Isle of Wight: Ellen MacArthur Foundation.

Ellen MacArthur Foundation. 2015b. *Growth Within: A Circular Economy Vision for a Competitive Europe*. Isle of Wight: Ellen MacArthur Foundation.

Ellen MacArthur Foundation. 2016a. *Intelligent Assets: Unlocking the Circular Economy Potential*. Isle of Wight: Ellen MacArthur Foundation.

Ellen MacArthur Foundation. 2016b. "Money Makes the World Go Round." The Netherlands. https://www.ellenmacarthurfoundation.org/assets/downloads/ce100/FinanCE.pdf.

Ellen MacArthur Foundation. 2018. "CE100—The Programme." https://www.ellenmacarthurfoundation.org/ce100/the-programme/enabling-collaboration.

European Commission. 2015. "Eco-Innovation in Poland." Eco-Innovation Observatory. https://ec.europa.eu/environment/ecoap/sites/ecoap_stay-connected/files/poland_eco-innovation_2015.pdf.

European Commission. 2017. "Report from the Commission to the European Parliament, the Council, the European Economic and Social Committee and the Committee of the Regions." Brussels. http://ec.europa.eu/environment/circular-economy/implementation_report.pdf.

Geng, Yong, and Brent Doberstein. 2008. "Developing the Circular Economy in China: Challenges and Opportunities for Achieving 'Leapfrog Development.'" *International Journal of Sustainable Development & World Ecology* 15 (3): 231–239. https://doi.org/10.3843/susdev.15.3:6.

Geng, Yong, Jia Fu, Joseph Sarkis, and Bing Xue. 2012. "Towards a National Circular Economy Indicator System in China: An Evaluation and Critical Analysis." *Journal of Cleaner Production* 23 (1): 216–224. https://doi.org/10.1016/j.jclepro.2011.07.005.

Ghisellini, Patrizia, Catia Cialani, and Sergio Ulgiati. 2016. "A Review on Circular Economy: The Expected Transition to a Balanced Interplay of Environmental and Economic Systems." *Journal of Cleaner Production* 114: 11–32. https://doi.org/10.1016/j.jclepro.2015.09.007.

Goldsby, Thomas, and Robert Martichenko. 2005. *Lean Six Sigma Logistics*. FL: J. Ross Publishing.

Gray, Rob. 2006. "Does Sustainability Reporting Improve Corporate Behaviour? Wrong Question? Right Time?" *Accounting and Business Research* 36: 65–88.

Gray, Rob, Richard Laughlin, Markus Milne, and David Owen. 2002. "Of Messiness, Systems and Sustainability: Towards a More Social and Environmental Finance and Accounting." *British Accounting Review* 34 (4): 357–386. https://doi.org/10.1006/s0890-8389(02)00105-1.

Gregson, Nicky, Mike Crang, Sara Fuller, Helen Holmes, Nicky Gregson, Mike Crang, Sara Fuller, et al. 2015. "Interrogating the Circular Economy: The Moral Economy of Resource Recovery in the EU." *Economy and Society* 44 (2): 218–243. https://doi.org/10.1080/03085147.2015.1013353.

Greyson, James. 2015. "A Glance at Waste-Free Economy." http://www.ecomena.org/tag/linear-economy/.

Hu, Jing, Zuobing Xiao, Rujun Zhou, Weijun Deng, Mingxi Wang, and Shuangshuang Ma. 2011. "Ecological Utilization of Leather Tannery Waste with Circular Economy Model." *Journal of Cleaner Production* 19 (2–3): 221–228. https://doi.org/10.1016/j.jclepro.2010.09.018.

Jowit, Juliette. 2008. "World Is Facing a Natural Resources Crisis Worse Than Financial Crunch." https://www.theguardian.com/environment/2008/oct/29/climatechange-endangeredhabitats.

Lacy, Peter, and Jakob Rutqvist. 2015. *Waste to Wealth*. Basingstoke, UK: Palgrave Macmillan.

Larrinaga González, Carlos, Francisco Carrasco Fenech, Francisco Javier Caro González, Carmen Correa Ruíz, and José María Páez. Sandubete. 2001. "The Role of Environmental Accounting in Organizational Change—An Exploration of Spanish Companies." *Accounting, Auditing & Accountability Journal* 14 (2): 213–239. https://doi.org/10.1108/09513570110389323.

Li, Nan, Tianzhu Zhang, and Sai Liang. 2013. "Reutilisation-Extended Material Flows and Circular Economy in China." *Waste Management* 33 (6): 1552–1560. https://doi.org/10.1016/j.wasman.2013.01.029.

Liker, Jeffrey. 2004. *The Toyota Way: Fourteen Management Principles from the World's Greatest Manufacturer.* New York, USA: McGraw-Hill.

McKinnon, Alan, Michael Browne, Maja Piecyk, and Anthony Whiteing (eds.). 2015. *Green Logistics*, 3rd ed. London: Kogan Page.

Ministry of Economy, Trade and Industry. 2004. *Handbook on Resource Recycling Legislation and Trends in 3R.* Tokyo: Recycling Promotion Divisions.

Murray, Alan, Keith Skene, and Kathryn Haynes. 2017. "The Circular Economy: An Interdisciplinary Exploration of the Concept and Application in a Global Context." *Journal of Business Ethics* 140: 369–380. https://doi.org/10.1007/s10551-015-2693-2.

Nadeem, Simon Peter, Jose Arturo Garza-Reyes, Anthony I. Anosike, and Vikas Kumar. 2017. "Spectrum of Circular Economy and Its Prospects in Logistics." In *Proceedings of the 2017 International Symposium on Industrial Engineering and Operations Management (IEOM)*, 440–451, Bristol, UK: IEEE.

Pauliuk, Stefan. 2018. "Critical Appraisal of the Circular Economy Standard BS 8001:2017 and a Dashboard of Quantitative System Indicators for Its Implementation in Organizations." *Resources, Conservation and Recycling* 129: 81–92. https://doi.org/10.1016/j.resconrec.2017.10.019.

Schulte, Uwe G. 2013. "New Business Models for a Radical Change in Resource Efficiency." *Environmental Innovation and Societal Transitions* 9: 43–47. https://doi.org/10.1016/j.eist.2013.09.006.

Singh, Jagdeep, and Isabel Ordoñez. 2016. "Resource Recovery from Post-Consumer Waste: Important Lessons for the Upcoming Circular Economy." *Journal of Cleaner Production* 134: 342–353. https://doi.org/10.1016/j.jclepro.2015.12.020.

Su, Biwei, Almas Heshmati, Yong Geng, and Xiaoman Yu. 2013. "A Review of the Circular Economy in China: Moving from Rhetoric to Implementation." *Journal of Cleaner Production* 42: 215–227. https://doi.org/10.1016/j.jclepro.2012.11.020.

The Danish Government. 2013. "Denmark Without Waste." Denmark. http://eng.mst.dk/media/mst/Attachments/Ressourcestrategi_UK_web.pdf.

UK Government. 2013. *The Waste Electrical and Electronic Equipment Regulations 2013.* London: Queen's Printer of Acts of Parliament. http://www.legislation.gov.uk/uksi/2013/3113/contents/made.

Unilever. 2016. "Independent Assurance." https://www.unilever.com/sustainable-living/our-approach-to-reporting/independent-assurance/.

Unilever. 2017. "Make Sustainable Living Commonplace." https://www.unilever.com/Images/unilever-annual-report-and-accounts-2017_tcm244-516456_en.pdf.

Unilever. 2018. "Lifecycle Assessments." https://www.unilever.com/sustainable-living/our-strategy/about-our-strategy/lifecycle-assessments/.

Velis, Costas A. 2015. "Circular Economy and Global Secondary Material Supply Chains." *Waste Management & Research* 33 (5): 389–391. https://doi.org/10.1177/0734242x15587641.

Webster, Ken. 2013. "What Might We Say About a Circular Economy? Some Temptations to Avoid If Possible." *World Futures* 69 (7–8): 542–554. https://doi.org/10.1080/02604027.2013.835977.

Webster, Ken. 2015. *The Circular Economy a Wealth of Flows.* Isle of Wight: Ellen MacArthur Foundation.

World Economic Forum. 2014. *Towards the Circular Economy: Accelerating the Scale-Up Across Global Supply Chains.* Geneva: World Economic Forum.

Zero Waste Scotland. 2016. "Zero Waste Scotland." http://www.zerowastescotland.org.uk/.

CHAPTER 4

Technology Challenges in Accounting and Finance

Liz Crookes and Elaine Conway

4.1 Introduction

The aim of this chapter is to introduce some of the many technological developments that are shaping the world of the accountant; Big Data, Cloud Computing, Artificial Intelligence (AI) and Blockchain. The focus of this chapter is to explain the effects of these emerging technologies on the role of the accountant from the standpoint of a management accountant working within a business or a financial accountant working either in practice or within a business.

In recent years, Big Data has transformed the business world and it has impacted both organisations and individuals. Huge datasets of structured, semi-structured and unstructured data gathered from sources such as the Internet, telecommunications and Global Positioning Systems (GPS) continue to grow second by second, creating a rich data source on virtually every aspect of life on the planet. This data is of immense value to businesses both for commercial reasons but also for developments within the worlds of medicine and science. It is vitally important that accountants understand the implications of this vast data in their own jobs and environment.

L. Crookes (✉) · E. Conway
Derby Business School, University of Derby, Derby, UK

E. Conway and D. Byrne (eds.), *Contemporary Issues in Accounting*,
https://doi.org/10.1007/978-3-319-91113-7_4

Linked to Big Data is the development of cloud computing, which allows businesses to pay for data storage and computer applications as they need them on the Internet, which has the potential to save considerable sums of money, but brings with it data security issues for accountants.

The chapter also discusses how AI is influencing business in its ability to carry out routine processes, but also to learn how to spot trends and interact with humans. Whilst still in its infancy, AI has the potential to transform many business processes, but we should be wary in relinquishing total control to machines until some of the broader implications of this technology have been adequately assessed.

Finally, this chapter provides an introduction to another potentially hugely disruptive technology, that of the blockchain. It discusses the principles behind blockchain and how it is already supporting the world's largest cryptocurrency, Bitcoin, but also how the technology itself is likely to transform the accounting and finance discipline in the future.

The chapter provides suggestions to (future) accountants on issues they may need to consider in their personal development and training in order to be equipped to leverage the benefits and challenges that these new technologies will bring.

4.2 Big Data

4.2.1 What Is "Big Data"?

The term Big Data emerged at the turn of the new century. As the name implies, it is a very large collection of records, some of which are unstructured such as images and which are too large to process using basic database management tools.

> Big data refers to the explosion in the quantity (and sometimes quality) of available and potentially relevant data. In this new and exciting world, sample sizes are no longer fruitfully measured in "number of observations" but rather in, say, megabytes. (Diebold 2003, p. 116)

Over the course of the twenty-first Century, there have been many advances in computer technology. Computer system hardware and bespoke software packages have become affordable to the smallest of companies. As more businesses have adopted computer systems, there has been a surge in the volume of data being recorded digitally. A simple example of this in the retail environment is Electronic Point of Sale Terminals (EPOST) and the more advanced Electronic Funds Transfer Point of Sale (EFTPOS) Terminals which record details about consumer purchases and behaviour from scanning barcodes of purchases and the checkout, and which are expected to increase in significant numbers in the next few years (Acute Market Research 2017). Additionally, cheaper digital storage developed in recent years has meant that more data can be stored (Russom 2011), whilst advances in software meant that this data could be retrieved and sorted with relative ease with the use of spreadsheets or database tools. Analysing data has become relatively quick and easy, particularly compared with manual record-keeping, however, it is often challenging to manage the sheer volume of data and gain any meaningful insights (Sundaresan 2008). This proliferation of data from retail terminals, Internet, mobile phone and social media activity, radio frequency identification (RFID) tags, business data feeds and GPS to name just a few data sources, has created huge datasets which are referred to generically as "big data", because of their size, which is often measurable in terabytes, or increasingly, petabytes or exabytes of data (Marr 2016).

By its very nature, accounting is "concerned with collecting, analysing and communicating financial data" (Atrill and McLaney 2017, p. 1). Arguably, it is the original Big Data in any organisation. Historically, the financial accounting records were kept manually. For a large organisation, this could mean rooms of people writing in ledgers. Extracting the details to construct a set of financial statements was a time-consuming task. Over the past 40 years, the process of recording records for financial accounting has been transformed by the use of computers. The collection and storage of records have become digitised. Double entry bookkeeping records are automatically generated. Software will produce an income statement and statement of financial position on demand.

Hence the role of the accountant is changing. There will always be a need for financial accountants to ensure companies comply with legislation and accounting standards to assure users of financial statements about the underlying performance of the business. Large organisations will still need financial accountants working internally to decide how best to account for different transactions and to continue to interact with other parts of the business. For the financial accountant working in practice, the nature of their work has changed as the nature of the economy has changed. Hence, the financial accountant has less work to do in terms of gathering the financial data when computer systems, such as Sage, Quickbooks and Xero are used by so many businesses. However, they now need to be able to handle much larger quantities of data and spot issues and trends in that data.

In a similar way to the changes to financial accounting, the function of the management accountant is changing. As reports become automated, the role is to provide better support for decision-making and performance management. The production of standard reports (such as end-of-month financials, variance analysis, Key Performance Indicators (KPIs) and regulatory filings) is becoming ever more automated. At the same time, due to the competitive environment, demand is growing for management accountants to provide ongoing "insight", not from financial data on its own but in combination with non-financial data as well, both internal and external to the business and sometimes including Big Data (Simons et al. 2013).

4.2.2 *Where Does Big Data Come from?*

Data collection and storage has been increasing exponentially over recent years. "According to IBM, companies have captured more data in the last two years than in the previous 2000 years" (Syed et al. 2013, p. 2248) and this trend has continued. Data is collected from virtually every transaction undertaken, sometimes without any human interaction at all. This can come from:

- activity data, such as reading eBooks or making a purchase on a credit card;
- conversation data, such as phone calls, Facebook and Twitter conversations;
- photo and video image data, such as the thousands of photos and videos uploaded from cameras, phone and even CCTV daily;
- sensor data, such a GPS sensor tracking movements; and
- Internet of things (IOT) data which comes from smart TVs, fridges, watches and alarms (Marr 2016).

Data collection in business is often used for marketing purposes (Michael and Miller 2013). The EPOST system introduced above can be extended with a customer loyalty card. For example, the Tesco Clubcard records personal information from the moment a customer provides personal details on registration and it is continually added to through data gathered on the card about where you shop, when you shop, items that you buy, the method of payment and more. This allows for targeted marketing to be carried out (Atkins et al. 2016). Equally, data is being constantly collected about you, your location and your preferences on the Internet through shopping websites (e.g., Amazon) or search engines (such as Google) whether through your computer or phone, even when you may not be aware of it (Collins 2017). Again, this information can be used to target you for particular products or services or to provide a rich dataset about consumer habits and preferences.

These purchasing activities can be linked through the supply chain, to pull inventory through the system once supplies are low or orders have been placed as part of a Just In Time (JIT) inventory management system. This can often be supported by other tracking devices or sensors, such as RFID tags which, together with GPS can monitor the movement of inventory throughout the supply chain, enabling it to be sent wherever it is needed (Want 2006).

4.2.3 *Making Sense of Big Data*

In order to make sense of Big Data, various authors have defined terms which explain its dimensions. Whilst there are various interpretations of them, the most commonly used are the 'V's: Volume, Velocity, Variety, Veracity and Value (Laney 2001; Shafer 2017; Marr 2016), which we will now explain in a little more detail.

4.2.3.1 Volume

In the early 2000s, Diebold (2003) discussed measuring data in megabytes. Megabytes or MB are 1024 KB which are 1024 bytes; a byte is 8 bits of data in binary code. A character is a byte. A kilobyte is a long paragraph. A megabyte might be about 4 books (plain text). A gigabyte or GB is 1024 megabytes. A GB could be about 4000 books and terabytes are 1024 GB. The list of terms continues to grow (such as petabytes and exabytes), like the data it describes. To put this into context, in the year 2000, the 3.5-inch floppy disk which held up to 1.44 MB of data was being phased out by rewritable CD holding 650 MB. The modern USB flash drive can hold from 1 GB to 128 GB and beyond. A 2 terabyte version is now available and Google routinely provides its users with 15 GB of free cloud storage. It was estimated in 2012 that about 2.5 exabytes of data were being created daily, and that figure doubles approximately every 40 months (McAfee and Brynjolfsson 2012).

For the accountant, this means that there is a huge amount of data available to work with. In terms of financial accounting, this data needs to be sorted into the financial transactions that are required to construct the published accounts. Arguably one set of accounts is not big data. But the accounts of all UK companies would be. For the management accountant, there are endless possibilities to use vast datasets (both internal and external to the company) to inform management and aid in decision-making.

4.2.3.2 Velocity

This is the rate at which data is generated on a continuous basis and processed in "real time" (Laney 2001). From a financial accounting perspective, this ability to process data in real time makes the production of the published accounts much faster. For the management accountant the month end process can be completed quickly, allowing better business decisions to be made. For example, if the report is produced two or more weeks after the month end and there are problems these can be up to six weeks old which can be detrimental to business performance. Identifying a problem sooner rather than later can make a difference to a business. This affects all areas of the company, not just accounting.

4.2.3.3 Variety

Data comes in many forms and from a range of sources. As mentioned earlier, data can be structured or unstructured. For example, a database is usually structured but the content of an email is often unstructured. Estimates from Cisco and IBM suggest that 90% of all data is unstructured (Cisco 2014). As more data is collected from different sources, the variety of data increases (Marr 2016). The problem then becomes extracting and making sense of the relevant data from these different sources (Marr 2016; McAfee and Brynjolfsson 2012). In many cases, humans are actually better at this than computers. For example, if a company receives two different invoices from two suppliers, a human will easily recognise the key features where a computer will still occasionally make a mistake, for example, not being able to identify the company name from a logo or reading a phone number as an invoice number. Conversely, computers are much better at sifting through data and searching for items if it is in a particular format: however, Big Data does not eliminate the need for vision or human insight (McAfee and Brynjolfsson 2012).

For the financial accountant, data has always arrived in different forms. A shoebox of receipts, a spreadsheet of clients, a box of invoices. For the financial accountant in practice, the client will usually have collated the data beforehand, either manually through inputs in a spreadsheet or by using software which can link to bank accounts to instantly summarise the cash position of the business. For the management accountant, the variety of data poses a challenge in terms of the extraction of relevant information. Receiving data from multiple sources means time must be taken to collate the data and present it in a manageable format. This is made more challenging as management accountants also typically deal with non-financial data as well as financial data.

4.2.3.4 Veracity

This relates to how “messy” or trustworthy data is, given the multiplicity of sources from which it comes and the forms it takes (Marr 2016). All data must be reliable, particularly, if it is being used to make decisions. As data collection becomes more autonomous, it could be argued that the human error element is being removed. However, where data comes in a variety of formats, collating the data into an understandable format adds a step which can reduce the reliability. Both humans and computers can (inadvertently) introduce errors, for example, voice recognition software which incorrectly interprets a speech pattern or accent.

For the financial accountant, data must be accurate and be reflective of the true performance of the company; the audit process (by having an independent review of the underlying figures and assumptions behind the financial statements) does add to the validity of the financial accounts, although even this is not infallible. For the management accountant, the quality of business decisions taken depends upon the validity of the data which underpins those decisions.

4.2.3.5 Value

Now that it is relatively inexpensive and straightforward to collect data, the challenge lies in analysing, spotting trends and interpreting the data to make sense and value from it. The sheer volume of data that has already been collected is staggering and very little of it is either being analysed at all or is not being analysed in ways which would allow companies to gain valuable insights from it (Sundaresan 2008; Jagadish et al. 2014). However, the ability of firms to exploit business information and analytics is now perceived to be a key differentiator in a competitive world, such that those who are skilled at it have used it to transform their businesses (Jagadish et al. 2014).

Whilst the datasets that the average financial accountant will be using will be small, the management accountant may well be tasked with looking at much larger datasets to spot trends, identify opportunities and support strategic decisions; this will require substantial data analytic knowledge and the support of additional data analysis tools beyond basic spreadsheets. It can also require a substantial change in mindset in firms to move from human experience to data-driven analytics to make decisions (Sundaresan 2008; Jagadish et al. 2014).

To elicit value from Big Data, firms need to invest into specialist data analytical tools, because they are designed to cope with the volume and variety of data which is now available, both in terms of storing the data but also in decoding it and manipulating it. There are various names of packages to support this such as Hadoop, HBase and Hive (Sagiroglu and Sinanc 2013). These packages carry out complicated searches of the data using such techniques such as text analytics (for standard, structured data), face recognition (for image and identifying people), sentiment analysis (using keywords used in social media messages to ascertain people's attitudes to certain things), and voice analytics (again to determine attitudes as well as content) of voice messages (Marr 2016). This can be used to predict new trends, highlighting products that could sell well in the future. However, it is important to remember that this knowledge can only be of use if there is a clear link between the opportunities which Big Data provides and the strategy of the firm (Jagadish et al. 2014).

4.2.4 The Application of Big Data

Apart from the marketing purposes and logistics purposes discussed above, Big Data can be used in medical disciplines by understanding disease and symptoms patterns (Michael and Miller 2013), including any links between lifestyles and health (Jagadish et al. 2014) or in the security services to track patterns of behaviour relating to terrorist activities (Marr 2016). It can be used to track traffic patterns in cities to ease traffic flow and design new public transport services around key areas of congestion (Marr 2016; Jagadish et al. 2014). Other uses include environmental modelling and even astronomy (Jagadish et al. 2014).

4.2.4.1 Big Data in Accounting

Accounting itself is the collection of data and the process of transforming that data into useful information. For the Financial Accountant, this is the production of the financial statements. For the Management Accountant, this is the production of monthly reports or financial information for projects. Although much of this will not change with Big Data, management accountants, in particular, will need to become more able to work with larger datasets with potentially new analytical tools than they do currently. This should complement the skills that most accountants have, to be enquiring and not afraid to challenge the sources of data and the analyses that have been carried out on it, to ensure that decisions based on it are reliable (McAfee and Brynjolfsson 2012). This does not mean that they will need to become data programmers themselves, but to have enough knowledge to be able to act as a bridge between the technical team and the rest of the business. As Simons, Masamvu and Parks (2013, p. 3) stated:

> To truly unlock the opportunities in big data, management accountants will need to partner more closely with three sets of key stakeholders: their colleagues in IT who capture much of the data; the data scientists who can perform advanced types of analysis on that data; and finally business leaders who can ensure new ideas are turned into concrete action. This requires financial professionals to have a broader range of management skills: clear communication, the ability to lead and influence, and a strategic understanding of the business – all of which are essential for the business partnering role that many firms want finance to play.

Big Data is already having and will continue to have an impact on business, leading to more accurate insights into the business environment and the changes happening within it. It will allow for better planning and forecasting, the identification of the root causes of costs in businesses, it can help detecting fraud and identifying risks and opportunities (Russom 2011), all activities in which accountants will need to be involved (Simons et al. 2013).

4.3 Cloud Computing

4.3.1 What Is "Cloud Computing"?

Linked to Big Data is the development of cloud computing. Cloud computing is simply a system of storing data and accessing processing applications on-demand through the Internet (the word "cloud" referring to the Internet [Bhardwaj et al. 2010]) rather than using the limited memory capacity of one's own device or network (Zhang et al. 2010). As defined by the US National Institute of Standards and Technology (2017):

> Cloud computing is a model for enabling convenient, on-demand network access to a shared pool of configurable computing resources (e.g., networks, servers, storage, applications, and services) that can be rapidly provisioned and released with minimal management effort or service provider interaction.

As the amount of data captured and stored has increased exponentially over recent years (see section on Big Data above), there is an increasing demand for more storage. Any single computer or network has a limited capacity of memory for storage, so rather than having to invest in large storage systems (Armbrust et al. 2010), end users can lease what space and applications they require as their needs change and then retrieve data and services when needed over the Internet.

There are generally two service providers in cloud computing, the infrastructure providers who manage the cloud platforms (often referred to as "Infrastructure as a Service" (IaaS) [Bhardwaj et al. 2010]) and lease space to service providers. This service includes management of computing power and memory and data storage in data centres. The service providers in turn lease the services required to end users (e.g., businesses or individuals) (often called "Software as a Service" [SaaS]) (Zhang et al. 2010; Bhardwaj et al. 2010). Examples of this include business applications and web services, such as Google Apps and Facebook. In between these two levels is a third-level called "Platform as a Service" (PaaS) (Armbrust et al. 2010; Bhardwaj et al. 2010) which provides operating system support and software frameworks needed by developers to develop applications based on technology such as .Net and Java, to provide services like Microsoft Azure or Google AppEngine (Liu et al. 2016). From an infrastructure point of view, the benefits of cloud computing are lower operating costs since resources can be quickly reallocated to manage demand and it is highly scalable as infrastructure providers can pool resources easily (Zhang et al. 2010; Armbrust et al. 2010). For businesses, applications and data can be easily accessed on a wide variety of devices such as phones and tablets anywhere, rather than just through a networked office-based computer (Bhardwaj et al. 2010). This reduces business risk since the risks of hardware failures are passed to the infrastructure providers who may have better skills to manage them and from a service point of view, the cost of updates, maintenance and staff training are reduced as a result of the sharing of these costs across many end users (Zhang et al. 2010).

From an accountant's and a business' point of view, cloud computing is undoubtedly a useful way in which to manage Information Technology (IT) resources as firms pay for the services as they use them, rather than in a single investment and they can store as much data as they need (Bhardwaj et al. 2010). It can also be a source of competitive advantage by collaborating with other firms across supply chains (Liu et al. 2016). However, the biggest concern around cloud computing is that of data security. As potentially all of a company's data could be held physically distant from the company in large data centres, businesses are dependent on the infrastructure provider to ensure data and access is both fully secure and auditable. These infrastructure providers must produce evidence that data is held confidentially (usually through some form of cryptography), and that there are robust safeguards around data access and transfer. Equally, they must be able to demonstrate that any security settings have not been altered without sufficient authorisation.

For accountants, as firms become more reliant on cloud-based IT with their business-critical data held in third-party (cloud) depositories, data security, business continuity and service availability are areas of crucial concern (Armbrust et al. 2010). To date, cloud services have been very robust and highly available (Armbrust et al. 2010), although this will need to be continually monitored as firms seek to ensure that business risks are appropriately managed.

In terms of data storage, new legislation (such as the General Data Protection Regulation (GDPR) in Europe [EU Parliament 2016]) keeps evolving to manage the rights of individuals whose data is kept in corporate databases. This legislation restricts the transfer of data across international boundaries and puts in place rules about the kind of data which may be kept, how long for and for what purposes. This clearly affects where firms (in particular, multinational corporations) may keep their data centres. Since the fines associated with breaches in these data protection regulations are becoming increasingly onerous, it is vital that accountants are aware of the impacts of distributed or cloud-based IT on corporate costs and risks.

4.4 Artificial Intelligence

AI is defined as "computational systems that attempt to mimic aspects of human intelligence" (Seshia et al. 2016), in other words, it is the idea of a machine or computer having human-like intelligence in order to learn, problem solve or take decisions.

The concept has been around since the 1950s (Kiruthika and Khaddaj 2017), first appearing in novels and movies and now becoming a real part of our lives, although perhaps not in the way the movies portrayed. It is embedded within self-driving cars, digital personal assistants such as Cortana and an AI computer has even won a game show (Jeopardy!) (Hawking et al. 2014). AI has the capacity to outsmart financial markets and produce new inventions, and ultimately may be of substantial benefit to humankind if it is able to cure diseases or solve social problems, but it needs appropriate controls to ensure that ultimately poor decisions are avoided (Hawking et al. 2014; Russell et al. 2015). Although AI is already capable of allowing machines to take decisions, this raises the ethical question: to what extent should humans allow them to do so without human intervention? This is particularly of concern in applications such as autonomous weapons systems which could select targets and engage with them without any human intervention and which to date, have been condemned by the UN (Russell et al. 2015).

Developments in AI currently are focused on building systems that are capable of thinking as well as, if not better than, humans, including both intelligence and reasoning (Kiruthika and Khaddaj 2017). This is done by building algorithms to "teach" computers to learn using a system of training, historic and live data. Any patterns which are learned by the computer are stored and when similar situations arise again, the computer uses its knowledge of the previous pattern to make the appropriate decision (Kiruthika and Khaddaj 2017).

There are three types of AI: process automation, cognitive insight and cognitive engagement, which will now be discussed. The main potential benefit of AI in the business world and the one most likely to impact on accountants is process automation (also known as robotic process automation), such as invoice processing (Castelluccio 2017), updating changes of address records, replacing lost credit cards and "reading" legal documents (Davenport et al. 2017). AI can also be used to detect patterns in vast quantities of data (such as Big Data) by the use of computer algorithms—this is cognitive insight AI (Davenport et al. 2017). This could assist in the prediction of customer demand for products, targeted marketing, the identification of fraud, analysis of warranty data and other similar processes where trends could be found. The final kind of AI, cognitive engagement, is where computers are able to engage with humans, such as employees or customers using natural human language, such as on chatbots. Clearly, this has the potential appeal for firms to have customer service, employee support programmes or health advice services available 24/7, but the technology is still not reliable enough to be extensively deployed at the current time, although doubtless, this is an area of significant future growth (Davenport et al. 2017).

Despite the hype around AI, few businesses outside of the technology sector currently use it significantly, although that number is increasing as the technology is developing (Bughin et al. 2017). Very large technology firms are clearly engaging in it since it will provide a competitive advantage for them: Internet search engines Google and Baidu both spend billions of dollars on research and development into AI (Castelluccio 2017). One example of an AI-enabled business application is behavioural analysis of potential customers when being asked to evaluate a new product. AI, together with other forms of technology, such as virtual reality, can elicit feedback from clients and their interaction with a potential new product and then use this to improve the product or to improve training or instructions for its use (Kiruthika and Khaddaj 2017). This has the potential to avoid wasting money on taking poorly designed products to market. It is also likely to improve sales and profit margins (Bughin et al. 2017). AI has also been used by a cancer centre in the US to recommend hotels for patient's families, identify which patients might need help paying their bills and solving other IT problems (Davenport et al. 2017). Whilst this may not seem revolutionary, it has improved the quality of life for many patients and is a tangible benefit of the technology. It may be initially the more repetitive and incremental applications of AI which will yield the initial impacts on business, but is likely in the long run to be a very disruptive but beneficial technology if the ethics of control are developed as well as the technology itself.

4.5 Blockchain

Blockchain is potentially a fundamental game changer in many spheres of digital life in the future. In the same way that electricity enabled telecommunications across the globe (McPhee and Ljutic 2017), blockchain has the potential to transform the way of doing business and interacting with other people globally in the future.

The most well-known use of blockchain technology currently is as the technology underpinning cryptocurrencies, which are currencies which operate online, without physical presence and without the support of any one nation or institution (like a bank). Bitcoin was the first of such currencies, launched in 2009 by an unidentified person or group of people under the name of Satoshi Nakamoto (2008) and it allows payments to be made globally using the virtual currency, where transactions are recorded on a decentralised public register. It is currently the largest public blockchain in commercial use (Swan 2015). By using blockchain, it is possible to move money across the world almost instantly and at low cost without the need to pay fees to a bank or wait for their internal processes to move the money around, which can often take days (Swan 2017).

4.5.1 What Is Blockchain?

Essentially, a blockchain is a network software protocol, which is a set of rules and conventions which allow network devices (e.g., computers) to communicate with each other (ICAEW 2017). A protocol specifies how devices are recognised and connected to the network and how data is formatted, packaged and sent between network devices. When data is packaged and sent over the network, it includes a small header and footer at the beginning and end of the data package to identify the sender and intended recipient of the data package. What differs with blockchain compared with other protocols is that these headers and footers are converted into cryptographic signatures or "hashes" which makes the likelihood of anyone tampering with the data virtually impossible.

Cryptography is a method of converting, storing or transmitting plain text in a form so that only those for whom it is intended are able to read it (Stinson 2006). As such it prevents data from being altered or stolen and aims to maintain confidentiality whilst authenticating permitted users. There are various techniques employed in cryptography, such as symmetric key (where the sender and recipient possess the same key to both encrypt and decrypt the message before and after transmission of the plaintext), public key (where the public key is widely distributed and is used to encrypt, but the private key used to decrypt is held secretly) and cryptographic hashing (where a fixed length hash value (a random collection of symbols) is embedded within the plain text) (Stinson 2006).

Transactions on a blockchain (e.g., a series of financial payments) are comprised of a series (or chain) of blocks of data and information which are linked to each other by these cryptographic "signatures" or hashes which link the last block with the next one. Each block is date and time stamped and blocks are added chronologically to the chain (Swan 2017). This updating is done by the devices attached to the blockchain, called "nodes" or "data miners". A data miner takes the hash from the last block in the chain and the new transactions which need to be added to the chain. The data miner then "hashes" this to match with the previous block once the transaction is authenticated and the new block (to record a new transaction) is added to the chain (Swan 2017). As transactions (or blocks) happen through the course of time and are added to the blockchain, then it grows in one direction. Once added the block is irrevocable. If a change needs to be recorded (e.g., the ownership of an asset needs updating), then a new block must be added to the chain (McPhee and Ljutic 2017). This creates an everlasting ledger of all transactions, which makes it eminently suitable to financial accounting records and the possibility of perpetual audit (Peze 2017).

Any authorised device granted access to the blockchain receives a copy of the entire blockchain, from the first initial block (called the genesis block) to the latest block to be added, hence why blockchain is also referred to as a "distributed" ledger technology: any changes made to the blockchain must be agreed by all participants who are allowed access to the chain and all transactions are visible to all (Swan 2015, 2017). All participants in the blockchain receive a copy of the whole blockchain and this is what makes it inherently different to other technologies—all transactions are seen and verified by all and no one person or organisation keeps a central copy—copies are updated and distributed approximately every ten minutes (depending on the kind and complexity of transactions in the blockchain).

By having this decentralised "peer-to-peer" approach reduces the need for the "middle man" such as brokers and potentially even governments (Wright and De Filippi 2015). Until blockchain technology emerged individual transactions over the Internet needed to be validated by a central authority, but that is no longer the case.

This distribution of data also effectively eliminates the need for a central repository of data (e.g., a bank (Swan 2015, 2017)) which can reduce cost and improve security as it is impossible for a hacker to gain access to and change the data from a single point of access (and failure) (McPhee and Ljutic 2017). This can facilitate the transfer of assets and information securely and more quickly than is currently the case when having to rely on the action of an intermediary such as a bank to validate the transaction and store records (Swan 2015, 2017).

4.5.2 *What Are the Potential Benefits of Blockchain?*

Technologies based on the blockchain are likely to drive efficiency and improvements in service delivery in both the public and private sector, due to their ability to verify and authenticate transactions and identities, leading to enhanced trust between service user and service provider (Wolfond 2017). The capability to verify genuine users and prevent fraud is a key strength in blockchain technology and it should lead to easier-to-use experiences for the user interacting with the service and reduce transaction costs for the provider.

One of the biggest advantages of blockchain technology is its security. Because of the cryptographic hashing used and the fact that there is no single-point-of-failure in the chain as everyone has a copy of the blockchain, then it is inherently more secure against hackers. In recent years, hackers have managed to infiltrate various financial institutions and companies which hold all their data in centralised databases, stealing passwords and confidential information about users (Swan 2017). This undermines public trust in such institutions and in their ability to maintain effective confidentiality. By replacing this "trust" with cryptography, blockchain is virtually impossible to tamper with.

Increased digitalisation of transactions and access to services such as banking, government and healthcare services has created increasing needs to verify users' identities and allow them access into a network, whilst keeping out "undesirables" such as hackers or persons seeking to commit fraud (Wolfond 2017). To enable more organisations to respond to consumers' desires to provide more digitally accessed services, it is necessary to ensure that digital identity can be robustly verified without the traditional reliance on paper-based documents such as passports or birth certificates or relying on users to remember multiple user names and passwords for every service they wish to access. These traditional systems are expensive to maintain and are relatively easy to abuse by creating forged documentation or data mining.

Currently, many service providers use identity management systems run through a centralised broker architecture to verify and authenticate the identity of a user. However, this relies on a single point of trust which is quite a weak system from a security standpoint as it can fail and can be tracked (and hence tampered with) quite easily (Wolfond 2017). Instead, having the ability to verify a user's identity through a decentralised blockchain-based model omits the need for a single intermediary and can allow for users' identities to be cryptographically protected to a much higher level than standard passwords and Personal Identification Numbers (PINs) do currently.

The potential cost savings associated with more secure, single-point user authentication alone are substantial. Martin (2016, cited in Wolfond 2017) estimated that it cost \$31 (Canadian dollars) to manage lost, forgotten or stolen passwords per transaction. Wolfond (2017) extrapolated that cost, assuming one lost, forgotten or stolen password incident per working Canadian per year, could result in a saving of \$572 million (Canadian dollars) annually. Clearly, this money could be spent elsewhere providing greater value and reducing the need for offices and staffing in all aspects of identity verification and authentication, again saving significant sums of money annually for many businesses.

For the user, a decentralised blockchain network will allow him/her to access services much more quickly, however, this will rely on the network and collaboration across multiple actors in the system to work. If organisations work together to agree how user identity can be verified, then it is a "win–win" for both the organisations providing the service and users who want the convenience to access services at minimal cost and effort to them. It would not be in an organisation's best interests to devise their own unique ways of verifying users since that would require users to use multiple access models, which they do currently and which can be a source of considerable frustration to users (Wolfond 2017). It is far more efficient for all organisations to agree user authentication collaboratively, through an "ecosystem for digital identity" to provide a better user service.

Another interesting potential with blockchain will be the ability to pre-program transactions to "self-execute" in accordance with an agreed contract, called smart contracts (Swan 2017). Whilst there are numerous examples of automated transactions currently in use such as direct debits and standing orders, blockchain smart contracts could have the rules and code written into them at the point of writing the contract, reducing the need for future interventions and reducing counterparty risk (ICAEW 2017).

4.5.3 *What Are the Potential Challenges to the Development of Blockchain?*

Despite the clear benefits of blockchain, there are still a number of barriers to be overcome before it becomes widely adopted beyond the current niche of cryptocurrencies. The underlying transaction processing of blockchain for the cryptocurrencies is for data miners (who validate and post transactions) to be rewarded with a fee (usually new bitcoins), so there would need to be agreement on the reward for data miners to validate many more transactions than are currently undertaken (ICAEW 2017).

A substantial growth in blockchain transactions would also cause issues for the timing and computing capacity of any network. It requires substantial computing power to validate and verify transactions using blockchain technology (ICAEW 2017). Currently, only approximately seven small transactions or three average-sized transactions can be carried out per second: Visa in comparison, carry out tens of thousands of banking transactions per second (ICAEW 2017).

Another concern is the potential need to encrypt data where the contents of the blockchain are confidential, since all participants in the blockchain have access to everything, which for some applications may not be appropriate. Equally, there is an issue of agreeing protocols between companies who may be competitors sharing a blockchain (ICAEW 2017).

For these reasons, it is unlikely that blockchain will have a sudden impact on the accounting profession; it is likely to be more of a gradual development over the next five years, once these issues are increasingly solved.

4.5.4 *Implications of Blockchain for Accountants*

The most significant effect of blockchain for accounting will be to eliminate the very basic data inputting and transaction processing work associated with bookkeeping. With smart contracts able to execute transactions embedded in the blockchain, the financial ledgers will require very little day-to-day interaction (Peze 2017). It will also mean that auditors will have access to the whole transaction records and the likelihood of errors and misclassifications should fall (LaFollette quoted in Hood 2018), reducing the need for complicated sampling, testing and verifying.

Hence, accountants and auditors (both internal and external) alike need to be well trained on the technology in order to be able to deliver value to their organisations and to continue to improve the operations of the organisation (Rooney et al. 2017). Currently, auditors' first point of departure in an internal audit is to review the ledger as maintained by the organisation and verify the transactions within it, including reconciling balances with external parties, such as customers, suppliers and banks. However, with blockchain technology, if there is one single record held and agreed already between the organisation and its partners, then there is no requirement to do this. This means that what internal auditors will need to do instead is ensure that the governance of the blockchains to which the organisation has access (and there could be several since it could interact with government and a myriad of other organisations) comply with the appropriate governance requirements of their own organisation—this will require collaborative working with auditors in these other organisations (Rooney et al. 2017). Equally, accountants and internal auditors will need to consider the implications of real-time data—since blockchains will simultaneously update once new transactions are entered into them and distributed—potentially eliminating the need for laborious month or year-end closure practices.

These changes will require auditors to have a good understanding of blockchain technology to be able to continue to provide assurance and value to their organisations (Hood 2018; ICAEW 2017). They should be involved in the creation of the blockchains within their organisation to ensure the governance, controls and risk management considerations are adequately addressed (Rooney et al. 2017). They should also leverage their knowledge of their organisation to consider the optimal benefits from adopting the technology, such as checking the validity of smart contracts at initial inception (Hood 2018).

Whilst audit will not disappear, it will need a new approach. For external auditors, this may mean more checking on the security of authentication keys and the more aggressive pursuit of fraud (Hood 2018), but it will also mean that they will need to add value to clients based on more of an advisory role than currently (Asgeirsson quoted in Hood 2017) and acting as a bridge between data technology specialists setting up the blockchains and the business world (ICAEW 2017).

Despite the fact that it may be some time before blockchain totally revolutionises accountancy and finance, it is undoubtedly a disruptive technology which has the power to change the practices and skillsets of future accountants. It is also quite high on the agenda of current professionals in the finance world. Wesley Bricker, the Chief Accountant of the Securities and Exchange Committee stated:

> it is important that those in the accounting profession invest the time to understand new trends and developments in technology and commerce to identify their potential effects on financial reporting to investors. (Bricker as reported in Cohn 2017)

4.6 Conclusion: Accounting and Technology

Technology has changed our lives and mostly for the better. It continues to develop at an ever-increasing pace. As we have discussed in this chapter, this has brought us unprecedented levels of data which requires making sense of, issues of storage and completely new ways of working. This will impact many jobs in the future, not least that of accountants—therefore it is imperative that accountants build on their analytical skills and inquiring nature to challenge and help develop the application of the technology to the business world in a sensible and ethical way. It will necessitate additional technical skills, but also communication and collaborative working on the part of the accountant to build and maintain bridges between the technology and data specialists on the one hand and the business world on the other.

References

Acute Market Research. 2017. "Global Electronic Funds Transfer Point of Sale (EFTPOS) Terminals Market Size, Market Share, Application Analysis, Regional Outlook, Growth Trends, Key Players, Competitive Strategies and Forecasts, 2017 to 2025." *Acute Market Reports.* http://www.acutemarketreports.com/report/electronic-funds-transfer-point-of-sale.

Armbrust, Michael, Ion Stoica, Matei Zaharia, Armando Fox, Rean Griffith, Anthony D. Joseph, Randy Katz, et al. 2010. "A View of Cloud Computing." *Communications of the ACM* 53 (4): 50. https://doi.org/10.1145/1721654.1721672.

Atkins, Kelly Green, Archana Kumar, and Youn Kyung Kim. 2016. "Smart Grocery Shopper Segments." *Journal of International Consumer Marketing* 28 (1): 42–53. https://doi.org/10.1080/08961530.2015.1082080.

Atrill, Pete, and Eddie McLaney. 2017. *Accounting & Finance for Non Specialists*, 10th ed. Harlow: Pearson.

Bhardwaj, Sushil, Leena Jain, and Sandeep Jain. 2010. "Cloud Computing: A Study of Infrastructure as a Service (IaaS)." *International Journal of Engineering* 2 (1): 60–63. http://ijeit.org/index_files/vol2no1/CLOUDCOMPUTINGASTUDYOF.pdf.

Bughin, Jacques, Brian McCarthy, and Michael Chui. 2017. "A Survey of 3,000 Executives Reveals How Businesses Succeed with AI," 2–7.

Castelluccio, Michael. 2017. "Artificial Intelligence in Business." *Technology Workbook* 98 (10): 55–57.

Cisco. 2014. *Big Data: Not Just Big, But Different*, vol. 2. https://www.cisco.com/c/dam/en_us/about/ciscoitatwork/enterprise-networks/docs/i-bd-04212014-not-just-big-different.pdf.

Cohn, M. 2017. "SEC Looks at Blockchain Technology for Accountants and Eyes Initial Coin Offerings." *Accounting Today*. https://www.accountingtoday.com/news/sec-looks-at-blockchain-technology-for-accountants-and-eyes-initial-coin-offerings.

Collins, Keith. 2017. "Google Collects Android Users' Locations Even When Location Services Are Disabled." *Quartz*.

Davenport, Thomas H., Rajeev Ronanki, Images by, James Wheaton, and Andrew Nguyen. 2017. "Artificial Intelligence for the Real World." *Harvard Business Review* (February): 108–117. https://doi.org/10.1016/S0016-3287(03)00029-6.

Diebold, Francis X. 2003. "'Big Data' Dynamic Factor Models for Macroeconomic Measuring and Forecasting." *Advances in Economics and Econometrics, Eighth World Congress of the Econometric Society*, 115–122. https://doi.org/10.1.1.12.1638.

EU Parliament. 2016. "General Data Protection Regulation (GDPR)." https://www.eugdpr.org/.

Hawking, Stephen, Max Tegmark, and Frank Wilczek. 2014. "Stephen Hawking: 'Transcendence Looks at the Implications of Artificial Intelligence—But Are We Taking AI Seriously Enough?'" *The Independent*. http://www.independent.co.uk/news/science/stephen-hawking-transcendence-looks-at-the-implications-of-artificial-intelligence-but-are-we-taking-9313474.html.

Hood, D. 2017. "Asgeirsson: See the Opportunity in Technology." *Accounting Today*. https://www.accountingtoday.com/news/asgeirsson-accountants-must-see-the-opportunity-in-technology.

Hood, D. 2018. "Brace Yourself for AI and Blockchain." *Accounting Today*. https://www.accountingtoday.com/news/accountants-need-to-brace-themselves-for-ai-and-blockchain.

ICAEW. 2017. "Blockchain and the Future of Accountancy." ICAEW. https://www.icaew.com/en/technical/information-technology/technology/blockchain/blockchain-and-the-accounting-perspective.

Jagadish, H.V., Johannes Gehrke, Alexandros Labrinidis, Yannis Papakonstantinou, Jignesh M. Patel, Raghu Ramakrishnan, and Cyrus Shahabi. 2014. "Big Data and Its Technical Challenges." *Association for Computing Machinery. Communications of the ACM* 57 (7): 86. https://doi.org/10.1145/2611567.

Kiruthika, Jay, and Souheil Khaddaj. 2017. "Impact and Challenges of Using of Virtual Reality & Artificial Intelligence in Businesses." *2017 16th International Symposium on Distributed Computing and Applications to Business, Engineering and Science (DCABES)*, 165–168. https://doi.org/10.1109/DCABES.2017.43.

Laney, Doug. 2001. "META Delta." *Application Delivery Strategies* 949 (February): 4. https://doi.org/10.1016/j.infsof.2008.09.005.

Liu, Sen, Yang Yang, and Yuan Liu Qu. 2016. "The Business Value of Cloud Computing: The Partnering Agility Perspective." *Industrial Management & Data Systems* 116 (6): 1160–1177. https://doi.org/10.1108/02635570710734262.

Marr, Bernard. 2016. *Big Data in Practice*, 1st ed. Chichester, UK: Wiley (The Audible book I listened to was this book on paper).

McAfee, Andrew, and Erik Brynjolfsson. 2012. "Big Data: The Management Revolution." *Harvard Business Review* (October): 1–9. https://doi.org/00475394.

McPhee, Chris, and Anton Ljutic. 2017. "Editorial: Blockchain." *Technology Innovation Management Review* 7 (10): 3–5.

Michael, Katina, and Keith W. Miller. 2013. "Big Data: New Opportunities and New Challenges." *Computer* 46 (6): 22–24. https://doi.org/10.1109/MC.2013.196.

Nakamoto, Satoshi. 2008. "Bitcoin: A Peer-to-Peer Electronic Cash System." www.bitcoin.org, 9. https://doi.org/10.1007/s10838-008-9062-0.

NIST. 2017. "Definition of Cloud Computing." National Institute of Standards and Technology, USA. https://csrc.nist.gov/Projects/Cloud-Computing.

Peze, J. 2017. "The Impact of Blockchain for Accountants." *Accounting Web*. https://www.accountingweb.co.uk/community/blogs/jerome-peze/the-impact-of-blockchain-for-accountants.

Rooney, Hugh, Brian Aiken, and Megan Rooney. 2017. "Is Internal Audit Ready for Blockchain?" *Technology Innovation Management Review* 7 (10): 41–44.

Russell, Stuart, Sabine Hauert, Russ Altman, and Manuela Veloso. 2015. "Take a Stand on AI Weapons." *Nature* 521 (7553): 415–418. https://doi.org/10.1038/521415a.

Russom, Philip. 2011. "Big Data Analytics." *TDWI Best Practices Report, Fourth Quarter* 19 (4): 1–34.

Sagiroglu, Seref, and Duygu Sinanc. 2013. "Big Data: A Review." *2013 International Conference on Collaboration Technologies and Systems (CTS)* (May): 42–47. https://doi.org/10.1109/CTS.2013.6567202.

Seshia, Sanjit A., Dorsa Sadigh, and S. Shankar Sastry. 2016. "Towards Verified Artificial Intelligence," 1–13. http://arxiv.org/abs/1606.08514.

Shafer, Tom. 2017. "The 42 V's of Big Data and Data Science." *Elder Research*. https://www.elderresearch.com/company/blog/author/tom-shafer.

Simons, Peter, Tarisai Masamvu, and Paul Parks. 2013. "From Insight to Impact - Unlocking Opportunities in Big Data." *CGMA*, 1–28. https://www.cgma.org/content/dam/cgma/resources/reports/downloadabledocuments/from-insight-to-impact-unlocking-the-opportunities-in-big-data.pdf.

Stinson, Douglas R. 2006. *Cryptography: Theory and Practice*, 3rd ed. Boca Raton: CRC Press.

Sundaresan, Venkat. 2008. "Bridging the Last Mile in Data Analytics." *ECN Electronic Component News* 52 (7): 37.

Swan, Melanie. 2015. *Blueprint for a New Economy*. Sebastopol: O'Reilly Media. https://doi.org/10.1017/CBO9781107415324.004.

Swan, Melanie. 2017. "Anticipating the Economic Benefits of Blockchain." *Technology Innovation Management Review* 7 (10): 6–11.

Syed, Abdul Raheem, Kumar Gillela, and C. Venugopal. 2013. "The Future Revolution on Big Data." *International Journal of Advanced Research in Computer and Communication Engineering* 2 (6): 2446–2451.

Want, R. 2006. "An Introduction to RFID Technology." *IEEE Pervasive Computing* 5 (1): 25–33.

Wolfond, Greg. 2017. "A Blockchain Ecosystem for Digital Identity: Improving Service Delivery in Canada's Public and Private Sectors." *Technology Innovation Management Review* 7 (10): 35–40.

Wright, Aaron, and Primavera De Filippi. 2015. "Decentralized Blockchain Technology and the Rise of Lex Cryptographia." *SSRN Electronic Journal*. https://doi.org/10.2139/ssrn.2580664.

Zhang, Qi, Lu Cheng, and Raouf Boutaba. 2010. "Cloud Computing: State-of-the-Art and Research Challenges." *Journal of Internet Services and Applications* 1 (1): 7–18. https://doi.org/10.1007/s13174-010-0007-6.

CHAPTER 5

The Contemporary Corporate Tax Strategy Environment

Juliet Hogsden

5.1 Introduction

Corporation tax is a material cost for companies, making corporate tax planning a crucial activity (Hardeck and Hertl 2014; Kubick et al. 2015). Traditionally the objective of companies' corporate tax strategy (CTS) was to minimise the tax cost, as part of the directors' fiduciary duty to their investors to maximise shareholder post tax profits (Wahab and Holland 2012). With this objective as the sole focus, the corporate tax function operated in isolation; it had little regard for the impact on other stakeholders. By reducing their tax burden, corporations (i) deprive governments of vital tax receipts, essential to funding key public services and (ii) potentially transfer the tax burden onto other tax payers such as small and medium sized enterprises (SMEs) and individuals. The traditional corporate tax reporting environment permitted such corporate tax behaviour to go unnoticed. Significant changes, however, in the contemporary tax environment mean that companies' CTS now need to embrace more than just good cost management of their corporation tax liability.

J. Hogsden (✉)
Derby Business School, University of Derby, Derby, UK

E. Conway and D. Byrne (eds.), *Contemporary Issues in Accounting*,
https://doi.org/10.1007/978-3-319-91113-7_5

Two other essential factors that this chapter will explore are the ethical stance of the CTS and the management of the increasingly stringent compliance and disclosure requirements of the tax regimes in which companies operate. With respect to the first factor, globalisation has increased the range of tax planning opportunities for companies that operate internationally. There are, however, large overseas operators which have made aggressive use of the tax planning opportunities presented. This has led to a very animated debate about whether companies pay their fair share of tax leading to intense public scrutiny of the ethical stance of companies' CTS. There is a great risk of damage to a company's legitimacy, reputation, brand relations and brand equity should the public perceive a company's CTS to be immoral. As for the stringent compliance and disclosure requirements, it is essential that companies proactively manage this aspect. There is a high risk of punitive penalties and sanctions where a company fails to comply with the compliance or disclosure regulations of the various tax regimes in which it operates.

Consequently, the CTS of corporations now must look beyond just efficient cost management of their corporation tax liability. They need to consider the ethics of the CTS and what measures to adopt to reduce the risk of failure and the associated consequences of not fulfilling the compliance requirements.

5.2 The Cost Component

The corporation tax cost to a company is based on its taxable profits, as calculated in accordance with the regulations of the tax regime where the value has been created and taxed at the prevailing corporation tax rate. It is potentially a significant cost for a company, reducing shareholder wealth (Hardeck and Hertl 2014; Kubick et al. 2015). It is the fiduciary duty of directors to maximise shareholder wealth, by managing their business costs; this includes the management of the corporation tax liability. As such it is appropriate that companies adopt tax planning activities to manage this cost efficiently. Not only is it a fiduciary duty for directors in some countries to promote the success of the company, but it can also be a legal duty; for example in the UK, under section 172 of the Companies Act 2006 "A director of a company must act in a way he considers, in good faith, would be the most likely to promote the success of the company for the benefit of its members as a whole" (Scott Slorach and Ellis 2017, p. 72).

Traditionally tax planning focused on the timing of revenues and expenses, and by companies making use of the tax reliefs and incentives available. This landscape began to change as companies started to expand their operations overseas. The internationalisation of business brought a proliferation of cross border transactions, an increase in capital and labour mobility, the growth of intellectual property and the associated royalties, as well as the rise of internationally active businesses, especially Multinational Enterprises (MNEs). As a result corporations are now able to operate in numerous tax jurisdictions all with different tax rules and regulations, all proactively competing for the foreign direct investment (FDI) these organisations bring. This has provided a wealth of new opportunities for corporate tax planning.

One such opportunity is exploiting the differences in international corporation tax rates. For example the lowest tax rate of Organisation of Economic Cooperation and Development (OECD) members as at April 2017 was levied by Switzerland, 8.5% in contrast the highest corporation tax rate levied was 35% by the United States (OECD 2017). Such differences have led to corporations, especially MNEs, establishing their taxable presence in locations with low or minimal tax rates, such as tax havens thereby "...significantly minimising their total tax payments" (Kyj and Romeo 2015, p. 298). According to these authors almost 15% of the world tax regimes are tax havens, providing many opportunities for companies to structure their operations so that taxable income is taxed in tax havens at much lower rates.

Another popular tax planning device is transfer pricing. Transfer pricing enables corporations to benefit from the different corporation tax rates across the world (Hardeck and Hertl 2014). Whilst it is based on commercial accounting practices, it has become a popular technique whereby group companies divert taxable profits to related companies located in lower tax jurisdictions (Kyj and Romeo 2015). An example of this tax planning device was used by Starbucks UK when they purchased the green coffee beans from a Swiss affiliate at much higher prices than normal commercial rates. Another example of transfer pricing is through the use of intra-group loans to subsidiaries. Finance costs for the borrower are often a tax allowable expense, although there may be criteria to be satisfied first. By ensuring that the lender is located in a lower tax rate jurisdiction, groups of companies can shift profits by charging interest rates above commercial arm length's rates. Starbucks is again an example of where this technique was used (Campbell and Helleloid 2016).

A third tax planning opportunity for companies, lies around the fact that many tax regimes have different definitions of corporation tax residency. This allows companies to generate income in a country without necessarily being classified as tax resident in that country and so the income escapes taxation. In the UK, companies that are either incorporated in the UK or centrally managed and controlled in the UK, are deemed to be UK resident for corporation tax purposes. In contrast the tax residency in Ireland is defined according to where the functional management of the company is, so companies can be incorporated in Ireland, but if their functional management is elsewhere the income arising in Ireland avoids taxation. In their study of Microsoft, Kyj and Romeo (2015) found that the company incorporated two interrelated subsidiaries in Ireland, but ensured the functional management and control of one of them was overseas in a tax haven. Known as the 'Double-Irish' it minimises the tax due by the companies involved in the arrangement; yet simultaneously the Irish subsidiaries provide the group with several commercial benefits, namely the free access Ireland gives to Euro-zone countries and access to a stable currency, the Euro, so there is less exposure to currency fluctuations. This technique has been used very effectively in reducing the corporation tax burden by software companies such as Microsoft Inc (Kyj and Romeo 2015). Kyj and Romeo (2015, p. 297) describe this technique as a "….method relies on Irish law, under which a company is taxed where it is functionally managed, but not necessarily where it is incorporated (territorial taxation). It requires two or more interrelated Irish companies to implement, with one of the companies in a tax-haven country such as Bermuda or the Cayman Islands." Lanis and Richardson (2015) identified that Apple Inc saved $US 2.4 billion of tax in 2011 using this residency device; in their research Payne and Raiborn (2018) found that Apple Inc generated $US 74 million between 2009 and 2012, but paid negligible tax on this income.

The rise of technology companies has generated another tax planning opportunity. Technology companies play a vital role in the economies of many countries, therefore numerous tax jurisdictions offer favourable tax incentives for research and development costs, such as the US and the UK. For technology companies, such as Microsoft Inc., innovation is vital to their long term survival, but the associated research and development expenditure is a significant part of their operating cost base.

According to Kyj and Romeo (2015) the research and development costs for Microsoft Inc. were 24% of total operating costs in 2009, reducing to 19% in 2014. In their analysis of the tax planning activities of Microsoft Inc., Kyj and Romeo (2015) found that the company's research and development activities predominantly occurred in the US, where the company benefits from the favourable tax treatment of these costs. The intellectual property rights to the resulting innovations were, however, distributed amongst the group's overseas companies, allowing Microsoft Inc. to keep the associate income to the intellectual property rights off-shore from the US and so avoid the higher US taxation rates (35%). A convoluted subsidiary structure meant most of the associated income was taxed in Bermuda, at significantly lower tax rates.

Microsoft is not the only group to manipulate intellectual property rights so that the associated royalty income is taxable in lower tax regimes whilst simultaneously tax relief for the associated costs is given in tax regimes with higher tax rates. Starbucks UK paid royalties to a Swiss affiliate for the use of the Starbucks brand and a range of business operations (Campbell and Helleloid 2016); the tax benefits of this arrangement are explained in more detail in the next section of this chapter.

These are just a few of the international tax planning opportunities presented to corporations. There are other opportunities such as the benefits of multilateral agreements (Klassen and LaPlante 2012), different definitions of various tax regimes of arms-length transfer prices, or individual tax jurisdictions offering favourable tax agreements such as Luxembourg and the Netherlands offered to Fiat and Starbucks respectively (Campbell and Helleloid 2016).

There are a vast array of tax planning opportunities available, to assist companies in efficiently and effectively managing their corporation tax costs, which are a material cost. However, the ability of large international companies, such as MNEs, to employ tax experts, has enabled them to 'cherry pick' from these tax planning opportunities, in a way Small and Medium Enterprises (SMEs), micro businesses and individuals cannot (Payne and Raiborn 2018). As Hardeck and Hertl (2014) point out this can lead to the burden of corporation tax shifting from the large international corporations to these other tax payers who do not have access to such tax planning opportunities. As people have become aware of such inequities there has been an increase in the scrutiny of the morality of the tax planning activities of corporations, especially international businesses such as MNEs. The bona fide use of the tax planning mechanisms as well as the tax reliefs and incentives available are considered to be morally acceptable. This is not so where a company's CTS involves aggressive tax planning; such CTSs are considered immoral, with stakeholders such as governments, consumers, public action groups, and the media, all willing to expose and tackle such unethical corporate behaviour. Consequently companies now need to consider not just managing their corporation tax cost but also the morality of the tax planning activities they adopt. As explored in the next section, companies who ignore the ethical component of their CTS risk adverse public reaction, negatively impacting their reputation, brand relations and brand equity.

5.3 The Ethical Component

There is no clear boundary between bona fide tax planning and aggressive tax planning. Neither are illegal. Both have the objective of reducing company's corporation tax liability, within the bounds of the relevant tax legislation (Datt 2014; Lavermicocca and Buchan 2015). Bona fide tax planning is morally acceptable for it merely seeks to release the benefit of the tax reliefs and incentives offered by the government under the tax legislation, in a way that is understood to be fair (Datt 2014). An underlying principle of UK tax legislation is that the "Taxpayers are entitled to organise their financial affairs in such a way so as their tax burden is minimised" (Melville 2018, p. 12).

In contrast, aggressive tax planning gives rise to tax avoidance, which is not illegal in itself, but in the words of Margaret Hodges, "immoral" (Datt 2014, p. 421). It involves the aggressive exploitation of loopholes in the tax legislation, as well as aggressive interpretation of the tax legislation. Tax avoidance has serious consequences for society. It erodes the tax base of governments thereby reducing their tax revenue, negatively impacting on public services provided (Lanis and Richardson 2015; Payne and Raiborn 2018). In addition, it transfers the burden of taxation from the tax avoiders to other tax payers such as SMEs, micro businesses and individuals who do not have access to the tax planning opportunities to which larger corporations have access (Hardeck and Hertl 2014).

The morality of the corporation tax strategies of corporations, especially large corporations, has come under increasing scrutiny by governments, the international community and the general public (Antonetti and Anesa 2017). These stakeholders expect corporations to be socially responsible, not to engage with tax avoidance, but to pay their fair share of tax (Lanis and Richardson 2015; Kanagaretnam et al. 2016). The revelations of the tax avoidance behaviour of such MNEs as Starbucks UK, Apple Inc., Google, and Amazon has given rise to a very emotive public debate as to whether corporations are paying their fair share of tax.

Yet what constitutes a 'fair share of tax' is a very hazy and subjective concept (Datt 2014). What is fair to one group of tax payers may not be fair on or to another group of taxpayers. For corporations the question is, 'is it fair for them to pay more tax than legally required just because of public sentiment?' For other taxpayers, the question remains, 'Is it fair that the tax burden gets shifted on them, because of unfair tax planning practices of some corporations?' It is a debate that is likely to run for years.

The numerous revelations about the aggressive tax planning behaviour of corporations, especially MNEs such as Amazon, Apple, Google, Microsoft, and Starbucks has put the CTS of many corporations under intense scrutiny by the international tax community, domestic tax authorities, and the general public (Kubick et al. 2015). Both the international tax community, through such bodies as the OECD, and domestic tax authorities have been proactively developing a wide range of measures to tackle tax avoidance, for many years. These include the Base Erosion and Profit Shifting (BEPS) programme by the OECD or the tax avoidance measures introduced in the UK such as Declaration of Tax Avoidance Schemes (DOTAS). Measures which some corporations (but not necessarily all) have been cooperating with, adapting their CTS over time.

Meanwhile the general public has also added its voice to the debate. Investigative journalism, public pressure groups, and consumers have each made it clear that they will not tolerate tax avoidance by companies. The case of Starbucks UK in 2012 is a good example of the adverse public response to the tax avoidance behaviour of a company.

Campbell and Helleloid (2016) record that by 2012, Starbucks UK had paid minimal UK corporation taxes since it began its operations in the UK in 1998, despite reporting large profits for its UK operations to its investors, as well as reporting billions of pounds of sales, and an 11% growth in revenue. In comparison, Dowling (2014) points out that Costa paid an effective UK tax rate of 30.5% for 2010–2011. The disparity between the high revenue receipts and the minimal corporation tax paid by Starbucks was reported by Reuters in late 2012 and investigated by a UK Parliamentary Investigative Committee.

According to Campbell and Helleloid (2016) this tax situation arose due to a combination of three tax planning mechanisms; (i) the use of intergroup royalty payments, (ii) the purchase of coffee beans from a Swiss affiliate at unusually high prices, and (iii) through intracompany financing arrangements. Firstly Starbucks made intragroup royalty payments so that it could use such intellectual property as the Starbucks brand and a range of business operations; this expense was tax deductible in calculating UK taxable income. These royalties were paid to various overseas affiliated companies diverting the associated taxable profits to tax regimes that had lower tax rates. This reduced the effective tax rate of the UK operations to less than 5% (Campbell and Helleloid 2016), at a time when the UK tax rate ranged between 31% in 1998 (HMRC 2009), reducing to 24% in 2012 (HMRC 2012, p. 16). The second method, transfer pricing, saw the purchase of its green coffee beans from an affiliated trading company whose legal address was in Switzerland. The green beans were purchased at unusually high prices, thereby significantly reducing the company's UK taxable income. The corresponding income of the Swiss affiliate was only taxed at 5%. The tax advantages gained were further enhanced by the fact that the green beans were then roasted in Netherlands by another Starbucks entity. The cost of the roasted beans to Starbucks UK was a major cost component to Starbucks UK products sold, reducing its taxable income, but the corresponding income of the Dutch affiliate was taxed at a lower rate because the Starbucks group had negotiated a preferential tax treatment with the Dutch tax authorities.

The third tax planning mechanism that the group aggressively deployed was the use of intercompany loans to Starbucks UK, where the interest rate charged on these loans being substantially higher than corporate bond rate. Again the interest payments were an allowable expense against the taxable income of Starbucks UK. This meant that in 2012, when the relevant UK corporation tax rate was 24%, Starbucks paid £1 million more interest than if it had paid at the corporate bond rate, saving UK tax of £240,000 (Campbell and Helleloid 2016). The combination of these three tax planning devices enabled Starbucks to generate a loss for UK corporation tax purposes and so Starbucks UK paid negligible UK corporation tax.

Once this knowledge was in the public domain, activists descended on UK outlets of Starbucks. Initially the company tried to defend this CTS, explaining it paid millions of pounds in other UK taxes such as NIC, as well as contributing to the economy by creating thousands of new jobs, and through the supply chain relationships, economic activities which themselves contributed to UK tax revenues. This did not appease the public feelings. In the end the company paid £20 million in voluntary tax repayments spread over 2013 and 2014 (Lavermicocca and Buchan 2015; Campbell and Helleloid 2016; Austen and Wilson 2017). Yet even this did not pacify the public outrage, seeing this tax sweetener as an unacceptable charitable donation. In a public statement on 8 December 2012 the organisation UK Uncut denounced the voluntary tax repayments, stating, “Offering to pay some tax if and when it suits you does not stop you being a tax dodger” (Campbell and Helleloid 2016, p. 48). The whole situation was further exacerbated by the fact that the Starbucks CTS strategy was not congruent with the rest of its Corporate Social Responsibility (CSR) strategy issued in 2001.

This aggressive CTS posed a serious threat to the viability of the company’s UK operations. In the fiscal year 2013 Starbucks experienced its first ever decline in sales (Campbell and Helleloid 2016). In order to restore and protect its reputation the company moved its regional head-quarters from Amsterdam to London, knowing that this would increase the UK company’s tax cost overall. In 2015 Starbucks UK reported a pre-tax profit of £34 million and paid taxes of just over £8 million (Campbell and Helleloid 2016).

The experience of Starbucks UK is a salutary lesson of the intolerance of tax avoidance practices both tax authorities and the public and the increasing scrutiny of these stakeholders (Antonetti and Anesa 2017). Lanis and Richardson (2015) and Kanagaretnam et al. (2016) all found that stakeholders, particularly governments and the public, are increasingly expecting corporations to be socially responsible corporate citizens, not engage with tax avoidance, but to pay their fair share of tax.

To continue devising CTSs that deploy aggressive tax planning techniques is likely to put the company’s legitimacy, reputation, brand relations and brand reputation at risk (Hardeck and Hertl 2014; Antonetti and Anesa 2017; Lavermicocca and Buchan 2015; Payne and Raiborn 2018; Austen and Wilson 2017). It is likely to lead to customer boycotts, as experienced by Starbucks UK in 2012. Research by Payne and Raiborn (2018) found that about one-third of British consumers were willing to boycott companies they perceive as not paying their fair share of tax and that 66% of Britons believe tax avoidance is morally wrong, with 57% believing it should be made illegal. Yet companies need to be aware that consumer behaviour is potentially asymmetric. Antonetti and Anesa (2017) found that whilst consumers are willing to boycott corporations who operate CTS they perceive to be immoral, they were much less willing to reward companies by paying a price premium because that company practices acceptable tax planning.

A further risk of aggressive tax planning, as Kubick et al. (2015) point out, is that it is likely to undermine the public trust in companies, exposing them to accusations of greed and dishonesty. The trust of stakeholders is an essential component of the relationship between a company and its stakeholders, as well as being vital to the company growth, but has been damaged in recent years, partly due to the 2007 financial crisis and partly due to the aggressive tax behaviour of companies (PwC 2013; Kubick et al. 2015).

The general public (particularly consumers, the media and public action groups) potentially have a powerful voice. In their report PwC (2013) noted that 97% of CEOs surveyed believed customers and clients are the most influential stakeholder. In their paper, Lavermicocca and Buchan (2015) identified that 40% of CEOs agreed that the media influenced the company's strategy and 12% acknowledged this influence was significant. In the same paper 76% of the CFOs surveyed were of the opinion that the media's focus on companies' CTS was detrimental to the company's reputation. In particular investigative journalism, together with the work of public action groups (such as The Tax Justice Network, Occupy Movement, Uncut UK, Uncut US, Action Aid), play a key role in identifying and exposing corporations who are considered to have not paid their fair share of tax or have been perceived to have practised aggressive tax planning (Datt 2014; Hardeck and Hertl 2014; Lavermicocca and Buchan 2015; Kanagaretnam et al. 2016). As Starbucks UK experienced in 2012, this voice can be immensely powerful.

When managing these risks to reputation, brand relations and brand equity companies need to be highly mindful of the risks posed by social media. As PwC (2013) and Eckert (2017) point out social media can see the rapid dissemination of negative information about a company on an extensive scale; the risk is further aggravated by the fact that social media messages tend be very succinct, blunt even brutal in their form and the information is readily available, often in great detail. This acute risk is difficult for companies to manage and the damage can be extensive (PwC 2013).

One of the by-products of all these risks is that investors, are now also becoming increasingly concerned about unethical corporate tax behaviour. Wahab and Holland (2012), building on the research of Desai and Dharmapala (2009) and Wilson (2009) (as cited in Wahab and Holland (2012)), concluded that UK shareholders no longer value tax planning. This is due to the information asymmetry between directors and shareholders in respect of tax planning, giving rise to either a moral hazard or a fear of a moral hazard. There is a risk, therefore, that tax planning is likely to reduce shareholder value. Wahab and Holland (2012), found that in UK corporates, good corporate governance procedures did not moderate this outcome (unlike Desai and Dharmapala (2009) and Wilson (2009), as cited in Wahab and Holland (2012), who found that in US corporations good corporate governance reduced shareholder concern and the risk to equity value).

The risks that all this poses to a company's reputation, brand relations and brand equity are risks that companies ignore at their peril; they need to be embraced as an essential part of their CTS. One approach advocated by Lanis and Richardson (2015) and Antonetti and Anesa (2017) is to adopt a more conservative CTS that is perceived to be fair and ethical, particularly if it is included in the company's CSR policy. For the public such an approach demonstrates the company is socially responsible and a good corporate citizen. Lanis and Richardson (2015), in their research of US listed companies, found that companies with a higher CSR were associated with a lower level of tax avoidance and so receive more public support. Research by Hardeck and Hertl (2014) similarly found that consumers with high tax morals are more likely to have a negative attitude towards a company they perceive to be operating an aggressive CTS, thereby undermining corporate success. Likewise Eckert (2017) found that new customers were more likely to form a relationship with companies perceived to have a positive CSR.

An alternative approach for UK companies is to seek to be accredited with the Fair Tax Mark (FTM). The objective of the FTM is to certify that the accredited company "…is paying the right amount of tax in the right place at the right time and applying the gold standard of tax transparency" (Fair Tax, n.d.-b). Founded in 2014 the FTM Ltd, as a not-for-profit organisation, was established to ensure a level playing field for firms to pay their fair share of tax and encourage businesses to show responsible tax leadership and improve transparency, ensuring taxable income is taxed in the place value is created, not shifted to lower tax regimes (Fair Tax, n.d.-a, b). The FTM is supported by the Tax Justice Network and assisted by the Ethical Consumer Research Association. It gives publicity to businesses operating a responsible and transparent CTS, providing a map so that consumers can easily locate them. It has helped build up trust between business accredited with a FTM, such that, for example: "64% of people trust a business with a Fair Tax Trade mark than one without it" and "77% of people would shop in favour of a company which can prove it is paying its fair share of tax" (Fair Tax Mark, n.d.-c). SSE was the first FTSE-listed business to achieve the FTM; other companies include Lush Cosmetics (UK's first high street retailer to achieve the Fair Trade Mark), the Co-Op group and now increasingly more.

Corporations now face increasing scrutiny of the ethical stance of their CTS by many stakeholders. Where such stakeholders perceive the company not to be paying their fair share of tax, the company risks significant damage to their legitimacy, reputation, brand relations and brand equity, as evidenced by the experience of Starbucks UK in 2012. The risk is heightened by such factors as the ready availability of information, and dissemination mechanisms such as social media. Such risks that cannot be ignored when devising a CTS. CTS can no longer just focus on managing their corporation tax cost, but need to embrace a more moral stance, that is transparent. The next section examinations the final aspect this chapter reviews, that is the management of compliance costs and risks that companies need to consider when adopting and operating a CTS.

5.4 The Compliance Component

The importance of taxation to governments cannot be underestimated. It is the biggest source of revenue for the government, the only practical means of raising the large amounts required to fund key public services and is a vital tool in managing their economy to ensure economic growth (Mirrlees et al. 2011; James and Nobes 2013; Datt 2014; Payne and Raiborn 2018; OECD 2017). Through the symbiotic relationship between taxation and the economy, governments can use their tax system to generate vital government revenue, promote research and innovation, productivity and inclusive growth. This is a challenging balance to achieve, especially post the 2008 financial crisis, as governments have tried to protect and nurture the fragile economic recovery, whilst simultaneously overcoming enormous fiscal debt and rebuilding their fiscal position.

In order to protect this source of revenue, tax jurisdictions, especially in advanced economies, operate a rigorous compliance environment. The purpose is not only to deter tax avoidance, but to ensure corporations make full and accurate declarations of their taxable income, as well as pay the associated corporation tax liability in full and on time. This is often enforced by stringent penalties and actions, alongside extensive investigative powers of the tax authorities.

To this end, individual tax jurisdictions and the international tax community have been developing tax systems that ensure corporations contribute fairly to the tax revenue of all the countries in which they operate and create value (Lavermicocca and Buchan 2015). This is principally achieved by establishing robust tax compliance environments, targeting harmful tax practices, tackling BEPS, and driving greater transparency and accountability. It is a challenging task for both the international tax community and for domestic tax jurisdictions, given the complexity of the business environment.

The OECD is the key agent working on behalf of the international community to tackle such issues as tax avoidance. The OECD has led the way in respect of international tax issues for over 50 years resulting in major advances in tackling tax avoidance, tax evasion and making the international tax system stronger and fairer (OECD 2017), successfully implementing a range of policies to improve tax disclosure, transparency and address tax avoidance. The OECD has developed standards for exchange of information between tax authorities, in particular the Common Reporting Standard (CRS). The CRS requires the automatic exchange of financial account information between tax authorities (AEOI) facilitated through a Common Transmission System; 98 members have committed to implementing the CRS in 2017 or 2018 (OECD 2017). Furthermore the OECD Global Forum on Transparency and Exchange of Information for Tax Purposes, which has 132 country members, is developing a tax transparency standard in respect of the Exchange of Information on Request (EOIR) (OECD 2017). Not only do these targeted measures on transparency tackle tax avoidance, but also encompass money laundering activities. In addition to the CRS, the AEOI and the EOIR, the OECD have pioneered other tax avoidance measures, including the BEPS project (Base Erosion and Profit Shifting) with over 100 jurisdictions involved; the OECD tax treaty model tax convention and tax inspectors without borders (OECD 2017).

Unilaterally, various tax jurisdictions have also been adopting a range of measures to achieve greater transparency and public accountability. In some instances these measures have been legislative such as in Australia and the UK. Australia have established the ASX Corporate Governance Principles which require companies listed on the Australian Stock Exchange, to act ethically and responsibly, including in respect of their CTS (Lavermicocca and Buchan 2015). The Australian Tax Office also requires mining companies with total income of $AU 100 million or more to publish a range of corporation tax information.

Another tax jurisdiction that has introduced accountability and transparency legislation is the UK. Under new measures introduced in the Finance Act 2016 Schedule 19 designated large businesses operating in the UK are required to publish their tax strategy in respect of their UK tax position and responsibilities. These designated businesses were qualifying UK companies, partnerships, qualifying UK groups, and qualifying UK sub-groups of foreign MNEs, which in the previous tax year had turnover that exceeded £200 million or the balance sheet exceeded £200 billion (Fair Tax 2017). It is aimed at increasing the transparency of the CTS of such companies, thereby discouraging aggressive tax behaviour. Designated businesses are responsible for the CTS, which must be published annually. Under the legislation designated businesses were required to publish their CTS, free of charge, on the internet before the end of the company's first financial year commencing after 15 September 2016. No publication will lead to penalties. The objective is to provide the general public with information, on a country-by-country basis, about the approach the company adopts in respect of the management of risk and governance of their UK tax position. In the published CTS the executive must disclose its attitude to tax planning and the level of risk the group is prepared to accept regarding their UK tax position. It must also detail the company's approach to their dealings with the Her Majesty's Revenue and Customs (HMRC).

At the time of writing it is difficult to evaluate the benefits of such legislation. Whilst aimed at improving transparency and accountability, there is no guarantee that legislation of this nature will provide sufficient assurance that the company is paying their fair share of tax. Furthermore there is a risk that the additional disclosures will be misunderstood by the public at large as the general public may not understand the legal and technical intricacies to properly evaluate the CTS information available. Certainly there is some evidence at the time of writing indicating poor compliance with Schedule 19. To date research published by Fair Tax Mark (2017) in October 2017 found that only 17 (34%) of the FTSE 50 companies had published their CTS online by 30 June 2017; the remaining two-thirds had failed to respond to the Schedule 19 requirements. Of the 17 that had published their CTS by 30 June 2017, 11 demonstrated basic compliance or less. Of the total FTSE 50 companies only 6 companies (12%) demonstrated compliance that was 'good' or better. On the face of this, this would appear to be a poor response to this mandatory legislation, but as yet companies may still be within the required timeline of publishing before the end of the company's first accounting period commencing after 15 September 2016.

There are other examples of tax disclosure requirements implemented by individual tax regimes, for example, the DOTAS regulations in the UK or the use by the tax authorities in New Zealand and Italy of questionnaires to target certain taxpayers in certain risk areas. Other countries have adopted advance rulings mechanisms, penalty linked disclosure rules (for example Ireland), co-operative compliance programmes (for example Australia, Ireland, The Netherlands, Italy, Spain, UK and the USA), or have additional reporting obligations (for example, The Netherlands, Italy, USA). Disclosure initiatives such as these promote greater compliance and create a more level playing field for all tax payers.

Such transparency and accountability legislation compounds the compliance risk to which corporations are now exposed. Many international tax regimes now have robust compliance regimes with stringent penalties and sanctions for non-compliance in respect of the accuracy, completeness and timeliness of the submission of tax returns and tax payments. Whether a company just operates in one tax jurisdiction, or several, they now operate in a complex international tax environment. They have a myriad of complex tax regulations to navigate across a range of different tax jurisdictions; the UK tax system alone contains over 8000 pages of tax legislation (Mirrlees et al. 2011). The corporate tax environment, especially for companies operating internationally, is a dynamic environment with tax regulations being constantly updated and revised in response to the constantly changing business environment and socio-economic and political influences. The risk of default, however unintentional and accidental, is now much higher, bringing unwelcome and costly penalties and sanctions. To avoid such punitive responses from the tax authorities, companies need to ensure their CTS secures the submission of tax returns and payments that are accurate, complete and timely in each and every tax jurisdiction they operate, as well as meeting all the requisite disclosure requirements. This requires a range of dedicated resources, including investment in the experience and training of high quality tax professionals, whether internally sourced or out sourced; tax professionals who are supported in keeping up to date with the frequent changes in tax legislation.

Another key investment is the need for reliable and rigorous accounting information systems and internal controls in place that enable them to effectively manage the compliance risks they face. Such systems and internal controls need to ensure that companies have calculated their tax position correctly; provide disclosure that is accurate, complete and timely, as well as provide assurance that tax payments are made properly and in a timely manner. Such systems and internal controls are essential to minimise the risk of non-compliance and need to be embraced as an essential part of contemporary CTS. This is especially true for those companies that operate in multiple jurisdictions, as the compliance regime in each one will have its own requirements. In addition, an inescapable aspect of tax compliance risk is ensuring access to professional tax advisors with the necessary expertise, whether that facility is in-house or out-sourced. It is a vital part of properly managing the tax compliance risk, escalating the dead weight of compliance costs.

Overall companies need to adopt a CTS that recognises and addresses the tax compliance risks to which corporations are exposed. This involves managing the compliance risks of correctly declaring their tax position in good time, and ensuring prompt and full payment of the associate tax liability in each tax jurisdiction, but it extends beyond this. Companies' CTS also need to recognise the need to co-operate with the transparency and accountability requirements of both individual tax jurisdictions and the international tax community, whether this is formal legislation, political enquiry or agreed international practice. These strands produce a complex tax compliance environment. It requires a robust response from corporations to efficiently and effectively manage the associated risks.

5.5 Conclusion

The traditional need of CTS to embrace efficient and effective tax planning still remains. The fiduciary duty of directors of maximising shareholder wealth remains a fundamental aspect (Datt 2014). It is now no longer, however, the only consideration. Now they must navigate through a much more complex corporation tax environment, particularly when they operate in more than one tax jurisdiction. Whilst globalisation has opened up a wealth of new tax planning opportunities, companies are now under immense pressure from the public and the government to deploy these opportunities in a fair manner that evidences they are paying their fair share of tax. These stakeholders now have a strong voice, requiring companies to be good corporate citizens and pay their fair of share of tax. Consumers, the media and public action groups are highly proactive in scrutinising the tax positions of companies. They are increasingly vocal if they suspect corporations have not been paying their fair share of tax, with a very powerful voice. If such stakeholders consider that the company have not paid their fair share of tax, then the company's legitimacy, reputation, brand relations and brand equity are at great risk. However, where corporations can demonstrate that their CTS is ethical and that they are good corporate citizens, then they reduce such risks. To that end companies that have highly acceptable CSR policies are often considered to be good corporate citizens.

A crucial element of managing this tax risk is controlling the information available. This is much easier said than done. Information about companies' tax position is much more readily available and disseminated. The media and public action groups are proactive in obtaining and publicising this information. Social media facilitates the instant, extensive and brutal dissemination of sensitive information that can be very damaging.

Another key element of CTS is the management of the tax compliance risk. The complexity of tax compliance legislation domestically and internationally makes this very challenging. It requires access to relevant, up-to-date expertise, plus the investment in appropriate accounting information systems with strong internal controls to minimise such risks. The risks surrounding tax compliance are not just restricted to timely disclosure and submission of accurate and complete information of the company's tax position and effecting prompt payments of the correct amount of tax. It must also recognise the risk of non-compliance with a wide range of disclosure and accountability measures adopted by both domestic tax regimes and the international community. Failure to fulfil the compliance requirements, however inadvertent, exposes the company to costly sanctions and penalties.

Today's contemporary reporting environment is much more exacting and unforgiving of companies and their CTS. To ignore the resultant tax risks would be folly indeed. Today the fiduciary duty of directors can no longer solely focus on reducing the corporation tax cost, in order to maximise shareholder wealth. Today there are other threats to shareholder equity, namely more stringent compliance regimes, greater intolerance by both tax authorities and the public of tax aggressive behaviour. To manage such threats, directors need to adopt a more proactive approach in devising an appropriate CTS, ensuring their corporate governance policy embraces such a need.

References

Antonetti, Paol, and Mattia Anesa. 2017. "Consumer Reactions to Corporate Tax Strategies: The Role of Political Ideology." *Journal of Business Research* 74: 1–10.

Austen, Chelsea Rae, and Ryan J. Wilson. 2017. "An Examination of Reputational Costs and Tax Avoidance: Evidence From Firms with Valuable Consumer Brands." *The Journal of the American Taxation Association* 39 (1): 67–93.

Campbell, Katherine, and Duane Helleloid. 2016. "Starbucks: Social Responsibility and Tax Avoidance." *Journal of Accounting Education* 37: 38–60.

Datt, Kalmen Hyman. 2014. "Paying a Fair Share of Tax and Aggressive Tax Planning—A Tale of Two Myths." *eJournal of Tax Research* 12 (2): 410–432. https://www.business.unsw.edu.au/research-site/publications-site/ejournaloftaxresearch-site/Documents/06_Datt_PayingFairShareOfTax.pdf. Accessed 9 Sept 2017.

Dowling, Graham R. 2014. "The Curious Case of Corporate Tax Avoidance: Is It Socially Responsible?" *Journal of Business Ethics* 124 (1): 173–184.

Eckert, Christian. 2017. "Corporate Reputation and Reputation Risk: Definition and Measurement From a (Risk) Management Perspective." *The Journal of Risk Finance* 18 (2): 125–158.

Fair Tax. 2017. *Tax Strategy Report Amongst the FTSE50—Slow to Emerge, Poorly Executed, but Some Examples of Excellence.* https://fairtaxmark.net/wp-content/uploads/2017/10/Tax-Strategy-Reporting-among-FTSE-50-FINAL.pdf. Accessed 24 Jan 2018.

Fair Tax. n.d.-a. https://fairtaxmark.net/who-we-are/team/. Accessed 24 Jan 2018.

Fair Tax. n.d.-b. https://fairtaxmark.net/getting-the-mark/. Accessed 24 Jan 2018.

Fair Tax. n.d.-c. https://fairtaxmark.net/supporters/. Accessed 24 Jan 2018.

Hardeck, Inga, and Rebecca Hertl. 2014. "Consumer Reactions to Corporate Tax Strategies: Effects on Corporate Reputation and Purchasing Behaviour." *Journal of Business Ethics* 123 (2): 309–326.

HMRC. 2009. *National Archives, A.6 Corporation Tax Rates.* http://webarchive.nationalarchives.gov.uk/20091102164614/, http://www.hmrc.gov.uk/rates/archive.htm. Accessed 5 Mar 2018.

HMRC. 2012. *Corporation Tax Statistics.* http://webarchive.nationalarchives.gov.uk/20121102170846/, http://www.hmrc.gov.uk/stats/corporate_tax/corporation-tax-statistics.pdf. Accessed 5 Mar 2018.

James, Simon and Christopher Nobes. 2013. *The Taxation of Economics 2013/14*, 13th ed. Birmingham: Fiscal Publications.

Kanagaretnam, Kiridaran, Jimmy Lee, Chee Yeo Lim, and Gerald J. Lobo. 2016. "Cross-Country Evidence on the Role of Independent Media in Constraining Corporate Tax Aggressiveness." *Journal of Business Ethics.* https://doi.org/10.1007/s10551-016-3168-9.

Klassen, Kenneth J., and Stacie K. Laplante. 2012. "Are U.S. Multinational Corporations Becoming More Aggressive Income Shifters?" *Journal of Accounting Research* 5 (5): 1245–1285.

Kubick, Thomas R., Daniel P. Lynch, Michael A. Mayberry, and Thomas C. Omer. 2015. "Product Market Power and Tax Avoidance: Market Leaders, Mimicking Strategies, and Stock Returns." *The Accounting Review* 90 (2): 675–702.

Kyj, Larissa S., and George C. Romeo. 2015. "Microsoft's Foreign Earnings: Tax Strategy." *Issues in Accounting Education* 30 (4): 297–310.

Lanis, Roman, and Grant Richardson. 2015. "Is Corporate Social Responsibility Performance Associated with Tax Avoidance?" *Journal of Business Ethics* 127: 439–452.

Lavermicocca, Catricha, and Jenny Buchan. 2015. "Role of Reputational Risk in Tax Decision Making by Large Companies." *eJournal of Tax Research* 13 (1): 5–50. https://www.business.unsw.edu.au/research-site/publications-site/ejournaloftaxresearch-site/Documents/01_LavermicoccaBuchan_RoleOfReputationalRisk.pdf. Accessed 9 Sept 2017.

Melville, Alan. 2018. *Taxation Finance Act 2017.* 23rd ed. Harlow: Pearson Education Ltd.

Mirrlees, James, Stuart Adam, Tim Besley, Richard Blundell, Stephen Bond, Robert Chote, Malcolm Gammie, Paul Johnson, Gareth Myles, and James M. Poterba. 2011. *Tax by Design.* Oxford: Oxford University Press.

OECD. 2017. *OECD Work on Taxation 2016–17.* Centre for Tax Policy and Administration. www.oecd.org/tax. Accessed 17 Aug 2017.

Payne, Dinah M., and Cecily A. Raiborn. 2018. "Aggressive Tax Avoidance: A Conundrum for Stakeholders, Governments and Morality." *Journal of Business Ethics* 147 (3): 469–487.

PwC 16th Annual Global CEO Survey. 2013. *Tax Strategy and Corporate Reputation a Tax Issue, a Business Issue.* https://www.pwc.com/gx/en/tax/publications/assets/pwc-tax-strategy-and-corporate-reputation-a-tax-issue-a-business-issue.pdf. Accessed 17 Aug 2017.

Scott Slorach, J., and Jason Ellis. 2017. *Business Law 2017–18.* Oxford: Oxford University Press.

Wahab, Nor Shaipa Abdul, and Kevin Holland. 2012. "Tax Planning, Corporate Governance and Equity Value." *The British Accounting Review* 44: 111–124.

CHAPTER 6

Corporate Reporting: From Numbers to Narrative

Parminder Johal

6.1 Introduction

Put simply, corporate reporting is all about the way in which an organisation reports what it has been doing over its preceding financial year. It is, therefore, a backward-looking exercise which is carried out by organisations so that their stakeholders can have confidence in decision-making, which in turn will benefit the organisation's internal operations and working capital position. In a broader sense, these decisions may contribute to the efficient working of capital markets so that strategic financial decisions can operate within a financial structure, more specifically, a structure which enjoys a lower cost of capital thus maximising shareholder wealth and contributing to the economic wealth of the nation.

The status of the reporting organisation can vary from sole trader/partnership and small and medium enterprises (SMEs) through to large and complex conglomerates. It is also the case that some organisations exist to create profit whilst others may exist, for example, to create social and or cultural value. Whatever the objective or legal status of the company, all of them are required to report on their financial performance

P. Johal (✉)
Derby Business School, University of Derby, Derby, UK

E. Conway and D. Byrne (eds.), *Contemporary Issues in Accounting*,
https://doi.org/10.1007/978-3-319-91113-7_6

and position. This reporting activity has taken the form of financial statements that are produced at the financial year-end and it is the large listed companies (companies that have shares which can be traded on a stock exchange) that have a legal obligation to publish these statements as part of their annual financial reports.

The preparation of the annual report is guided by the Conceptual Framework for Financial Reporting, developed by the International Accounting Standards Board (IASB), a comprehensive set of accounting standards and company legislation. Historically the core information produced in the annual reports has been of a quantitative nature supported by a narrative section that was limited to the disclosure requirements as set out by the statutory and accounting regulations. The numbers reported in the annual reports reflect the financial information from within the company, which is adapted and transmitted to the final external published set of accounts, to be presented in the company's annual report.

Over the last two decades, however, the quality and scope of what is reported has been debated and as a consequence, action has been taken to encourage companies to embrace a broader approach to corporate reporting, one that transitions focus from the numbers to the narrative. A very recent example of this is the EU Non-Financial Reporting (NFR) Directive on disclosure of non-financial and diversity information. A further example, albeit in a very different context, is evident in the recent changes to the Corporate Reporting syllabus for the Association of Certified Chartered Accountants (ACCA), which now places greater emphasis on the broader responsibility of corporate reporting. This chapter will, therefore, provide an overview of the changing shape of annual reporting, starting with an understanding of narrative reporting in its broader sense and then to explore the shift from numbers to narrative within the corporate reporting function. Its purpose is to inform both academics in their knowledge and teaching and to aid organisations in their knowledge and practice.

6.2 The Changing Shape of Corporate Reporting

The sole purpose for the need to change the way in which companies report their business and, therefore, changes to the annual report, is to deliver the information that the users want. It is noteworthy that a company's annual report is probably, even in today's digital environment, the most important medium of communication. A study carried out by the American Institute of Certified Public Accountants (AICPA 1994), researched the information needs of specific stakeholder groups and in their final report, also known as the Jenkins report, made recommendations for businesses so that they could improve their reporting function. The recommendations focused on forward-looking, longer term value, non-financial measures and better alignment of internal and external information. It is not surprising that the same focus is evident in the definitions of and references to narrative reporting decades later.

According to The UK Corporate Governance Portal (2017) "Narrative reporting describes the non-financial information included in annual reports to provide a broad and meaningful picture of the company's business, its market position, strategy, performance and future prospects. This includes the strategic report, the directors' report, the chairman's statement, the directors' remuneration report and corporate governance disclosures". A definition by PWC also defines narrative reporting as non-financial information and also makes reference to the need for reporting to address the 'future':

> Narrative reporting is shorthand for the critical contextual and non-financial information that is reported alongside financial information to provide a broader, more meaningful understanding of a company's business, its market position, strategy, performance and future prospects. It includes quantified metrics for these areas. (PWC 2017)

Narrative reporting is, therefore, the umbrella under which organisations can manage their communication of non-financial information, that which will set the context for the organisations operations so that stakeholders can establish strategic fit and a more holistic view of the organisation's future direction. For the purposes of this chapter, narrative reporting will, therefore, envelope terms such as non-financial information, environmental reporting, corporate social responsibility (CSR), sustainability and integrated reporting. All of which have secured a place on the corporate reporting agenda over the last two decades.

It is widely agreed that the aim of corporate reporting in the form of published annual reports is to provide useful information to its users (ACCA 2011). However, this vehicle in its traditional role as an accountability document (Stanton and Stanton 2011) has also extended its function to that of a vehicle for corporate communication (Adams and Harte 1998), one that can communicate with all of the stakeholder groups of an organisation. Such reports are starting to be recognised as a tool via which companies can communicate the company's personality and philosophy (Anderson and Imperia 1992) and create their desired image (Neu et al. 1998).

Interestingly though, corporate reporting is the result of an accounting function, one that has been primarily regulated by the law and by accounting standards. The regulation of company annual reports which typically represented the historical picture of an organisation, predominately through the use of numbers, with narrative limited to statutory disclosure requirements, has begun to take a very different shape. A shape that resembled the form of a marketing document (Bekey 1990). Or a document that comprises not only of the financial statements required by statute but also voluntary non-regulated disclosures. The simplicity of the voluntary narrative serves the purpose of presenting information in a way that is understood by the user and whilst it may have been felt that this form of communication was not tenable, it was a "....forum to communicate information to shareholders in a language they understand" (Anderson and Epstein 1996, pp. 56–57). This inclusion of user-friendly narrative meant that the published annual reports had grown in volume to serve as a public relations document. Research by Campbell et al. (2006) found that the length of the annual report has increased from 37 pages to 90 pages over the last four decades. Whilst some of this increase in volume may be due to company legislation and accounting regulation around financial information, a considerable amount is due to the rise in narrative reporting. The increased volume of information does not, however, automatically result in information that is decision-useful.

A research exercise by the ASB (2009, p. 3) found that when reporting on the matter of CSR, annual reports were populated with "immaterial clutter". The report revealed that this content did not necessarily lend itself to information that could be used to make important decisions, such as how to decide on resource allocation, for example. This notion of clutter and information overload is further supported by an international survey carried out by ACCA (2010). Whereby preparers of the annual reports were asked about their thoughts on the current and future challenges for narrative reporting. The findings revealed that preparers felt the reports were not only more costly to produce but also more complex. Consequently, this complexity detracted from the transparency that the narrative sections were set out to deliver on. Other research has recognised that narrative reporting is necessary if financial reporting is to fully reflect the performance of modern day organisations (AICPA 1994; Beattie et al. 2002; IASB 2009). Furthermore, not only has the information content changed but so too has the mode of delivery. Company web sites are now often the first point of call for stakeholders looking for information about a company (Campbell and Slack 2008).

The shape and scope of the annual report is, therefore, undergoing a change and continual reshaping to try and capture the perfect balance of financial and non-financial information. This is to the point where bodies such as the Investors Relations Society (IRS) are prepared to give out awards for the "Best Annual Report", the criteria for which is based around effective communication, insight into company objectives and for UK companies, adherence to the Financial Reporting Council (FRC) guidance (IR 2017), as part of the 'clear & concise' initiative launched in June 2014.

6.3 Narrative Reporting in Practice

In light of the growing emphasis on improving the quality, transparency and decision—usefulness of company annual reports, there is some evidence of how this is playing out in practice. Research studies in the 1980s of how companies in the UK were engaging with narrative reporting have been somewhat limited (Gray et al. 1987; Gray 1990; Guthrie and Parker 1989). These studies showed that the information relating to social and environmental issues was limited to what was required by statute. Other research by professional firms such as Coopers Lybrand Deloitte and Touche Ross (Harte and Owen 1991) supported the dearth of social and environmental reporting. However, a focus on the 1990 annual reports for a group of companies showed that reporting of an environmental nature had increased (Harte and Owen 1991), albeit with a public image focus rather than an impact and or accountability focus. The increased importance of responsibly reporting on the environmental issues is further supported in a later study by Parker (2005).

As narrative reporting has evolved and gained prominence in the corporate reporting debate, it has done so, as mentioned earlier on in the chapter, to include a number of areas such as non-financial information, environmental reporting, CSR, sustainability and integrated reporting.

There are so many versions of what constitutes narrative reporting, some are more specific and relevant to particular business sectors. Therefore, this has meant that there has been an increase in the reporting of some areas more than others. For example, there has been an increase over the last two decades in sustainability reporting (KPMG 2011; Kolk 2008; Owen 2006) and as working beyond the 1990s and into the millennium years the number of top UK companies reporting on social and environmental issues has doubled (KPMG 2011). Reporting of this type is not specific to the UK. A comprehensive report by the Centre for Strategy and Evaluation Services (CSES) (2011), analysed the publication of non-financial information by seventy-one countries across eight different countries. The non-financial content related to a sustainability or CSR type of report. Most of the companies used the Global Reporting Initiative (GRI) framework and almost all reported on the environmental issues, with only half of the participating companies reporting on economic impact or human rights. The research also found that, whilst not required to by law, the SMEs in the sample produced comparatively less non-financial information than the larger companies in the research sample. Whilst this may be expected, it is interesting that SMEs are volunteering any non-financial information at all, particularly as all companies identified that providing this additional information resulted in a cost, with larger companies having to deal with a greater cost range than the SMEs. However, the research revealed that all companies associated this optional 'extra' information with increased credibility, more transparent reporting and brand identity. However, there was little agreement with the idea that this manner of reporting would result in increased sales and, therefore, performance (CSES 2011).

In contrast, research by De Klerk et al. (2015), examined the association between CSR disclosure by large UK firms and their performance. It was found that there was a positive correlation between the two and the research supported the notion that such non-financial disclosure added information value for investors. It seems, therefore, that despite the extra costs that are incurred by companies in meeting the requirements of narrative reporting (Chaidal and Jones 2017; ACCA 2010), some companies are seeing the value of this type of reporting.

This silo nature of narrative reporting has, however, paved the way for the idea that the areas under narrative reporting are not only interrelated but are not separate from financial reporting (Jenson and Berg 2012). This school of thought has been responsible for the emergence of integrated reporting (IR), with the aim to shift the corporate mindset from short-term financial returns to a long-term business picture that commits to a sustainable future. The focus of IR is, therefore, concerned with the idea of value creation over time and is based on the business model of six capitals which capture qualitative and quantitative information to assess value creation. The framework identifies these capital as financial, manufactured, intellectual, human, social and relationship and natural capital. Although South Africa is the first to formalise the adoption of IR, there is evidence of a number of other countries including the UK which are using IR (De Villiers et al. 2014) but are doing so on a voluntary basis. Companies such as Glaxo SmithKline and BT are examples of companies where IR has been adopted. On embracing this approach to reporting, these companies advocate IR as a means of value creation (Deloitte 2015). Despite a general feeling of support for the idea of IR, there is some scepticism around the decision-usefulness of IR. In addition, there is, in some sectors, a resistance to the notion of IR as a potential future reporting framework. In particular, fund managers and equity analysts are signalling low confidence in the adoption of IR as a reporting framework. It may be the case that IR, for some, may be nothing more than a fad (Slack and Tsalavoutas 2017).

6.4 Reporting Requirements

Changes in reporting requirements have supported the move towards the inclusion of narrative sections in the annual report. For example, in April 2005, the Operating and Financial Review (OFR) was introduced, so that companies could include more explicit narrative content in their annual reports, content that explained the financial health of the company in light of future prospects and risks. This narrative was intended to support the quantitative content of the annual report and to provide content for all stakeholders and not just the investors. The OFR was not prescriptive and instead it offered directors of the company the flexibility to pick and choose their content so that competitive advantage was not compromised. This led to much longer annual reports, being dominated by non-standardised narrative reporting (Anderson 2000; Smith and Taffler 2000). This increase in volume in the annual reports is further supported by the research of Campbell et al. (2006).

It was not, however, certain that this extra volume met the objectives of the OFR. A major study carried out by Rutherford (2003) focused on analysing the use of the OFR in practice. The findings of the study revealed that there was an overreliance on the use of external consultancy companies in the preparation of the narrative sections of the report. In addition, it was found that the guidance for environmental issues and social policies was limited. As a final point, it was felt that there needed to be a better balance between the level of flexibility and the amount of prescribed information in the annual reports. Such a balance would provide a more structured and organised narrative, that could potentially enable better and more meaningful comparative data for its users. After much debate and lobbying around the contents and purpose of the OFR, in March 2005 company directors were required by statute to prepare an OFR. The contents of the OFR must include narrative on environmental, employee and social issues as part of the annual reports, but this requirement was limited to listed companies only.

The dramatic shift from allowing directors to be flexible in their narrative reporting to a position of over prescription on the one hand, may have resulted in a balanced document that enhances relevance and comparability for its users. However, on the other hand, it introduced the risk that companies may operate "creative compliance" reporting. The practice of this kind of creative reporting aimed to seek out loop holes so that companies can reflect their position in the best light (McBarnet 2006). In November 2005, however, the UK Government, as a move to deregulate, reduce the cost burden for companies and create a space for narrative reporting, not only for listed companies but also for unlisted companies, abruptly withdrew the OFR legislation. It was then replaced with a new legal requirement for all but small UK and European Union (EU) companies. The new requirement was to provide a Business Review, again with directors having the discretion to choose their content, under the advisory guidance provided by the ASB, a situation not too dissimilar from the choice available under the OFR.

Therefore, at present all companies other than those that fall under the definition of 'small', as per Companies Act 2006, are required to produce, as part of their annual report, a strategic review of the company's operations, in the form of a strategic report. Companies that are listed have additional disclosure requirements, which include the requirement for a Management Report or a Business Review. In addition to these reporting requirements relevant to UK companies as of the year ending 30 September 2013, listed companies are also required to include information on greenhouse gas emissions (GHG) within their directors' report. These disclosures are not subject to an audit and the reason for inclusion is to address the noise around the purview and quality of information in annual reports.

Alongside the changing legal requirements, what is considered as relevant content in the annual reports is also being heavily influenced by the guidance from professional bodies, committees, political lobbyists, boards and frameworks, all of which have an increased focus on narrative reporting. Annual reports, therefore, comprise a mixture of mandatory and voluntary non-financial information. Companies have received guidance on how they can report their impact on the environment, society and the economy. The G4 Sustainability Reporting Guidelines have been replaced by the GRI Sustainability Reporting Standards which will be effective from 1 July 2018. The Integrated Reporting Framework is another framework, created in 2013 by the International Integrated Reporting Council (IIRC). This was designed with the objective to demonstrate how organisations create value by integrating financial and non-financial information, rather than focusing on the latter in isolation. Other guidance to facilitate companies in their narrative reporting function includes the Sustainability Accounting Standards Board (SASB). Further afield, a US organisation that develops accounting standards for social and environmental issues also offers ISO 26000 (international standard for organisations), a voluntary standard on CSR.

The need for changes as to how and what is to be reported by companies has also been strongly influenced by the increased use of corporate websites. The website has become a popular vehicle via which companies communicate. Another factor influencing the financial reporting function has been the periodic corporate scandals that have occurred over the years. Some of these have been country specific, whilst the 2008 financial crisis had its impact felt across the globe. Such corporate scandals have highlighted the importance of and drawn attention to the quality of financial reporting (Clarke and Dean 2007; Donoher et al. 2007). Narrative reporting can, therefore, be regarded as a way of plugging the information needs gap and a means to provide a solution to issues such as the agency problem, methods of measurement that impact corporate valuations, safeguarding of investors interests, that is, the kind of issues that have contributed to many corporations making the headlines in the news for all the wrong reasons. By complementing the traditional style of financial accounting reporting with the inclusion of a strategic review, a management report, risk assessment, narrative to explain the company's position on CSR, the environment and so on, narrative reporting lends itself to the creation of greater transparency in the annual report. According to Yeoh (2010), this transparency will enable the market to better evaluate and assess corporate performance. Furthermore, the inclusion of a greater breadth of mandatory and voluntary information leading to transparency is gaining popularity. The UK, in particular, has embraced the idea of addressing the interests of a company's broader set of stakeholders. Not only to address poor governance that feeds financial scandals but also to ensure the UK market remains competitive in the face of capital mobility and is visible as a safe and transparent market that is open for business.

At a global level, narrative reporting is evident but some countries are progressing at a faster pace than others. A survey carried out by ACCA in partnership with Deloitte revealed that preparers of financial reports across the globe recognised increased regulation around narrative reporting as both costly and time-consuming and the plea is very much in favour of increased discretion and less regulation. Furthermore 88% of those surveyed felt that the most important audience for annual reports is the shareholder, in which case it was suggested that a different problem lies ahead and that "The future of narrative reports may, therefore, depend on resolving the preparers' predicament in trying to fulfil the different needs of the primary users, i.e. shareholders and regulators" (ACCA 2010, p. 8).

Research by Professor Tomo Suzuki Shozaburo (2012), however, created an argument for narrative reporting based on his belief that the purpose of accounting went beyond just the needs of reporting to satisfy the needs of the investors. His research revealed that the International Financial Reporting Standards (IFRS) did not address issues such as the environment, human rights or the stakeholders beyond the financial market. His report led to the Indian government expressing strong reservations regarding convergence of accounting standards with IFRS and also led to him contributing to further work to help create standards that are relevant to specific countries and business industries. Although the issue of global convergence of accounting standards is a separate one, the work of Professor Tomo Suzuki Shozaburo does recognise a space for narrative reporting in an era of global business and political economy. Further research by ACCA, this time seeking the views of a range of stakeholders across the UK, United States and Canada on the value of information within the annual reports, revealed that 50% of the respondents still looked to these reports as their primary or only source of information. This research amongst other findings also reported that 59% felt that "… inclusion of social and environmental data through an integrated report would add value" (ACCA 2011, p. 4). It is evident that companies have been and are subject to mandatory regulation and voluntary guidance to assist them to move away from the traditional annual report to a report that better reflects the needs of today's global audience.

6.5 Recent Events

6.5.1 EU Non-financial Reporting (NFR) Directive

A recent example of the increasing pressure on corporate reporting to move away from the traditional annual report is the adoption by the European Commission (EC) of non-binding guidelines on the disclosure of non-financial information by companies. This is consistent with all other initiatives to assist companies in providing information on: employee aspects, human rights, anti-corruption, bribery, boardroom diversity and information of an environmental and social nature. The aim is that this level of information will address a wider group of stakeholders in a consistent and comparable manner. The guidelines are set out in the EU NFR Directive (Directive 2014/95/EU), on disclosure of non-financial and diversity information and are effective as of 1 Jan 2017.

It is noteworthy that in the directive, the emphasis on what needs to be included in the annual report is stipulated as a "description" (Symons and Epsom 2017). This lends itself to the provision of true qualitative, narrative reporting. Again the burden of disclosure rests on companies of a large size but this time in both the public and private sectors and again allowing flexibility around what is included to enable relevance to the company and the needs of its audience. It is also noteworthy that this flexibility may be an obstacle to achieving the overarching objective of companies providing comparable information. This is further intensified by the fact that companies have the choice of applying national, European or international frameworks. The EU directive, however, would argue that the choice of framework allows the continued use of existing good practice and could potentially bridge the gap between national and international reporting. A bridging which would result in greater comparability of narrative sections in the annual reports (Federation of European Accountants 2016).

As mentioned previously the introduction of the latest EU directive does not sit in isolation to the guidance and legislation that is already in place. Since its introduction, the EU Directive has triggered a number of changes. In particular, the FRC's work on the guidance that was issued for companies following the initial introduction of the requirement for certain companies to produce a strategic report, is being revisited. Following the introduction of the new EU directive, effective as of 1 Jan 2017, the FRC is amending its existing guidance on the strategic report, to ensure that the new EU directive is taken into account. In line with the FRC's Clear & Concise initiative, the focus of the guidance will continue to encourage companies to reflect and report on how they impact society. It aims to address the impacts which affect how sustainable they are as a future going concern. The amendments to the guidance are to ensure the cohesion of financial and non-financial information in the strategic and annual report. As always the objective is to enhance quality and transparency in the annual report. The idea that a level of cohesion is needed between non-financial and financial information, in order to achieve this, presents a strong case for narrative reporting.

In addition to amending the guidance on strategic reports to account for the new EU directive, the FRC is also proposing changes to the strategic report so that it is more aligned to the legislation on Section 172 of the Companies Act 2006 (Deloitte 2017a). The legislation initially required directors to 'promote the success of the company', this has now been extended to include how companies do this. The FRC would, therefore, like companies, through their narrative in the strategic report, to demonstrate *how* this duty is being fulfilled. There is pressure on companies to consider the broader remit, linking activities to the reputation and brand value of the company. As a consequence, the Government and the Department for Business, Energy and Industrial Strategy (BEIS) are in support of the FRC and consultation has taken place. However, since the consultation, it has been announced that legislative changes relating to reporting on Section 172 are likely to take place and to be expected in March 2018 (FRC 2017). It follows, therefore, that any amendments proposed by the FRC to the existing guidance on strategic reports, will wait until the legislative changes have been published.

It is hoped that the efforts of the various institutions (FRC, EU, UK Government, ASB, BEIS), to emphasise the need for a cohesive strategic report will result in companies taking a broader view of their responsibilities and their audience. Certainly, from the government's perspective;

> ...The hope is that 'more transparency will also help to reassure investors, creditors and others that companies are being run with a view to their long-term sustainability'. And there is another goal, a hoped-for knock-on effect. 'Better reporting should improve the visibility of good boardroom practice', the BEIS says, 'allowing it to be replicated and adopted more widely'. The end result should be greater clarity all round. (Deloitte 2017b)

The FRC in its clear and concise initiative is focused on the provision of transparent reporting. It is aware of and involved in the implementation, consultation and lobbying of many initiatives that are keen to expand annual reporting to beyond the numbers. It does, however, urge the government to consider a joined-up approach when looking at potential initiatives. This is evident in the FRC's recent response to the consultation on Streamlined Energy & Carbon Reporting (FRC 2018). Not only is it evident that the demand for a more narrative type of reporting is increasing but according to the FRC there is a need to focus on by who and how this 'additional' reporting will be delivered.

Directives from the EU and guidelines from the ASB have governed much of UK reporting practice in an attempt to address the need for greater transparency, which it is believed, has been and will be achieved through the narrative sections of the annual reports.

Looking ahead at the unknown political roadmap, the UK's position with the EU is amidst negotiation. How much of future reporting guidance and regulation for companies will be influenced by the EC, is an unknown quantity. Not only for UK companies, but also for standard setters, professional bodies and other interest groups alike.

6.5.2 Brexit

On 23 June 2016, the UK experienced a massive turnout of 72.2% of registered voters, amounting to 33.6 million people casting a vote on the EU referendum. The turnout was just 0.1% below the voting turnout for the 1992 general election (Henderson 2016). Since the referendum vote, Article 50 has been invoked and the UK parliament has until 29 March 2019 to conclude negotiations to exit the UK from the EU. The recent UK Government's repeal bill will have implications for business and their reporting:

> ...the repeal bill will repeal the 1972 European Communities Act, which took Britain into the EU and meant that European law took precedence over laws passed in the UK Parliament. It will also end the jurisdiction of the European Court of Justice. All existing EU legislation will be copied across into domestic UK law to ensure a smooth transition on the day after Brexit. (Newbury 2017)

Whilst assurances are being given by the government that disruption to businesses will be minimal, it is necessary to consider that in the spirit of retaining quality corporate reporting, companies will now need to communicate how this turning point in the Brexit negotiations will impact their future strategies so that uncertainties are addressed and risks are considered and disclosed. Such communication is likely to be presented in the narrative parts of the company's annual report and more importantly its inclusion will be expected by the stakeholders. The FRC in July 2016 issued a reminder to companies to this effect, in particular for the inclusion of narrative under the headings of: Business model, Principle risks and uncertainties and Viability statement. Furthermore, the uncertainty of the impact of Brexit on accounting standards and, therefore, reporting of financial performance still remains. The narrative may, therefore, be an obvious opportunity to ensure that the stakeholders are aware of how such events may impact the company's strategy. For companies to simply say 'they don't know' may no longer be good enough.

6.6 Conclusion

Corporate reporting in annual reports has had a lot of attention over the last few decades. This has been driven by a combination of repeated corporate scandals and the emergence of a wider global audience as far as company annual reports are concerned. In response, regulators and statute have responded through contributions via accounting standards and or EU directives/company law. The impact of these responses is visible in the changed structure and scope of company annual reports with the financial sections now neatly settled to the rear of the report and the narrative sections occupying the front end. In addition, the mode of delivering this information is increasingly based on digital competency. In the future, we may see a move to the use of a more central digital space where topical narrative reports may sit.

Emphasis has been placed on the contents of the reports to be decision-useful and relevant to its audience. Interestingly, changes so far have increased the amount of information that is being made available to stakeholders and it is the large listed companies who are falling under the pressure to change their reporting habits. This does of course raise the question about the reporting position of SMEs. This is an area that has not been fully addressed, nonetheless it is worth making the point that over 99% of UK businesses are small- or medium-sized businesses—employing 0–249 people (Federation of Small Businesses 2017) and, therefore, not required to adhere to recent narrative reporting requirements. It is clear through the numerous initiatives, both mandatory and voluntary, that there is an appetite amongst investors and other stakeholders for information on environmental, CSR and sustainability matters. Surely these are not matters specific only to large listed companies? There appears, therefore, to be an innate inequity, as UK PLCs are required to follow narrative reporting directives in order to ensure transparency but smaller companies are not.

Whilst it may be the case that the scrutiny over corporate reporting, which in the UK, has been influenced all the way by EU directives, has resulted in the combined narrative and financial sections of the annual report, presenting a more balanced picture for the wider stakeholder groups. It is possible that the debate around what goes into the annual reports may still have some way to go, particularly if it decides to realign itself with the political appetite for a more national focus. Is it possible, therefore, that the UK will take the opportunity to change corporate reporting to reflect national interest, abandon existing directives post-Brexit, only to create UK specific law/guidance? Or will the UK retain EC/EU guidance and influence? Either way, it is likely that the debates over narrative reporting are not yet over.

References

ACCA. 2010. "Hitting the Notes But What's the Tune?" http://www.accaglobal.com/content/dam/acca/global/PDF-technical/narrative-reporting/hitting_the_notes.pdf. Accessed 5 Sept 2017.

ACCA. 2011. "Re-assessing the Value of Corporate Reporting." http://www.accaglobal.com/content/dam/acca/global/PDF-technical/financial-reporting/reassessing-value.pdf. Accessed 5 Sept 2017.

Adams, Carol A., and George Harte. 1998. "The Changing Portrayal of the Employment of Women in British Banks and Retail Companies Corporate Annual Reports." *Accounting, Organisations & Society* 23 (8): 781–812.

AICPA. 1994. *Improving Business Reporting—A Customer Focus: Meeting the Information Needs of Investors and Creditors.* New York: American Institute of Certified Public Accountants.

Anderson, Arthur. 2000. *Spice Up the Story: A Survey of Narrative Reporting in Annual Reports:* London: Arthur Anderson.

Anderson, Claire, J., and Giovanna Imperia. 1992. "The Corporate Annual Report: A Photo Analysis of Male and Female Portrayals." *The Journal of Business Communications* 29 (2): 113–128.

Anderson, Ray, and Marc Epstein. 1996. *The Usefulness of Corporate Annual Reports to Shareholders in Australia: An International Comparison:* Greenwich, CT: JAI Press.

ASB. 2009. "Rising to the Challenge." https://www.icaew.com/en/archive/technical/corporate-governance/non-executive-directors/corporate-reporting/asb-rising-to-the-challenge. Accessed 6 Sept 2017.

Beattie, Vivien, Bill McInnes, and Stella Fearnley. 2002. *Through the Eyes of Management: A Study of Narrative Disclosures.* London: ICAEW.

Bekey, Michelle. 1990. "Annual Reports Evolve into Marketing Tools." *Financial Manager* 3: 50–60.

Campbell, David, Geoff Moore, and Phillip Shrives. 2006. "Cross Sectional Effects in Community Disclosure." *Accounting, Auditing & Accountability Journal* 19: 96–114.

Campbell, David, and Richard Slack. 2008. *Analysts' Perspectives on the Materiality of Voluntary Narratives in Annual Reports.* London: ACCA.

Chaidal, Panagioula, and Michael Jones. 2017. "It's a Matter of Trust: Exploring the Perceptions of Integrated Reporting Preparers." *Critical Perspectives on Accounting* 48: 1–20.

Clarke, Frank, and Graeme Dean. 2007. *Indecent Disclosure: Gilding the Corporate Lily.* Melbourne: Cambridge University Press.

CSES. 2011. "Disclosure of Non-financial Information." http://ec.europa.eu/internal_market/accounting/docs/non-financial-reporting/com_2013_207-study_en.pdf. Accessed 12 Jan 2018.

Deloitte. 2015. "Annual Report Insights 2015: The Reporting Landscape." https://www2.deloitte.com/content/dam/Deloitte/uk/documents/audit/deloitte-uk-annual-report-insights-2015-full-survey.pdf. Accessed 27 Aug 2017.

Deloitte. 2017a. "The Bruce Column—Making S172 More Accessible." https://www.iasplus.com/en-gb/news/2017/10/bruce-column-s172. Accessed 20 Jan 2018.

Deloitte. 2017b. "FRC Proposes Amendments to Its Guidance on Strategic Reports." https://www.iasplus.com/en-gb/news/2017/08/frc-amendments-guidance-on-strategic-report. Accessed 20 Jan 2018.

De Klerk, Marna, Charl De Villiers, and Chris Van Staden. 2015. "The Influence of Corporate Social Responsibility Disclosure on Share Prices: Evidence from the United Kingdom." *Pacific Accounting Review* 27 (2): 208–228. https://doi.org/10.1108/PAR-05-2013-0047.

De Villiers, Charl, Leonardo Rinaldi, and Jeffrey Unerman. 2014. "Integrated Reporting: Insights, Gaps and an Agenda for Future Research." *Accounting, Auditing & Accountability Journal* 27 (7): 1042–1067.

Directive 2014/95/EU. https://eur-lex.europa.eu/legal-content/EN/TXT/?uri=CELEX:32014L0095. Accessed 1 Dec 2017.

Donoher, William J., Richard Reed, and Susan F. Storrud-Barnes. 2007. "Incentive Alignment, Control and the Issue of Misleading Financial Disclosures." *Journal of Management* 33 (4): 547–569.

Federation of European Accountants. 2016. "EU Directive on Disclosure of Non-financial and Diversity Information. Achieving Good Quality and Consistent Reporting." https://www.accountancyeurope.eu/wpcontent/uploads/FEE_position_paper_EU_NFI_Directive_final.pdf. Accessed 10 Sept 2017.

Federation of Small Businesses. 2017. Accessed 23 Dec 2017.

FRC. 2017. "Strategic Report Guidance to Follow Government Legislation." https://www.frc.org.uk/news/december-2017/strategic-report-guidance-to-follow-government-leg. Accessed 15 Dec 2017.

FRC. 2018. https://frc.org.uk/getattachment/f827020b-4b8c-445b-9e16-7a03ab901c31/FRC-response-to-DBEIS-Carbon-reporting-consultation-4-Jan-2018.pdf. Accessed 20 Jan 2018.

Gray, Rob. 1990. "Corporate Social Reporting by UK Companies: A Cross-Sectional and Longitudinal Study—An Interim Report." Paper Presented to British Accounting Association, University of Dundee, April.

Gray, Rob, Owen, David, and Maunders Keith. 1987. *Corporate Social Reporting: Accounting and Accountability*. Hemel Hempstead: Prentice Hall.

Guthrie, James, and Lee David Parker. 1989. "Corporate Social Reporting: A Rebuttal of Legitimacy Theory." *Accounting and Business Research* 19 (76): 343–352. https://doi.org/10.1080/00014788.1989.9728863.

Harte, George, and David Owen. 1991. "Environmental Disclosure in the Annual Reports of British Companies: A Research Note." *Accounting, Auditing & Accountability Journal* 4 (3): 51–61.

Henderson, Barney. 2016. "Huge Turnout of 72.2 Per cent for EU Referendum with 33.6 Million Voting." *The Telegraph*. https://www.telegraph.co.uk/news/2016/06/23/high-turnout-for-eu-referendum-vote-could-break-uk-records/. Accessed 3 Dec 2017.

IASB. 2009. "Management Commentary ED/2009/6." London: IASCF.

IR. 2017. "IR Society." http://irsociety.org.uk/events/best-annual-report-20161#SmallCap.

Jenson, Julia Catherina, and Nicola Berg. 2012. "Determinants of Traditional Sustainability Reporting Versus Integrated Reporting. An Institutionalist Approach." *Business Strategy and the Environment* 21: 299–316.

Kolk, Ans. 2008. "Sustainability, Accountability and Corporate Governance: Exploring Multinationals' Reporting Practice." *Business Strategy and the Environment* 18: 1–15.

KPMG. 2011. "International Survey of Corporate Responsibility Reporting." http://www.econsense.de/sites/all/files/Survey-corporate-responsibility-reporting-2011.pdf. Accessed 14 Sept 2017.

McBarnet, Doreen. 2006. "After Enron Will 'Whiter Than White Collar Crime' Still Wash." *British Journal of criminology* 46 (6): 1091–1109.

Neu, D., H. Warsame, and K. Pedwell. 1998. "Managing Public Impressions: Environmental Disclosures in Annual Reports." *Accounting, Organizations and Society* 23 (3): 265–282.

Newbury, Deborah. 2017. European Union (Withdrawal) Bill. http://www.kennedyslaw.com/article/european-union-withdrawal-bill/.

Owen, Daniel. 2006. "Emerging Issues in Sustainability Reporting." *Business Strategy and the Environment* 15: 217–218.

Parker, Lee David. 2005. "Social and Environmental Accountability Research: A View from the Commentary Box." *Accounting, Auditing and Accountability Journal* 18 (6): 842–860.

PWC. 2017. https://www.pwc.com/, http://www.pwc.com/gx/en/services/audit-assurance/corporate-reporting/frequently-asked-questions/what-is-corporate-reporting.html. Accessed 10 Aug 2017.

Rutherford, Brian. 2003. "Half the Story: Progress and Prospects for the OFR." London: ACCA.

Shozaburo, J. 2012. http://www.ox.ac.uk/research/research-impact/revealing-hidden-impact-international-financial-reporting-standards-ifrs-0. Accessed 12 Sept 2017.

Slack, Richard, and Ioannis Tsalavoutas. 2017. "Integrated Reporting Decision Usefulness: Mainstream Equity Market Views." https://papers.ssrn.com/sol3/papers.cfm?abstract_id=2959745. Accessed 2 Dec 2017.

Smith, Malcolm, and Richard. J. Taffler. 2000. "The Chairman's Statement: A Content Analysis of Discretionary Narrative Disclosures." *Accounting, Auditing & Accountability Journal* 13 (5): 624–646.

Stanton, Patricia, and John Stanton. 2011. "Researching Corporate Annual Reports: An Analysis of Perspectives Used." https://www.researchgate.net/publication/252830779_RESEARCHING_CORPORATE_ANNUAL_REPORTS_AN_ANALYSIS_OF_PERSPECTIVES_USED. Accessed 15 Oct 2017.

Symons, David, and Robbie Epsom. 2017. "EU Non-financial Reporting Directive: New Requirements For Mandatory Environmental Reporting for UK Companies." http://www.wsp-pb.com/PageFilesn/80407/NFRD%20White%20Paper.pdf. Accessed 10 Aug 2017.

The UK Corporate Governance Portal. 2017. Accessed 23 Mar 2018.

Yeoh, Peter. 2010. "Narrative Reporting: The UK Experience." *International Journal of Law and Managemnt* 52 (3): 211–231.

CHAPTER 7

Contemporary Challenges in Audit

David Thompson

7.1 Introduction

Audit services account for approximately 42% of the revenues of the "Big 4" audit firms; PWC, Deloitte, KPMG and EY. This proportion is significantly higher than any other service line. Advisory services contribute 35% and taxation services 23% (ICAS 2016b). The landscape faced by auditors is changing by increased innovation within the profession and from external factors affecting the nature of financial reporting. It is therefore important for audit firms to implement clear strategies to deal with contemporary challenges affecting the profession. The aim of this chapter is to set out some of the key challenges likely to impact on audit in the coming years and discuss the steps audit firms may undertake to deal with such issues. This chapter will primarily focus upon the need to enhance audit quality as an overarching principle. It will go on to discuss the evolving skill sets required of auditors in light of changing technologies. It will also discuss the effect on audit of the emergence of narrative reporting. Finally, the issues affecting the audit standards are discussed in a consideration of whether these remain fit for purpose given the changing landscape.

D. Thompson (✉)
Derby Business School, University of Derby, Derby, UK

E. Conway and D. Byrne (eds.), *Contemporary Issues in Accounting*,
https://doi.org/10.1007/978-3-319-91113-7_7

7.2 Current Challenges

For an individual company, the audit process results in an independent opinion on the truth and fairness of the company's financial performance and position as reported in its annual financial statements. This provides reasonable assurance to the shareholders that the directors are adhering to their fiduciary duty in their capacity as stewards of the company. In a broader sense, audit is a key driver in ensuring investor confidence in markets and maintaining appropriate share values on international markets. Historically, audits in the UK were guided by the Auditing Practice Board (APB)'s own audit standards, Statements on Auditing Standards (SAS) for use in the UK. The audit process is now guided by the International Standards on Auditing (ISAs) which, whilst adoption has been varied, has helped to achieve some standardisation in the audit process around the world through international harmonisation. The International Audit and Assurance Standards Board (IAASB)'s Clarity Centre lists 125 jurisdictions around the world that use the ISAs or are committed to using them in the near future (IAASB 2018).

Readers of the business press will see that the business world can harbour people with dubious underlying ethics. This then transpires to cause fraud and scandal on a seemingly regular basis. In such instances, the perception of blame is often subjectively apportioned between directors and auditors; the most infamous case in history being the collapse of Arthur Andersen (Oppel and Eichenwald 2002), then one of the "Big 5" audit firms in the world. Cases may to some extent be regarded as part of the expectations gap and residual ambiguity over the auditor's accountability. Nevertheless, as a consequence, over recent years considerably more emphasis has been placed on the issue of enhancing audit quality to restore the reputation of the profession.

In 2004 the UK professional body, the Institute of Chartered Accountants in England and Wales (ICAEW) set up the Audit Quality Forum (AQF) at the instigation of the UK Government to promote debate and progress on this issue (ICAEW 2018). In academic circles, the focus of research has been on the issue of promoting audit quality. Recent examples of efforts to enhance audit quality include the increasingly stringent rules requiring mandatory audit firm rotation and restrictions on provision of non-audit services such as fee caps and prohibitions. This is to strengthen the auditor's independent position, for example, the adoption of the 2015 EU audit directive requiring mandatory tender after ten years and mandatory rotation after twenty (PWC 2015).

Most recently, the challenge to demonstrate less tangible traits such as professional scepticism has placed emphasis on ethical considerations in the pursuit of quality (FRC 2017b).

Another key issue affecting audit is the emergence of "Big Data", which presents an opportunity for auditors to become more sophisticated in their data analysis, for example, using data mining techniques to predict trends in a large database. This however poses a challenge to "skill sets" in facilitating the necessary analytics. Information systems are becoming more complex and internal controls more sophisticated, often embedded invisibly into clients' systems. Auditors need the mathematical and IT skills to handle these fast-changing technologies. There is debate over whether an accounting background alone is adequate, and whether an IT background may be more suitable to cope with such demands. Increasingly the recruitment net is being widened to bring in talent with more diverse backgrounds.

The increasing emergence of narrative reporting also poses new challenges for the auditor. The primary purpose of an audit of financial statements, derived from Agency Theory to report to the principal shareholder is perhaps receding in importance to the secondary objectives of providing information to wider stakeholders. This poses interesting challenges for an auditor in recognising their fundamental aim and indeed, establishing liability. The requirements of an audit performed from a financial perspective may be required to widen in scope to capture the other forms of capital in the integrated reporting movement. Again, this places debate over the skill set of the auditor. It also gives rise to the need to establish auditable performance indicators to reasonably substantiate the increased narrative being reported.

Challenges are also being posed to the standard setters, primarily IAASB, in terms of the adequacy of current audit standards. It could be argued that in the light of rapidly advancing opportunity for innovation created by technological advancements, the existing standards could be seen more as an inhibitor rather than an enabler of future best practice. Innovation is being demanded by intended users and practitioners in the developed economies. As an example, the concept of sampling could be rendered obsolete if the ability to test entire data sets is achieved.

Though certainly not exhaustive, this chapter will provide an overview of some of the current issues facing the audit profession and the challenges this poses to the required skill sets of the auditor and consider the fundamental approach to the audit process going forward.

7.3 The Focus on Audit Quality

In a practical sense, quality audits in the UK are enforced by making firms accountable through monitoring measures. The Financial Reporting Council (FRC) was established as the designated Competent Authority for Audit in 2016/17 and they perform Audit Quality Review Inspections (AQR). The largest audit firms are inspected annually whilst other audit firms are inspected once every three years (FRC 2016a). Other monitoring visits are performed by the professional accounting bodies themselves such as the Quality Assurance Department (QAD) of the ICAEW. Serious breaches could result in sanctions or removal of the firm's licence to practice under the umbrella of that Recognised Supervisory Body (RSB) (ICAEW 2017c). These monitoring measures are useful to provide a deterrent and curtail weak or unethical practice in audit firms. An Independent Review of the FRC's enforcement sanctions in 2017 showed that the total fines issued to audit firms by the FRC amounted to £12.8m, with the largest individual fine being £5.1m (FRC 2017c). Despite the total fines having doubled since the previous year, there are calls for larger fines going forwards. Amounts less than £10m are seen as little deterrent to Big 4 firms (FRC 2017c). It is therefore very likely that the FRC fines will rise significantly in the future, but it is unlikely that a Big Four entity would collapse in the manner Arthur Andersen did given the improved governance regimes that exist, nor would any government wish to see this given the lack of subsequent competition that would arise.

From a more theoretical standpoint, audit quality is pursued by the ICAEW's "Audit Quality Forum", who promote debate on quality issues in audit. The debate series in November 2017 was given the ominous title "Do We Still Need Auditors?" (ICAEW 2018). Audit has played such a pivotal role for many years and forms an integral part of the regulatory framework that it is generally accepted that auditors will always have a role to play. However, the landscape is changing on the primary function of a set of accounts and this may necessitate significant evolution in the audit process to remain relevant in the modern business world. This "relevance debate" is a driving force behind the audit firms' desire to innovate. It is also a key risk to the regulators and drives their motivation to invite discussion on potential changes to standards to remain fit for purpose.

Another relatively recent addition is the Audit Firm Governance Code which applies to a small number of audit firms who audit greater than 20 listed companies (ICAEW 2017c). Other audit firms can also follow its guidance on a voluntary basis. The 2016 iteration of this Code has introduced measures such as the requirement for Independent Directors to be present within the governance structure of the audit firm. The Code also requests more communication between the audit firm and the investors of the listed entities. This is similar to the principles within the "Relations with Shareholders" section of the UK Corporate Governance Code. This should go some way to alleviate the problem of governance vacuums where large institutional investors buy large portions of share capital in listed firms but have little motivation to exercise responsible ownership rights. This can lead to quick gains from myopic management through unsustainable practices. The Audit Firm Governance Code would therefore seem to dovetail in well with the FRC's Stewardship Code which has similar aims and promotes responsible ownership. The FRC is clearly a key driving force behind the promotion of good quality practice, underpinned by ethical principles. They have good experience following development of the UK Corporate Governance Code, which celebrated its 25th anniversary in 2017 (FRC 2017a).

It is likely that the FRC will promote further advancement in quality in their ethical code for auditors. The current iteration is entitled "Revised Ethical Standard 2016" and combines the existing ES1–ES5 provisions with the requirements of the recent EU Audit directive (FRC 2016b). The current code appears to have been hastily assembled, as the new EU regulations came into effect from 17 June 2016. It can therefore be expected that a more polished and coherent set of ethical guidance will be produced at the next iteration. It is also likely that this will place more prominence on the idea of visibly promoting the ethical values. New students studying audit have always been taught that auditors need to "be and be seen to be" independent. This remains a current issue with the perception being key. Going forwards auditors will also need to "possess and be seen to possess" professional scepticism. Simply being ethical and exercising professional scepticism is no longer sufficient. Auditors will need to "be and be seen to be" ethical in terms of all of the key principles; integrity, objectivity, professional behaviour, confidentiality, professional competence and due care. The "perception" of ethics is crucial. The challenge is to find ways of developing and demonstrating these qualities. New recruits to the profession need to be exposed to situations where they may develop these traits and the culture of the firm must place these traits at the heart of their culture. Upon reading this passage from the FRCs report "Developments in Audit 2016/17", the words that stand out are "demonstrably" and "perceptions":

> Auditors carrying out high quality audit act with integrity and objectivity, are demonstrably independent and do not act in a way that risks compromising stakeholders' perceptions of that. (FRC 2017b, p. 2)

Demonstrating audit quality is an ongoing challenge. Improving the perception of quality by more visibly emphasising "professional scepticism" has been brought to the forefront of the debate. The FRC produce a comprehensive report on issues affecting the profession "Developments in Audit" on an annual basis in July each year. The 2016/17 report emphasised the current debate around skill sets that auditors new to the profession may lack (FRC 2017b). Very high on the list was scepticism, with audit firms hesitant to place these individuals in demanding positions where they can readily develop this trait. Even for those who naturally possess a good level of scepticism and apply this in their work, the challenge remains one of perception and it is not very readily demonstrable. A key challenge for employers is therefore to adequately expose new and inexperienced recruits to situations where they can develop professional scepticism. This is a key current issue around audit quality. Audit firms need to demonstrate good systems for mentoring staff (Schilder and Koktvedgaard 2017). They may also use case study simulations to help develop critical thinking. This is perhaps a significant area where those from a higher education academic degree route background may have advantage over those from a professional exam route background. This is due to the high level of criticality required in the deep learning styles of higher education and the requirement to substantiate statements similar to the manner in which auditors seek corroborative evidence (Leopold and Vickerman 2010). A clear strategy to implement a mechanism to enable those to develop a sceptical mindset and promoting this visibly may help to shift perceptions. The ICAEW have begun to develop immersive, cinema quality productions as training materials to help to develop sceptical thought processes. Films such as "False Assurance" and "Without Question" have been introduced with the remit "Through education we aim to help firms make the right decisions about ethical issues" (ICAEW 2017a). Arnold Schilder, IAASB Chairman commented that there is a strong link between professional scepticism and the role of the "tone at the top" and the "tone at the middle" (Schilder 2017). This suggests that as the Audit Firm Governance Code takes more of an effect, it will lead to improved professional scepticism.

7.4 Evolving Skills Requirements for Auditors Due to Changing Technologies

An aside from the author:

> Back in 2003, I undertook my first role as a trainee auditor. The team of audit staff used A3 sized paper analysis pads with gridlines to conduct their work. Calculations that needed a written record were performed on till roll machines. All audit work was recorded on paper and stored in lever arch files. Along the corridor was a room called "The Computer Room" because it had a computer in it. In 2009, the audit firm I worked for adopted a computerised audit package (CaseWare) and the audit files became "paperless".

The modern technological landscape is in some respects very exciting in terms of the opportunities available to the auditor. Going beyond the capabilities of a basic Excel spreadsheet, auditors now have the opportunity to design algorithms to perform complex data analytics. This can allow the auditor to audit entire population sets of data and mine deep into the data set to perform detailed stratifications. This ability challenges the existing audit methodology required by the ISAs which asks for "sampling" to be performed. This is one of the key criticisms of current regulations governing audit being an inhibitor of progress and innovation (Schilder 2017). Predictive analytics may be used to revolutionise the manner in which risk assessments are performed. Modelling techniques and simulations may be used to predict best expected and worst-case scenarios in a manner more sophisticated than ever before. A human auditor will still be required at the end of the process to exercise professional judgement in the interpretation of results.

Continuous or perpetual auditing is another area in which the innovative auditor can offer more than the current standards require (Shilts 2017). For example, the need to perform a year-end inventory check is lessening as the auditor can gain assurance over the operational effectiveness of the client's live inventory system. Audit software can be embedded into client's systems to flag up erroneous data in real time. Auditors will need the IT skills to embed the audit tests into the client's systems. The challenge this places to the current audit standards and the blurring of the role of the external auditor is discussed in a later section.

Another exciting area is Artificial Intelligence (AI) applied in the audit process. Audit firms are experimenting in this area in the present time. This technology represents an extension of Computer Assisted Audit Techniques (CAATs). The technology can, for example, examine large data sets and apply algorithms which simulate judgement in the detection of anomalies. PWC successfully used this technology and became the winners of the Digital Accountancy Forum and Awards' Audit Innovation of the Year in 2017 (PWC 2017). Interestingly, PWC partnered with a leading IT company to develop this capability. This suggests that the development of such technology may be beyond the skill set and development capabilities of the audit firms themselves and that significant expertise is needed in bringing these innovations to market. Whilst that is the case such innovations are likely to remain within the domain of the larger firms, who have the financial clout to engage in such joint ventures. Conversely, we may see more and more computer software firms entering the audit arena. These companies will likely seek to link up with audit firms to access their client base.

Increasingly, new recruits to audit are being drafted in from non-accounting backgrounds (King 2016). This has more often been the case historically in internal audit roles where the scope is more varied. However, a wider skill set is increasingly needed in external audit roles. A challenge exists though to make audit an attractive proposition for those with more unique specialisms such as in IT, who could thrive in their own industries. Audit has commonly been seen as a stepping stone along the career pathway into other positions. Many novice auditors are attracted by the experience potential. They know they will gain a wide breadth of experience as they visit company after company with rights of access that enable them to see how different businesses make their money and operate their systems. After a few years, many in senior audit positions choose to focus on one specific area of accounting as they progress in their career. Many will settle down to working for one company in their finance team and use their breadth of knowledge to enhance that function. Only a small proportion will progress through the audit ranks to manager and partner/director positions in practice. It is therefore difficult to entice those with specific niche skills into being "career-auditors", when they could go into positions such as IT consultants or similar.

As the challenges facing the auditor continue to increase, there is concern amongst a number of stakeholders that the profession of audit is going to become increasingly less attractive to new recruits (Irvine 2016). Many in the auditing community, supported by the professional bodies, have introduced a rather novel way of challenging this notion through the introduction of the "Auditor Proud day" where on one day of the year in late September auditors around the world unite through social media via the hashtag "#auditorproud" in a demonstration of their pride for the profession. The campaign is designed to generate a buzz and online conversations about audit and its exciting career opportunities for next-generation auditors.

Some current developments in technology have implications for the continuance of traditional means of bookkeeping and this could lead to uncertainty if the rate of change out-paces the audit community. In the mid-nineties financial instruments became headline news, with seemingly unethical parties taking advantage of their complexity. This led to allegations of fraud and scandal, excessive risk-taking, poor monitoring mechanisms and the collapse of entities such as Barings Bank. This was in some part due to complex types of financial instrument being created. This led to what was referred to as "black box" accounting, where regulators could not keep pace with the rate of change in the financial markets (BBC 2011). Similar effects could be seen around the time leading up to the financial crisis in 2008, as new debt instruments were created such as Collateralised Debt Obligations (CDOs) (Treanor 2008). The lack of regulation, and excessive lending created an unsustainable bubble, followed by financial collapse. Regulators were either unable or unwilling to keep pace with the innovations in these instruments (BBC 2011). It is possible that new technologies, such as digital currencies like BitCoin and applications of blockchain technologies, may have similar effects. These innovations are being brought to market so quickly that the regulators are unlikely to have robust systems in place to regulate their use in the first instance. It is likely there will be a reactive approach from regulators in response to some future scandals.

Blockchain is a technology disruptor in that it proposes the use of distributed ledgers. Whilst in principle blockchain offers an audit trail by its inherent nature, it may lead to different forms of exchange which move away from those captured under traditional audit processes (Rae 2017). This is likely to go hand in hand with digital currency exchange which eliminates the need for the bank. Auditing of blockchain is likely to become "real time" and adds to the debate over the role of the auditor as an independent opinion maker following the year-end, or as an extension of the firm's systems and internal controls. Blockchain is unlikely to become mainstream in the short term and is likely to be implemented alongside traditional means when introduced. The large audit firms will need to keep a close eye on developments to ensure that they have the capability to keep pace with this innovative and disruptive technology.

On a more imminent practical front there are many opportunities in technological advancements that will benefit systems and controls such as Radio Frequency Identification (RFID) (Leavins and Ramaswamy 2013). Businesses are embracing this technology to streamline their operations. The auditor must conduct tests of control to ensure this technology is in place and operating effectively throughout the accounting period. For example, physical verification of assets can be done from a computer screen if the auditor can be assured that the operating effectiveness of the system is sound throughout the reporting period.

Data Analytics and the capturing of useful insights from Big Data will provide additional information to auditors to utilise in analytical procedures. Results may be generated that were not conceived when the existing audit standards were created. Audit firms are likely to act as pioneers in driving forward innovation in audit processes. Firms are eager to do so as this will act as a key competitive advantage. Audit firms are keen to go over and above the minimum service standards required by the Audit Standards. Users of accounts in the developed economies are also requesting innovation to satisfy their increasing information needs (Gambier and Jeffrey 2016). The benefits of utilising data analytics are clearly highlighted by Arnold Schilder, IAASB Chairman, who states that the use of data analytics in the audit can lead to better-informed risk assessments, through understanding the business of the auditee, and more available evidence to support professionally sceptical behaviour (Schilder 2017).

7.5 The Effect on Audit of the Emergence of Narrative Reporting

The nature of the audit profession may be required to change to meet the needs of narrative reporting. This has an impact on standard setters, audit process and the skill sets required. Standard setters such as the IAASB are impacted by narrative reporting as the current standards are designed to audit the financial aspects only. New standards will certainly be needed to cope with the audit of other forms of capital.

This will have a significant effect on the audit methodology, with a greater focus on overall value creation rather than on profitability and solvency. Auditors will also have to develop their skill sets to audit new and emerging performance criteria to judge whether new narrative disclosures are reasonable. Auditors cannot form a clear view on the requirements at present as narrative reporting is in its developmental stages (ACCA 2015). Regulators have begun to gather data and promote discussion on the issues.

Audit has always been a challenging career choice. The prospect of dealing with the increased demands stemming from narrative reporting is even more challenging. In 2017, ICAS inferred that new potential recruits may be reluctant to become an auditor going forward (ICAS 2016b). The study infers that the perception of audit as a desirable career choice is being affected by the increased demands on skill set within the role. This is due to the increased demands of changing technologies, as mentioned previously, but also due to the increase in narrative reporting. The accounting profession continues to experiment with narrative reporting in a number of ways. Some firms have increased the size of the annual report with more and more disclosures. Others have experimented with Integrated Reports which at present are voluntary alongside the Annual Report. Going forward it may be necessary for the auditor to be capable of auditing not just the figures but this extended narrative as well. This will necessitate significant evolution in the audit process. This is substantiated by research from the professional body of Chartered Accountants (ICAS) "if audit is to evolve beyond the traditional financial statement audit, then the skill set of auditors needs to evolve to execute the audit of the future" (ICAS 2016b).

One of the challenges of producing and validating content for narrative reporting is the development of key metrics and performance indicators. These need to be capable of capturing and presenting performance in the various forms of capital. The challenge for the auditor will be to give an opinion on the reasonableness (truth and fairness) of conclusions drawn from these indicators. Exercising such a level of subjectivity on subject matter of this nature has proven difficult in the past in Corporate Social Responsibility (CSR) reporting. This, like many forms of voluntary reporting, is notoriously fraught with marketing spin and hyperbole. The auditor will therefore need to exercise a significant degree of professional scepticism when judging whether the narrative statements represent a faithful representation.

Auditors in the UK are currently required to peruse sections of narrative supporting information in the Annual Report and report by exception on any contradictive wording. This is part of the enhanced reporting regulations in the UK, required by International Standard on Auditing (ISA) 700—Forming an Opinion and Reporting on Financial Statements (Revised June 2016) (IFAC 2009). Auditors may therefore feel adept at spotting contradicting wording. The challenge may come in the scale of narrative and the subjective judgement of what constitutes good performance in the measurement of other forms of capital.

The practice of "flagging" sections of the financial statements which are incapable of being audited will likely be necessary. This is often done in Environmental audits where many of the performance measures do not have tangible and quantifiable source data by which to substantiate the claim being made. Such flagging arguably diminishes the value of the audit opinion. The auditor has little power to solve this problem and it is for researchers in the areas of performance indicators to devise new Key Performance Indicators (KPIs) that are auditable. The Integrated Reporting movement is growing and has over 1500 companies globally producing Integrated Reports to communicate with stakeholders on a voluntary basis (IIRC 2018). It is unlikely to be made mandatory in the short term due to the difficulty in finding quantifiable and verifiable measures on which to base the narrative included in them, but nevertheless demonstrates the direction of travel for corporate reporting.

The International Audit and Assurance Standards Board (IAASB) has recognised the need for new guidance for assurance providers to help with ensuring the credibility of narrative reporting. IAASB's Integrated Reporting Working Group is stimulating debate at the preliminary discussion paper stage (IAASB 2016). The discussion paper identifies 10 key challenges for providing assurance on "Emerging forms of External Reporting" (EER).

The ten key challenges for supporting credibility and trust in Emerging Forms of External Reporting identified in the Integrated Reporting Working Group's Discussion Draft (IAASB 2016, p. 8) are:

1. Scoping EER assurance engagements
2. Suitability of criteria
3. Materiality
4. Building assertions in planning and performing the engagement
5. Maturity of governance and internal control processes

6. Narrative information
7. Future orientated information
8. Professional scepticism and professional judgement
9. Competence of practitioners performing the engagement
10. Form of the assurance report

The broadness of these challenges suggests that the work is at a very early stage. The discussion paper explains that the challenges are not insurmountable but identify a clear need for developing guidance for practitioners and that further conceptual analysis is needed to develop appropriate responses to them (IAASB 2016). IAASB also note that "the EER frameworks and entities' reporting systems, controls and oversight that underpin their preparation of EER reports are at an early stage of development and are likely to mature further" (IAASB 2016, p. 8). This adds weight to the view that it is the performance measures that need developing. They go on to state that "it may be too early to develop a definitive subject matter specific standard to address EER assurance engagements" (IAASB 2016). From an audit perspective, IAASB are therefore watching and waiting, but audit is likely going to be led by the developments in financial reporting on this.

The Financial Reporting Lab is an entity set up and funded by the Financial Reporting Council. Their purpose is to invite and conduct debates around emerging issues in accountancy. The Financial Reporting Lab routinely survey auditors, professional bodies and academics upon their choice of issue to target (FRC 2017e). In February 2018, it was reported that the result of the most recent survey was to target the issue of Performance Measures (Fisher 2018). This is most likely due to the fact that new, auditable performance measures are needed to help substantiate narrative reports. This is not just a look to the future. Reliable indicators are also needed in the present to help substantiate existing narrative in the annual report. The annual report is becoming increasingly lengthy, as aspects of developing theory on narrative reporting finds their way into the extended voluntary narrative. Another reason why increased research is needed on Performance Indicators is the latest proposed revision to the UK Corporate Governance Code. For example, the proposed change to wording of the Performance Related Pay (PRP) principle to a more generic, "Pay in line with successful performance relating to meeting the company's strategic objectives" principle (FRC 2017d). This is a positive step in that it will be more difficult to justify excessive pay based upon the bottom line figure, however, it could be challenging to measure the performance against strategic objectives in a clear and objective manner.

Until such time as it becomes mandatory there is no call for a statutory audit of narrative reporting with reasonable assurance levels. Ironically it cannot become mandatory until it is capable of being audited and this is dependent upon innovations in performance measurement. In the meantime, it may be possible to undertake limited assurance engagements on narrative subject matter. Audits of narrative reports are likely to fall into the domain of "other assurance engagements" for some time to come. Opinions are unlikely to carry much more weight than assurance engagements on CSR reports. However, it is important for audit firms to be developing processes in how to conduct such engagements and the changing methodologies that will be needed.

7.6 Audit Standards

Pressure on auditors is likely to grow as increasing demands are placed on them. In developing economies, the call is for stability in audit standards (ACCA 2017). Countries benefit from having a clear benchmark from the traditional financial statements audit. This helps to achieve conformity and stability and raises standards over time. Conversely, in developed economies there is clamour for evolution in the audit profession. Audit firms can provide more value and user groups want more value from the process. A round-table debate was conducted by Grant Thornton and ACCA in which the main finding was that stakeholders of listed entities are wanting more than a pass/fail opinion. There were three main findings in the report; frustration that the audit report is only addressed to shareholders, only covers "historical" financial information and is a single standardised report (Gambier and Jeffrey 2016). The fundamental characteristics of an audit are therefore being challenged.

An immediate response to previous similar findings was the development of ISA 701—which contained guidance on a new extended audit report (ICAEW 2017b). The auditor must now publicly detail their view of the key risk areas, their response to addressing these key areas and a justification of their decisions on materiality levels. No longer can these factors be brushed off under the secrecy of it being a matter of the auditor's professional judgement, due to their skill experience and qualifications. This increased transparency arguably enhances audit quality. The audit report has grown from a small number of relatively standardised pages to over ten pages in length to accommodate this additional detail. This is a demonstration of the increased pressures placed on auditors as users demand more added value from the service.

Addressing the audit report to a wider group of stakeholders than just the shareholders could give rise to liability and responsibility debates. Specific disclaimer statements in audit reports will become more important. In response to the claim regarding infrequent and historical communications, the auditor could react by innovating to produce assurance reports at more regular intervals. This could tie in well with the new innovative capabilities of audit firms, particularly the Big 4, in terms of the movement towards perpetual auditing, by embedding audit CAATs into the client's systems. These CAATs flag up erroneous information on an ongoing basis. This would however fundamentally change the role of the auditor as an independent examiner post year end. This also blurs the role of the external and internal auditor. Perhaps the clamour is in fact for more visible internal audits, rather than placing this burden on external auditors. When auditors report on an ongoing basis and comment on matters which could be acted upon to shape the future direction of the business this poses a threat to their independence. The auditor will become a part of the system, an additional internal control, rather than an independent entity commenting on the controls. The challenge here is that the more relevant the auditor becomes, the less independent they may be perceived. The same criticism could be applied to the third finding, i.e. the call for more than one single standardised report that does not meet the needs of users. This would also change the role of the auditor, but again is perhaps more within the remit of the internal audit profession.

Interestingly, it is the strength of the regular financial information that the shareholders are already receiving throughout the financial year that is rendering the external audit report "old news and merely confirmatory" (ACCA 2017, p. 7). Companies that comply well with Corporate Governance practice will be regularly "relating with shareholders" throughout the year. Gone are the days that they eagerly await the audit report in trepid anticipation of the results. This would suggest that the external audit report should indeed contain more, to provide value for money. This has been achieved to some extent with the ISA 701 revision requiring extended narrative (ICAEW 2017b).

The audit thresholds increased from 1st January 2016 (ICAS 2016a) and this will likely have caused a loss of income for smaller audit firms. This trend is likely to increase to relieve the burden on smaller entities requiring an audit. Audits may be seen as less and less relevant due to increased information flow and media channels enabling communication from companies to their stakeholders. It may well be "self-preservation" of the profession that will be a key driver for the audit regulators as they endeavour to evolve to stay relevant. "The overwhelming feeling is that both the traditional audit and the traditional auditor need to respond more promptly to change if they are to remain fit for purpose. This poses a challenge for auditors: how to meet the needs of users without compromising the independence that is at the heart of auditors' professional standards" (ACCA 2017, p. 10).

7.7 Conclusion

A balance must be found between independence, innovation and regulation. There is a call from stakeholders in developed economies for audit reports to evolve further and there is the skill required from the largest audit firms to deliver innovative solutions. Some of these solutions hinder the independent position of the auditor and blur the lines between external and internal auditing. The regulators must balance this with the stable audit standards which are called for in less developed economies. The challenge for regulators is to have a set of standards that are fit for purpose for both sets of user needs. Innovation is clearly needed in the profession and it is likely that the audit firms will be drivers of this change. Furthermore, the regulators are currently searching for conceptual answers to address the issue of emerging forms of external reporting. It is unlikely that such forms of narrative reporting will become mandatory until such a time as their creditability can be assured.

"Self-preservation" is likely to be the key driving force that ensures audit firms keep pace with the change in technology. Differentiation from competitors in the market may be achieved with bold claims of futuristic data analytics and harnessing the power of Big Data. Whether this has any substance in terms of methodology and practice will be revealed over time. Similarly, the regulators are likely to take a step back and allow the audit firms to be innovative as they recognise the importance of staying relevant. They must do this whilst maintaining strong levels of ethics to ensure independence and professional scepticism are demonstrably maintained to satisfy public perception.

References

ACCA. 2015. "The Challenges of Assuring Integrated Reports: Views from the South African Auditing Community." http://www.accaglobal.com/content/dam/ACCA_Global/Technical/integrate/ea-south-africa-IR-assurance.pdf.

ACCA. 2017. "The Future of Audit." http://www.accaglobal.com/content/dam/ACCA_Global/Technical/audit/ea-future-of-audit.pdf.

BBC. 2011. "Nick Leeson on Newsnight with Jeremy Paxman." https://www.youtube.com/watch?v=lsZ5RlBail4.

Fisher, Liz. 2018. "Pathology of Reporting." *AB Magazine*.

FRC. 2016a. "Audit Quality Review." https://www.frc.org.uk/auditors/audit-quality-review.

FRC. 2016b. "Ethical Standard (2016) Integrity, Objectivity and Independence." https://www.frc.org.uk/getattachment/0bd6ee4e-075c-4b55-a4ad-b8e5037b56c6/Revised-Ethical-Standard-UK-June-2016.pdf.

FRC. 2017a. "25th Anniversary of the UK Corporate Governance Code." https://www.frc.org.uk/directors/corporate-governance-and-stewardship/uk-corporate-governance-code/25th-anniversary-of-the-uk-corporate-governance-co.

FRC. 2017b. "Developments in Audit." https://www.frc.org.uk/getattachment/915c15a4-dbc7-4223-b8ae-cad53dbcca17/Developments-in-Audit-2016-17-Full-report.pdf.

FRC. 2017c. "Independent Review of the Financial Reporting Council's Enforcement Procedures Sanctions Review Panel Report."

FRC. 2017d. "Proposed Revisions to the UK Corporate Governance Code Appendix C—Summary of Changes from 2016 UK Corporate Governance Code."

FRC. 2017e. "The Lab." https://www.frc.org.uk/getattachment/e3d916ce-c13a-415e-9633-01c93218f79e/The-Lab-at-a-glance-April-2017.pdf.

Gambier, Andrew, and Nick Jeffrey. 2016. "The Future of Audit." https://www.ifac.org/global-knowledge-gateway/audit-assurance/discussion/future-audit.

IAASB. 2016. "Supporting Credibility and Trust in Emerging Forms of External Reporting: Ten Key Challenges for Assurance Engagements." https://www.ifac.org/system/files/publications/files/IAASB-Discussion-Paper-Integrated-Reporting_0.pdf.

IAASB. 2018. "Support and Guidance." https://www.iaasb.org/clarity-center/support-and-guidance.

ICAEW. 2017a. "ICAEW Educational Films." https://www.icaew.com/en/learning-and-development/icaew-educational-films.

ICAEW. 2017b. "The Start of a Conversation the Extended Audit Report." https://www.icaew.com/-/media/corporate/files/technical/audit-and-assurance/audit-and-assurance-faculty/publications/extended-audit-report.ashx?la=en.

ICAEW. 2017c. "Your Audit Monitoring." https://www.icaew.com/-/media/corporate/files/technical/audit-and-assurance/audit-monitoring-visits.ashx?la=en.

ICAEW. 2018. "Audit Quality Forum (AQF)." https://www.icaew.com/technical/audit-and-assurance/audit-quality-forum-aqf.

ICAS. 2016a. "Audit Exemption: What Are the New Rules?" https://www.icas.com/technical-resources/audit-exemption-update-what-are-the-new-rules.

ICAS. 2016b. "Auditor Skills in a Changing Business World." https://www.icas.com/__data/assets/pdf_file/0010/259516/Auditor-skills-ICAS-FRC-20.9.16-Final.pdf.

IFAC. 2009. "International Standard on Auditing 700 Forming an Opinion and Reporting on Financial Statements." *Auditing* 700 (June): 653–681.

IIRC. 2018. "Integrated Reporting—When? Advocate for Global Adoption." https://integratedreporting.org/when-advocate-for-global-adoption/.

Irvine, Julia. 2016. "FRC Survey Reveals Fears That Audit Profession Becoming Less Attractive." *Economia*. https://economia.icaew.com/news/july-2016/frc-survey-reveals-fears-that-audit-profession-becoming-less-attractive.

King, Agnes. 2016. "KPMG's New Auditors Don't Have Accounting Degrees." *Financial Review*. http://www.afr.com/business/accounting/kpmgs-new-auditors-dont-have-accounting-degrees-20151208-gliczy.

Leavins, John R., and Vinita Ramaswamy. 2013. "Improving Internal Controls over Inventory with Radio Frequency Identification Technology." *Review of Business Information Systems* 17 (2): 59–64. http://journals.cluteonline.com/index.php/RBIS/article/view/7844/7905.

Leopold, Teresa, and Philip Vickerman. 2010. "Learning and Teaching Guide on Critical Thinking." https://www.heacademy.ac.uk/system/files/ssg_leopold_critical_thinking.pdf.

Oppel, Richard, and Kurt Eichenwald. 2002. "Enron's Collapse: The Overview; Arthur Andersen Fires An Executive for Enron Orders." *NY Times*, January. http://www.nytimes.com/2002/01/16/business/enron-s-collapse-overview-arthur-andersen-fires-executive-for-enron-orders.html.

PWC. 2015. "EU Audit Reform—Mandatory Firm Rotation Summary of Adopted Legislation on Mandatory Audit Firm Rotation (MFR) for Public Interest Entities." https://www.pwc.com/gx/en/audit-services/publications/assets/pwc-fact-sheet-1-summary-of-eu-audit-reform-requirements-relating-to-mfr-feb-2015.pdf.

PWC. 2017. "Harnessing the Power of AI to Transform the Detection of Fraud and Error." https://www.pwc.com/gx/en/about/stories-from-across-the-world/harnessing-the-power-of-ai-to-transform-the-detection-of-fraud-and-error.html.

Rae, David. 2017. "Blockchain: Accountancy's Transformer." *AB Magazine*. http://www.accaglobal.com/uk/en/member/member/accounting-business/2017/04/insights/blockchain-17.html.

Schilder, Arnold. 2017. "The Future of Audit: Technology." https://www.icaew.com/en/technical/audit-and-assurance/faculty/the-future-of-audit/the-future-of-audit-technology.

Schilder, Arnold, and Kristian Koktvedgaard. 2017. "Professional Scepticism: Inside the Mind of the Auditor." http://www.accaglobal.com/content/dam/ACCA_Global/Technical/eventinvitations/Professional-scepticism-17-October-2017-REPORT.pdf.

Shilts, Josh. 2017. "A Framework for Continuous Auditing: Why Companies Don't Need to Spend Big Money." https://www.journalofaccountancy.com/issues/2017/mar/continuous-auditing.html.

Treanor, Jill. 2008. "Toxic Shock: How the Banking Industry Created a Global Crisis." *The Guardian*. https://www.theguardian.com/business/2008/apr/08/creditcrunch.banking.

CHAPTER 8

Why Do We Need to Measure Performance? A Local Government Perspective

Hilary Coyle

8.1 Introduction

In this chapter, we will look at some of the issues that surround the measurement of performance. Should we measure performance at all? Surely if you have the right people in the right jobs they will do what they need to and there will be no need to measure anything? Just think if your lecturer does not turn up for your class on time—what do you do? Do you get your books out, set up and start to do some work or do you say, "I'll give her five more minutes then I'm leaving"? You may smile but this is often the case in a working environment that productivity slows down when managers and supervisors are not present. So then the issue is how much do you need to measure and what do you measure? There are also further complications within the public sector due to the fact there are many more stakeholders who are interested in their performance, particularly since it is public money that is being spent. Many governments are keen to show their public that the money is being spent wisely and fairly. Whether the public agrees with them or not is entirely another issue. We will review some of the literature on performance measurement and examine some of the tools that are currently used.

H. Coyle (✉)
Derby Business School, University of Derby, Derby, UK

E. Conway and D. Byrne (eds.), *Contemporary Issues in Accounting*,
https://doi.org/10.1007/978-3-319-91113-7_8

8.2 Measuring Performance

Balabonienė and Večerskienė (2015, p. 317) state that "it is not possible for any organisation to act effectively without having its performance measured". Nath and Sharma (2014, p. 2) believe the "use of performance indicators is important because they are an essential part of the monitoring of programs and employee performance".

Is this correct? Do we need to measure our performance at all? There are some theorists that believe if you employ the right people in the right roles, then there is no need to measure their performance as they will always do the right thing. This is the view of Stewardship theory. There is no extrinsic or monetary motivation but a sense of achievement when a job is well done (Glinkowska and Kaczmarek 2015). This also supports the view of McGregors' Theory Y that staff will work on their own and without line management (Seddon 2008). However, the view of the general public that the public sector is lazy and inefficient means that the electorate will not leave the staff to their own devices but require targets to prove that public money is being used fairly. This is also supported by the command and control view of management from Seddon (2008).

8.3 Target Setting

There are two schools of thought regarding the use of target setting according to Bourne and Franco-Santos (2010, p. 29); "Good" or "Divisive and counterproductive". Evidence from management literature believe that having a realistic and achievable target is better than no target at all but with just an overall focus of work hard or do your best. On the other hand, there is the dysfunctional behaviour that can "create fear, undermine teamwork and destroy performance improvement" (Bourne and Franco-Santos 2010, p. 29). If your targets create intense competition within teams, then they will not be focussing on the goals of the organisation. They will be channelling their energy into beating their colleagues. This will have an adverse effect on performance. Performing well as part of a team means that all parts of the team have to work together, which cannot happen if individuals are competing against each other. If teams do not gel, then it is hard to deliver performance targets (Bourne and Franco-Santos 2010). Opposing this is the view from the control theorists that peer pressure can help everyone achieve their targets. People will work together to achieve their goals as they do not want to let down their colleagues (Merchant and Van der Stede 2012).

Organisations should not just look at individuals' performance. It has to be the whole team. The whole team creates the synergy which is not there if they are kept separate as individuals. Recruiting the right team is vital. Managers who inspire are needed to bring out the best in staff supported by Human Resources to train, coach and mentor (West and Blackman 2015). "All levels of management and employees ... must drive the change" (West and Blackman 2015, p. 76). This is a theme that runs through a successful organisation, that to achieve your performance goals you need to work together as a team and all move in the same direction. So the most obvious purpose of a performance measurement system (PMS) is to improve performance, whether this is to improve and increase funding, or to control costs, or even to identify defunct processes or procedures (Lewis 2015).

However, as soon as people are measured, their behaviour changes and the deviousness of people's characters can come out (Lewis 2015). Bevan and Hood (2006) agree with this sentiment as they believe that gaming occurs and people begin to adapt and look out for themselves. Do you agree with this? If you are being watched or filmed are you self-conscious? Do you behave differently? This is one of many side effects of measuring performance. Lewis (2015) feels that all the dysfunctional consequences of measuring performance cannot be pre-empted and there will always be some non-intended side effects. However, we should not be scared to measure our performance because of the actions of a few people. Pavlov et al. (2017) believe that performance measurement does influence performance in a good way as it provides focus for managers and means they can organise and coordinate resources together.

8.4 What Is Performance Measurement?

Performance measurement was being discussed in 1956 by Ridgway (Ridgway cited in Neely 2005) and it has been reviewed many times. However, in the 1980s and 1990s, it became a fashionable topic to research and many authors devised frameworks (Neely 2005). Ghobadian and Ashworth (1994) noted that it also became a topic of interest for local governments around this time as they were being pressurised from central government, the public and new competitive market strategies, amongst other pressures. Organisations are "clearly searching for performance measurement solutions" (Fitzgerald in Hopper et al. 2007, p. 223).

Thus, there is agreement across many academics that performance measurement is a subject for discussion and has been for several decades. "Performance measurement has for a long time been one of the crucial issues among scholars and business managers" (Larimo et al. 2016, p. 877). The business environment is constantly changing and thus performance measurement, too, has to change and continuously update itself (Yadav and Sagar 2013). Globalisation and the increase in the capability of technology are some of the factors that are pushing organisations to analyse their performance in greater detail (van der Meer-Kooistra and Vosselman 2004). The journal Management Accounting Research created a special issue, number 25 in 2014, to look at the issues in performance measurement. Bourne et al. (2014) describe performance measurement as being at a crossroads. No one is sure of which road to take. The literature has been inconsistent in their findings when trying to link performance to performance measurement. They suggest that there are still gaps in knowledge about the effect performance measures have on the overall performance of organisations. Yet performance measurement will still not prevent organisations from collapsing. So where does performance measurement go next academically?

Neely et al. (1995, p. 80) comment that the term "performance measurement" is not very often defined as it can mean different things to different people depending on what discipline you are coming from. However, they do produce a short definition:

> Performance measurement can be defined as the process of quantifying the efficiency and effectiveness of action. (Neely et al. 1995, p. 80)

Hall (2008 cited in Franco-Santos et al. 2012) states that performance measurement systems

> translate business strategies into deliverable results [...] combining financial, strategic and operating business measures to gauge how well a company meets its targets. (p. 80)

Other authors suggest that performance measurement can be used to rank different initiatives to see which one performs the best and which one will be the one the organisation focusses on (Ittner et al. 2003 cited in Franco-Santos et al. 2012).

Melnyk et al. (2014) define PMS as

> the process for setting goals (developing the metric set) and collecting, analysing and interpreting performance data. (p. 175)

A PMS, if designed well, can be used to translate the goals of an organisation into an action plan to deliver. However, it can also identify if the strategy is the right one for the organisation. It can point out any gaps or confusion as the behaviour it creates may deviate from what the organisation intended (Franco-Santos et al. 2007). So there are many different interpretations of what performance measurement is. How far organisations go in terms of data collection will depend. Some will have very basic manual systems and some will develop complex data bases (Franco-Santos et al. 2007). Quite often staff feel very comfortable with collecting and analysing data and collect huge amounts. "Measuring the shadow of the shadow" is a quote that stood out from some recent research the author completed. Staff are unwilling to let go of measures and often collect data "just in case". At some point, the number of measures needs to be reduced to maintain focus and efficiency. Thus how can organisations structure their performance measurement to obtain the optimum amount of data?

Franco-Santos et al. (2007) have suggested a process for a business PMS:

1. Selection and design of measures
2. Collection and manipulation of data
3. Information management
4. Performance evaluation and rewards
5. System review. (Franco-Santos et al. 2007, p. 798).

Micheli and Manzoni (2010) believe that strategic performance measurement (SPM) processes have a positive effect on the performance of a business. However, it has almost turned into an industry of its own with:

> UK government departments estimating that they spend over £150m per year solely to monitor progress on national targets. This is without the data gathering costs of front line organisations. (Micheli and Manzoni 2010, p. 466)

The benefits of a SPM are that there is a consistent message and communication and this will strengthen the corporate brand and reputation. It can also help to improve motivation by generating a performance improvement culture. However, if it is not implemented properly, it can fail and end up costing the organisation a lot of money. The key to success is the link to the strategy. Firms with just a PMS show no difference in performance to firms without a PMS (Micheli and Manzoni 2010). So your organisation will not grow and improve just because you measure it.

8.5 What Are the Current Trends in Performance Measurement?

Radnor and Barnes (2007) have completed a detailed review of performance measurement and management systems with regards to operations management, however, the techniques are transferrable to other disciplines. In the early twentieth century at the time of the industrial revolution factories were starting to expand with new machinery and managers were starting to think about economies of scale and time and motion studies or how to get the maximum output from your labour force. Taylor (citied in Radnor and Barnes 2007) started to measure the performance of individual workers to be able to incentivise them to work even harder and to produce even more. Cost accountants would produce figures based on the financials of the factory. Seal et al. (2012) comment that more emphasis was based on financial accounting at this time due to the fact that factory owners were looking to finance their expansion plans by borrowing funds. To prove that they were reliable, the owners would have to produce audited accounts and thus the accountants' time was spent on this type of accounting more than the management accounting discipline.

The 1920s saw the growth in techniques such as Return on Investment and the Pyramid of Financial Ratios as tools to measure the performance of an organisation. At this time, traditional management accounting costing techniques were being used but were inadequate at tracing costs of products and focussed mainly on control of resources (Yadav and Sagar 2013).

After the Second World War, the Japanese developed tools such as Total Quality Management (TQM) and Just in Time (JIT) manufacturing with their focus directed towards efficiency and effectiveness. Japanese companies were seen to be outperforming western businesses. Western businesses had focussed on the efficiency to the detriment of being effective. Long production runs and stock piling products took the emphasis away from what the customer wanted. As western organisations started to examine their effectiveness, they found that improved quality would drive this forwards (Radnor and Barnes 2007).

The change in emphasis for performance measurement tools over the last 30 years has moved away from being purely financially focussed to also include non-financial information. There will always be financial information included but it is now recognised that it is not enough on its own (Yadav and Sagar 2013). Organisations started to see the issues and problems that arose from directing a business from purely financial data (Bourne 2008). This has seen organisations incorporating both non-financial and financial measures into frameworks that also link into the strategy of the organisation.

Neely (1999, p. 207) refers to this time as the "Performance Revolution". Thousands of articles have been written about performance measurement and the membership of the various accounting institutions has increased by huge amounts as more and more businesses look to improve their PMS.

When reading extensively about performance measurement, a reoccurring concept emerges, called the Balanced Scorecard. Kaplan and Norton were the authors of the original "Balanced Scorecard" which emerged from the research institute linked to KPMG in the early nineties (Kaplan and Norton 1996). Kaplan and Norton had originally designed the balanced scorecard framework for performance measurement for profit-making companies. However, Chang et al. point out that Kaplan and Norton also believed it could be adapted for Not-for-Profit Organisations (Chang et al. 2002).

Often these techniques are referred to as frameworks as the balanced scorecard is above. Folan and Browne (2005, p. 665) define framework as "the active employment of particular sets of recommendations". The frameworks can be split between a procedural one and a structural one. Once you have these you can then start to develop a PMS. Sharma and Gadenne (2011, p. 167) support this view by commenting that the balanced scorecard has "long been recognised as a performance measurement framework".

8.6 What Is the Balanced Scorecard?

The balanced scorecard is a tool that helps to translate the strategy of the organisation into a set of targets and measures. These targets are then filtered down through the whole organisation so all staff are working towards the same objectives. As no two organisations have the same strategy, it follows that all balanced scorecards are different. Kaplan and Norton (1996) originally visualised four sections to the scorecard which covered financial, customer, internal and the combined learning and growth perspectives. As the scorecard has developed over the years, organisations have been adapting it for their own needs and creating their own versions. Along with the four perspectives, Kaplan and Norton (2001) give guidance on how to translate the vision of the organisation, how to obtain feedback and learn from their existing procedures, how to communicate and link the strategy to the measures for everyone at all levels in the organisation. This then becomes a framework with which the organisation can begin to use to improve its performance (Folan and Browne 2005).

The balanced scorecard has the advantages of the mix of the different types of measures with both monetary and non-monetary. Bourne (2013) also comments that the balance comes from how you look at the scorecard. Both Financial and Customer perspectives are outward looking and this balances with the inward-looking Internal Processes and Learning and Growth. Yet you can also look at it as now and the future, with "what we have done" as the lagging measures, and those which will affect the future as the leading measures. The balanced scorecard has several advantages. It is very simple and easy to understand. It has also survived the test of time as it has been around for over twenty years (Bourne 2013). It is also useful because it has everything in a snapshot on one page which is often vital for busy senior management teams (Drury 2015). It also does force organisations to look at their long-term plans and to develop a strategy if they do not have one or to fine-tune a strategy they already have. However, it is not a panacea and it does have its limitations such as it can become very complicated with far too many measures. Neely and Adams (cited in Ryan 2012) believe that management are obsessed with measurements. They feel that they must be controlling their organisations because they are measuring everything they can. This is also made possible by the sophisticated computer systems that businesses can use to slice and dice the data. "What should we measure?" is often a question asked and it is tempting to measure what is already known and what is easy to measure rather than challenging this and asking the difficult questions (Ryan 2012). Melnyk et al. (2014) support this view as they discovered that often when organisations changed their strategy they did not change their measurement system.

Norreklit (2003) takes the disadvantages further and produced an article that claims that the balanced scorecard is all hype with no substance. That there is no theoretical underpinning to Kaplan and Norton's views. Bessire and Baker (2005) support this view and feel that the scorecard does not address the political issues well enough and thus will never reach its potential. However, there are many other authors that feel that the scorecard is a worthwhile tool whilst recognising that it is not a panacea (Neely 2005; Northcott and Taulapapa 2012, amongst others). Arnaboldi et al. (2015) believes that the balanced scorecard is just a management fad that has had its time, due to the issues of the complexity of organisations and how the balanced scorecard tries to simplify the issues. Equally, there is no integration with the accounting system.

Yadav and Sagar (2013) claim the largest influence on performance measurement, was the Balanced Scorecard. This is supported by Bourne et al. (2002, p. 1288) as they write that the Harvard Business Review cites the balanced scorecard as the "most important management tool in the last 75 years". It changes the way organisations measured their performance. Neely (1999) asks the question why now? Why in the early nineties should scholars become interested in new ways of performance measurement? Whilst some traditional PMS are less intuitive, the balanced scorecard approach with its flexibility has been able to adapt to some of challenges of traditional management accounting methods which Neely (1999) identified as:

- The changing nature of work
- Increasing competition
- Specific improvement initiatives
- National and International awards
- Changing organisational roles
- Changing external demands and
- The power of information technology.

(Neely 1999, p. 210)

Organisations want to understand more clearly how they can translate their strategy and objectives into targets for their people to use to ensure the organisation performs well and is successful. The balanced scorecard is constantly evolving to address these challenges. Kaplan and Norton are still heavily involved in the process so they are still regarded as experts. They have developed the tool to include "strategy mapping" where the cause and effect linkages are shown clearly in pictorial form (Ross 2011). One of the issues with the original balanced scorecard was that there were too many measurements and it was difficult to choose the correct ones for an organisation's strategy (Drury 2015). With this strategy mapping technique, the measures that are not driving the organisation towards its goals can be identified and removed (Ross 2011). Nevertheless, Kaplan and Norton (2004, p. 5) see the balanced scorecard as a "powerful management tool. A measurement system that gets everyone's attention". Neely and Adams (cited in Ryan 2012) have taken the balanced scorecard further and created their "Performance Prism". They have added more dimensions to the scorecard and advocate the need for the organisation to analyse the needs of all their stakeholders before finalising their strategy (Ryan 2012).

Neely and Bourne argue that the emphasis has moved from the issue in the 1980s of organisations measuring the "wrong things" to organisations now measuring "too much" (Neely and Bourne 2000, p. 6). There are too many measurements to be of any real use. In particular, this could be exacerbated in Not-for-Profit Organisations as they often have many varying objectives and multiple stakeholders (Ross 2011). Designing a performance measurement framework that works to achieve these many goals is a complex task that covers many disciplines, not just accounting (Neely and Bourne 2000).

Even though performance measurement has been a topic researched for many years, it is constantly evolving. The tools need to be adapted to move with the changing organisations. There is more data available to be collected than ever before. Neely suggests that the;

> challenge for the research community [...] is to take the performance measurement agenda forward. If we fail to do so then we risk becoming trapped by solutions proposed for problems of the past. (Neely 2005, p. 6)

8.7 Local Government and Performance Management

Local Government have their own set of issues when it comes to measuring performance. The issues that Cartwright (1975) was discussing in the seventies are still relevant today. Authorities needed to define the objectives of their organisation. Elected members of these authorities needed time to think about what they wanted their organisation to achieve. Time was spent analysing how much money had been spent but not about what it had been spent on. How did members allocate scarce resources between different projects? What were the long-term objectives and how could they be planned for rather than just looking at the short term? Did members have a choice of options for the key areas they needed to make decisions for? All these comments are still relevant in the public sector today forty years later.

In the 1980s and 1990s, the public sector underwent a modernisation strategy that is often referred to as "New Public Management (NPM)" (Williams and Lewis 2008, p. 655). Chief executive officers were encouraged to use some of the tools that were being used in the private sector, such as benchmarking, six sigma and the balanced scorecard. Williams and Lewis (2008) believe the motivation for using these tools were increasing competition, performance directives from central government such as the benchmarking standards and also the fear of being sued if the level of performance was unacceptable. Dreveton (2013) believes that the excitement that the private sector has shown for the balanced scorecard has seeped into the public sector. This is where the public sector is moving to be more "Business Like". It will not be the same as a free market but it can move towards the characteristics of business.

Lowe (2013) delves into the realms of measuring the outcomes of social policy. The aims of the public sector are very complicated and not easily converted into measurable outcomes. How do you measure the effect an action has on a person's life? It cannot be measured by one thing but by understanding the individual and this would take an enormous amount of resource to collate the evidence. Thus, an easy-to-calculate measure is used and the impact is not really understood.

Bevan and Hood (2006, p. 518) compare the "governance by targets and performance indicators theory of the public health care system" to the pre-cold war Soviet regimes where those in charge ruled by "terror"; so much so that it encouraged a gaming mentality to ensure that as a manager you survived but never exceeded at your role. Evidence of manipulation of hospital waiting lists and schools focussing on those pupils that may not pass to ensure they will pass their exams are two of the many examples available to support Bevan and Hood's views. These are classed a deviant or dysfunctional behaviours and do not help the organisation achieve its goals (Fryer et al. 2009).

Many implementations of the balanced scorecard fail which could be another reason why local government have not invested in this tool.

Can authorities justify more performance measures on top of the existing KPIs especially if there is evidence to suggest that "70 per cent of balanced scorecard implementations fail" (Neely and Bourne 2000, p. 6). Fryer et al. (2009) suggest that the reasons why the balanced scorecard fails in the public sector is that they have not invested enough time into changing and adapting it to the needs of their particular organisation. Nath and Sharma (2014) suggest the issues with implementation of the balanced scorecard in the public sector come from trying to link it to the multidimensional organisation strategy.

Kaplan and Norton adapted their balanced scorecard for the public sector and started by moving the financial perspective further down the scorecard and promoting the customer perspective to the top. However, who are the customers of a public organisation? Is it those who provide the money or those who consume the services? In a private organisation, these are often one and the same. However, for the public sector, there will be donors who have specific goals as to what they want their money to achieve and there are the consumers who use the services and products.

8.7.1 *What Is Performance in Local Government?*

Franco-Santos et al. (2007) believe that it is incredibly important to define what is meant by performance. For the public sector, it is the 3 E's: Economy, Efficiency and Effectiveness. Economy is about the best value for money. It may not be the cheapest option but the ones that gives the best value. Efficiency is making the most out of the resources you have and Effectiveness is about doing what is needed (Drury 2015). There could be a fourth option of Equity, to ensure that resources are spread over the whole community (Wilson and Game 2011). However, value for money and the 3 E's have "failed to deliver a global model of performance measurement" (Arnaboldi et al. 2015, p. 9). Arnaboldi et al. (2015) believe that just because the organisation has saved money and can deliver a balanced budget does not mean they have been effective and met all the service demands or efficient. "The idea of 'more with less' has become a slogan" (Arnaboldi et al. 2015, p. 1). Say it too many times and it means very little.

Again the question emerges of how are the outcomes measured? What outcomes should we be measuring and how can we determine what is good performance and what is poor performance? (Sharma and Gadenne 2011). Public sector organisations have tried to measure their performance with varying degrees of success. Some have looked at input–output models and some have followed instructions from central government as to what they should be measuring.

Many models of performance measurement "fail to tackle efficiently the communication of the strategy across all organisational levels" (Marinho and Cagnin 2014, p. 50). Pandey (2005) feels that if the scorecard fits in with the strategy and is aligned with it, the communication and motivation will follow naturally and thus produce improved performance. Marinho and Cagnin (2014) feel that a lot of effort goes into the design of the strategy and very little into the implementation. Hamid et al. (2016) believe that the reason why there are so many poor implementations of performance measurement strategies come from the fact that the employees have a lack of knowledge. Employees focus on their statutory tasks and fail to engage with the performance measurement strategy.

In the past it was believed that tools used in the private sector could not be transferred to the public sector. Now there is evidence that this is not true are there are some successful implementations of the balanced scorecard in the public sector (Hamid et al. 2016). Areas of performance that are measured tend to be the areas that people focus in on. More effort is expended when it is known that the results will be published or individuals performance will be targeted (Drury 2015). Jääskeläinen and Laihonen (2014) found in their research that staff in the middle management levels liked the measures that they could have an impact on. This supports the view that when people understand the measures and they are clear they will work towards them with more vigour than when they are not "bought into" the measures, irrespective of whether the measures work towards the goals of the organisation.

Some researchers have suggested that the measures chosen can have a key impact on the performance of the firm. Success or failure could depend on the measures chosen (Larimo et al. 2016). Performance measures can be linked to goal theory, "conscious goals impact action" (Marginson et al. 2014, p. 64). This supports the theory of what you measure is what you get. Although goal theory suggests that people can create their own goals as well as having goals imposed on them. Some people are motivated by "the need to achieve a sense of personal satisfaction" (Marginson et al. 2014, p. 64). These people will strive to achieve their goals and keep going even when they miss achieving them. These people will respond positively to stretch targets whereas others will wilt under the pressure. Nevertheless, the evidence suggests that defined goals work better than just an overall pledge of "we must all work to a high standard" (Marginson et al. 2014, p. 64).

However, in all the guidance of how to create a PMS, it is rare that authors offer advice on how to design the performance measures themselves. There are many offers of advice regarding dysfunctional behaviour but not a lot regarding how to avoid it and create the right measures (Bourne and Neely 2002).

Bourne and Franco-Santos (2010, p. 30) have produced a checklist for good target setting to make sure targets are:

1. Clearly defined
2. At the correct level—not too high or too low
3. Shared out appropriately
4. Consistent with the strategy and economic environment
5. Based on rigorous data—not just on past history
6. Reviewed regularly
7. Owned
8. Supported by a specific action plan.

This is a lot of work but as the authors say "If you can't spare the time and effort then maybe it would be better not to set targets at all" (Bourne and Franco-Santos 2010, p. 30).

Performance measurement practices are often centralised. Jääskeläinen and Laihonen (2014, p. 355) comment that when choosing what to measure "strategic choices are often made without careful consideration and/or comparison of alternatives". They also believe that "academic literature has only a few studies investigating how public performance approaches have evolved to meet the changing information needs of public managers" (Jääskeläinen and Laihonen 2014, p. 355).

Evans (2017, p. 35) sees local government actors over-complicate matters and "develop a complex solution to an issue without the pragmatism or common sense to strip out the irrelevant and keep things simple". Balabonienė and Večerskienė (2015, p. 315) feel that public sector organisations are "oriented to the processes and not the results". Going through the motions of a regular process is safe and easy to measure that the process has been completed. Evans (2017, p. 35) wants a "performance culture based on regular specific feedback and good conversations rather than a sterile, box-filling exercise once or twice a year". Just measuring what we have always measured will not produce any different results. Jääskeläinen and Laihonen (2014) support this view that it is a tick box exercise rather than a useful management tool that can support the organisation.

The ways the results are measured need to be consistent otherwise the results will become meaningless (Bourne and Bourne 2002). If people in the organisation do not believe that the methods of data collection are valid, then the targets will lose their value. If the measurements are inaccurate or inconsistent, then staff will not be committed to them and become less motivated to achieve them if they know they are wrong. Elg (2007 cited in Antonsen 2014) likened the measurement of results with no communication to someone measuring the outside temperature: You can measure it but you cannot change it. Arnaboldi et al. (2015) feel that there is a lot of research on performance measurement but it has not achieved anything or produced any solutions for the issues of performance management. "We are fabulous at firing arrows into walls, drawing targets around them and then saying it was a brilliant shot" (Ezzamel et al. 2007 cited in Arnaboldi et al. 2015, p. 9).

The public sector is so varied as it covers 196 countries which are all shaped differently with different influences (Arnaboldi et al. 2015). Often it ends up with results focussed measurement systems. Arnaboldi et al. (2015, p. 2) believe we have created a "performance measurement industry". The theory of performance measurement sounds simple and easy to implement. However, what are the issues that affect organisations and their use of performance measurement tools? "Why do some organisations outperform others?" (Tegarden et al. 2003, p. 133). Just having a PMS does not automatically mean you will become successful or better at what you do. "Measurement just keeps the score" (Bourne 2008, p. 68); it is how you change the way you work and improve your processes that will lead to the overall performance increasing. It is hard to decide on what to measure. Often it is easier to take the measures that are already collated and try to fit them around a tool like the balanced scorecard. This then misses the key point of linking the strategy to the targets. This can also happen when departments are able to create their own targets and often miss the vital strategy link (Bourne 2008).

Managers look at the organisation and try to allocate resources. What needs to be done? How many staff are available? Timed targets such as how fast is the phone answered becomes a major focus. However, the question here should be what value does the customer receive rather than how fast can an operator answer the phone? Often in these targets very little is mentioned about the quality of the answer that the customer received (Seddon 2008).

The staff of an organisation are key to performance and all staff members should be engaged and motivated to work for the good of the organisation and not just finding a work around to meet their targets. Data manipulation does not usually have a positive effect on the organisation. There are many examples in the public sector to support this, for example National Health Service (NHS) waiting times (Bourne 2008). Organisations also wait until they need to save money or processes have deteriorated before they start to manage the issues through using the information from the measures. The key finding from Bourne's (2008) research is to learn from Japanese companies' kaizen performance and look to continually improve performance. However, most issues with performance measurement in the public sector are based on "conflicting influences … political interferences and ambiguous objectives" (Nath and Sharma 2014, p. 2). A cynic would say that politicians do this deliberately so they cannot be held to account easily.

Performance measurement should be a logical and rational process. Identifying criteria to achieve and then measuring the results to see how much has been achieved. However, Lewis (2015) believes many complex issues lie behind the process.

> If information is power the performance measurement is surely tightly linked to the creation and use of power. (Lewis 2015, p. 1)

Governments worldwide are fascinated by performance measurement, trying to prove that the bodies they fund are providing the right services and are doing what they are supposed to be doing. Many questions are asked about the technical data and the goals of the organisation. However, the key question is who chooses the measures? Who decides who wins and who loses (Lewis 2015)? How is this power used? Is it to confirm the existing hierarchy and structure, thus giving directors more power? Is it used as a control mechanism? Budget funding will follow the decisions. Linking into the transparency argument the public sector has lost the trust of the general public so now finds the need to measure everything to prove that it is using its resources wisely. In times of austerity, the public need to be reassured that the allocation of scarce resources is fair. The politicians then hope the public will continue to support them (Lewis 2015).

Central government will also use the framework of performance measurement to change the behaviour of local agencies. The national data set was an example of central government dictating what the local areas should focus on. "Measurement is assumed to change behaviour" (Lewis 2015, p. 6). Bourne (2008) queries the usefulness of the academic research in such practical areas as performance measurement. Academics talking to themselves, via journal articles, in a language only they understand will not solve the problems. However working with practical managers will increase their knowledge of what is actually happening and how things are done in the field. More research is needed on longitudinal studies rather than surveys to really understand what is needed.

8.8 Thoughts for the Future

What measures are suitable for a local government authority? Who should be the ones choosing them? Leaders, staff or combinations of both. The literature talks a lot about strategy mapping (Kaplan and Norton 1992) but how in practice can this be achieved successfully?

There is still not enough evidence to see what measures work. Jackson (2011) comments that it needs longitudinal studies to work out what makes a policy work. However politicians are only focussed as far as the next election so invariably they will ensure they have some "quick wins" in the short term to stay in power.

Councils will have to make the decisions of what to measure and how this will affect the behaviour of their staff. This is crucial as dysfunctional behaviour can easily occur if a person follows their targets religiously. Choosing the targets that provide goal congruence and not just measuring because it is easy to do. Clearly, the right things need to be measured and these will be different for each organisation. A rule of thumb often used by management accountants is that is should cost less to collate the information than the benefits that the information can bring. Jackson (2011) asks the same question about the new performance measures. Have they facilitated improved performance? Can the cost of producing the measures really be justified? Hoque (2014) comments that the balanced scorecard is the best we have at the moment and we will continue to use it until something better comes along.

So we have discussed many issues that occur with measuring performance in the public sector. Hopefully this will stimulate your thinking and help you to formulate challenges in the future. Setting targets and measuring performance has been shown to be a complicated topic with further research needed. There is no right or wrong way to measure performance and each organisation will be different. The key is to learn from your choice of measures and adapt them to encourage improved performance.

References

Antonsen, Yngve. 2014. "The Downside of the Balanced Scorecard: A Case Study from Norway." *Scandinavian Journal of Management* 30 (1): 40–50. https://doi.org/10.1016/j.scaman.2013.08.001.

Arnaboldi, Michela, Irvine Lapsley, and Ileana Steccolini. 2015. "Performance Management in the Public Sector: The Ultimate Challenge." *International Journal of Public Sector Management* 31 (1): 1–22. https://doi.org/10.1111/faam.12049.

Balabonienė, Ingrida, and Giedrė Večerskienė. 2015. "The Aspects of Performance Measurement in Public Sector Organization." *Procedia—Social and Behavioral Sciences* 213: 314–320. https://doi.org/10.1016/j.sbspro.2015.11.544.

Bessire, Dominique, and C. Richard Baker. 2005. "The French Tableau de Bord and the American Balanced Scorecard: A Critical Analysis." *Critical Perspectives on Accounting* 16 (6): 645–664. https://doi.org/10.1016/j.cpa.2004.01.004.

Bevan, Gwyn, and Christopher Hood. 2006. "What's Measured Is What Matters: Targets and Gaming in the English Public Health Care System." *Public Administration* 84 (3): 517–538. http://dx.doi.org/10.1111/j.1467-9299.2006.00600.x.

Bourne, Mike. 2008. "Performance Measurement: Learning from the Past and Projecting the Future." *Measuring Business Excellence* 12 (4): 67–72. https://doi.org/10.1108/13683040810919971.

Bourne, Mike. 2013. "What Is Balanced Scorecard." https://connect.som.cranfield.ac.uk/p7m07c9otnu/.

Bourne, Mike, and Pippa Bourne. 2002. *Balanced Scorecard in a Week*. London: Hodder & Stoughton.

Bourne, Mike, and Andy Neely. 2002. "Cause and Effect." *Financial Management*, September.

Bourne, Mike, and Monica Franco-Santos. 2010. "Performance Management." *Financial Management*, March.

Bourne, Mike, Steven A. Melnyk, Umit Bititci, K. Platts, and B. Andersen. 2014. "Editorial: Emerging Issues in Performance Measurement." *Management Accounting Research* 25: 117–118.

Bourne, Mike, Andy Neely, Ken Platts, and John Mills. 2002. "The Success and Failure of Performance Measurement Initiatives Perceptions of Participating Managers." *IJOPM International Journal of Operations & Production Management* 2211 (11): 1288–1310. https://doi.org/10.1108/01443570210450329.

Cartwright, John. 1975. "Corporate Planning in Local Government—Implications for the Elected Member." *Long Range Planning* 8 (2): 46–50. https://doi.org/10.1016/0024-6301(75)90004-7.

Chang, L, S.W. Lin, and D.N. Northcott. 2002. "The NHS Performance Assessment Framework: A 'Balanced Scorecard' Approach?" *Journal of Management in Medicine* 16 (5): 345–358.

Dreveton, Benjamin. 2013. "The Advantages of the Balanced Scorecard in the Public Sector: Beyond Performance Measurement." *Public Money & Management* 33 (2): 131–136. https://doi.org/10.1080/09540962.2013.763425.

Drury, Colin. 2015. *Management and Cost Accounting*, 9th ed. Andover: Cengage.

Evans, S. 2017. "A Refreshing Approach." *The Municipal Journal (The MJ)*: 35. 20 April.

Folan, Paul, and Jim Browne. 2005. "A Review of Performance Measurement: Towards Performance Management." *Computers in Industry* 56 (7): 663–680. https://doi.org/10.1016/j.compind.2005.03.001.

Franco-Santos, Monica, Lorenzo Lucianetti, and Mike Bourne. 2012. "Contemporary Performance Measurement Systems: A Review of Their Consequences and a Framework for Research." *Management Accounting Research* 23 (2): 79–119. https://doi.org/10.1016/j.mar.2012.04.001.

Franco-Santos, Monica, Mike Kennerley, Pietro Micheli, Veronica Martinez, Steve Mason, Bernard Marr, Dina Gray, and Andrew Neely. 2007. "Towards a Definition of a Business Performance Measurement System Article Information." *International Journal of Operations & Production Management.* 27 (8): 784–801.

Fryer, K., J. Antony, and S. Ogden. 2009. "Performance Management in the Public Sector." *International Journal of Public Sector Management* 22 (6): 478–498.

Ghobadian, A., and J. Ashworth. 1994. "Performance Measurement in Local Government—Concept and Practice." *International Journal of Operations & Production Management* 14 (5): 35–51.

Glinkowska, Beata, and Bogusław Kaczmarek. 2015. "Classical and Modern Concepts of Corporate Governance (Stewardship Theory and Agency Theory)." *Management* 19 (2): 84–92. https://doi.org/10.1515/manment-2015-0015.

Hamid, Siti Mardinah Binti Abdul, Jamil Bin Haji Hamali, and Firdaus Abdullah. 2016. "Performance Measurement for Local Authorities in Sarawak." *Procedia—Social and Behavioral Sciences* 224: 437–444.

Hopper, T., Deryl Northcott, and R. Scapens. 2007. *Issues in Management Accounting*, 3rd ed. Essex: Pearson Education.

Hoque, Zahirul. 2014. "20 Years of Studies on the Balanced Scorecard: Trends, Accomplishments, Gaps and Opportunities for Future Research." *British Accounting Review* 46 (1): 33–59. Elsevier Ltd. https://doi.org/10.1016/j.bar.2013.10.003.

Jääskeläinen, Aki, and Harri Laihonen. 2014. "A Strategy Framework for Performance Measurement in the Public Sector." *Public Money & Management* 34 (5): 355–362. https://doi.org/10.1080/09540962.2014.945807.

Jackson, Peter M. 2011. "Governance by Numbers: What Have We Learned over the Past 30 Years?" *Public Money & Management* 31 (1): 13–26. https://doi.org/10.1080/09540962.2011.545542.

Kaplan, Robert S., and David P. Norton. 1992. "The Balanced Score Card Measures That Drive Performance." *Harvard Business Review* 70 (1): 71–79.

Kaplan, Robert S., and David P. Norton. 1996. *The Balanced Scorecard. Translating Strategy into Action*. Boston, MA: Harvard Business School Press.

Kaplan, Robert S., and David P. Norton. 2001. "Transforming the Balanced Scorecard from Performance Measurement to Strategic Management: Part II." *Accounting Horizons* 15 (2): 147–160. https://doi.org/10.2308/acch.2001.15.2.147.

Kaplan, Robert S., and David P. Norton. 2004. *Strategy Maps. Converting Intangible Assets into Tangible Outcomes*. Boston, MA: Harvard Business School Press.

Larimo, Jorma, Huu Le Nguyen, and Tahir Ali. 2016. "Performance Measurement Choices in International Joint Ventures: What Factors Drive Them?" *Journal of Business Research* 69 (2): 877–887. https://doi.org/10.1016/j.jbusres.2015.07.003.

Lewis, Jenny M. 2015. "The Politics and Consequences of Performance Measurement." *Policy and Society* 34 (1): 1–12. Policy and Society Associates Ltd Partnership. https://doi.org/10.1016/j.polsoc.2015.03.001.

Lowe, Toby. 2013. "New Development: The Paradox of Outcomes—The More We Measure, the Less We Understand." *Public Money & Management* 33 (3): 213–216. https://doi.org/10.1080/09540962.2013.785707.

Marginson, David, Laurie McAulay, Melvin Roush, and Tony van Zijl. 2014. "Examining a Positive Psychological Role for Performance Measures." *Management Accounting Research* 25 (1): 63–75. https://doi.org/10.1016/j.mar.2013.10.002.

Marinho, Sidnei Vieira, and Cristiano Cagnin. 2014. "The Roles of FTA in Improving Performance Measurement Systems to Enable Alignment between Business Strategy and Operations: Insights from Three Practical Cases." *Futures* 59: 50–61.

Melnyk, Steven A., Umit Bititci, Ken Platts, Jutta Tobias, and Bjorn Andersen. 2014. "Is Performance Measurement and Management Fit for the Future?" *Management Accounting Research* 25 (2): 173–186. https://doi.org/10.1016/j.mar.2013.07.007.

Merchant, Kenneth A., and W. Van der Stede. 2012. *Management Control Systems. Performance Measurement, Evaluation and Incentives*, 3rd ed. Harlow: Prentice Hall.

Micheli, Pietro, and Jean-Francois Manzoni. 2010. "Strategic Performance Measurement: Benefits, Limitations and Paradoxes." *Long Range Planning* 43: 465–476.

Nath, Nirmala, and Umesh Sharma. 2014. "Performance Management Systems in the Public Housing Sector. Dissemination to Diffusion." *Australian Accounting Review* 24 (1): 2–20.

Neely, Andy. 1999. "The Performance Measurement Revolution: Why Now and What Next?" *International Journal of Operations & Production Management* 19 (2): 205–228. https://doi.org/10.1108/01443579910247437.

Neely, Andy. 2005. "The Evolution of Performance Measurement Research." *International Journal of Operations & Production Management* 25 (12): 1264–1277. https://doi.org/10.1108/01443570510633648.

Neely, A., and Mike Bourne. 2000. "Why Measurement Initiatives Fail." *Measuring Business Excellence* 4 (4): 3–7.

Neely, A., M. Gregory, and K. Platts. 1995. "Performance Measurement System Design—A Literature Review and Research Agenda." *International Journal of Operations & Production Management* 15 (4): 80–116. https://doi.org/10.1108/01443579510083622.

Norreklit, Hanne. 2003. "The Balanced Scorecard: What Is the Score? A Rhetorical Analysis of the Balanced Scorecard." *Accounting, Organizations and Society* 28 (6): 591–619. https://doi.org/10.1016/s0361-3682(02)00097-1.

Northcott, Deryl, and Tuivaiti Ma'amora Taulapapa. 2012. "Using the Balanced Scorecard to Manage Performance in Public Sector Organizations: Issues and Challenges." *International Journal of Public Sector Management* 25 (3): 166–191.

Pandey, I. 2005. "Balanced Scorecard: Myth and Reality." *Vikalpa* 30 (1): 51–66.

Pavlov, Andrey, Matteo Mura, Monica Franco-Santos, and Mike Bourne. 2017. "Modelling the Impact of Performance Management Practices on Firm Performance: Interaction with Human Resource Management Practices." *Production Planning & Control* 28 (5): 431–443. https://doi.org/10.1080/09537287.2017.1302614.

Radnor, Zoe, and D Barnes. 2007. "Historical Analysis of Performance Measurement and Management in Operations Management." *International Journal of Productivity and Performance Management* 56 (5): 384–396.

Ross, L. 2011. *Public Sector Performance. A Global Perspective.* London: CIMA.

Ryan, Nick. 2012. "The Performance Prism." *ACCA Student Accountant.* http://www.accaglobal.com/uk/en/student/exam-support-resources/professional-exams-study-resources/p5/technical-articles/performance-prism.html.

Seal, W., R.H. Garrison, and E.W. Noreen. 2012. *Management Accounting*, 4th ed. Berkshire: McGraw Hill.

Seddon, John. 2008. *Systems Thinking in the Public Sector. The Failure of the Reform Regime… and a Manifesto for a Better Way.* Axminster: Triarchy Press.

Sharma, Bishnu, and David Gadenne. 2011. "Balanced Scorecard Implementation in a Local Government Authority: Issues and Challenges." *Australian Journal of Public Administration* 70 (2): 167–184. https://doi.org/10.1111/j.1467-8500.2011.00718.x.

Tegarden, Linda F., Yolanda Sarason, and Catherine Banbury. 2003. "Linking Strategy Processes to Performance Outcomes in Dynamic Environments: The Need to Target Multiple Bull's Eyes." *Journal of Managerial Issues.* http://ezproxy.lib.ucf.edu/login?URL=http://search.ebscohost.com/login.aspx?direct=true&db=psyh&AN=2003-99718-001&site=ehost-live.

van der Meer-Kooistra, J., and E.G.J. Vosselman. 2004. "The Balanced Scorecard: Adoption and Application." In *Advances in Management Accounting*, edited by Mark Epstein and John Y. Lee, 287–310. Oxford: Elsevier.

West, Damian, and Deborah Blackman. 2015. "Performance Management in the Public Sector." *Australian Journal of Public Administration* 74 (1): 73–81. https://doi.org/10.1111/1467-8500.12130.

Williams, Wil, and Duncan Lewis. 2008. "Strategic Management Tools and Public Sector Management." *Public Management Review* 10 (5): 653–671. https://doi.org/10.1080/14719030802264382.

Wilson, David, and Chris Game. 2011. *Local Government in the United Kingdom*, 5th ed. Basingstoke: Palgrave Macmillan.

Yadav, Neetu, and Mahim Sagar. 2013. "Performance Measurement and Management Frameworks: Research Trends of the Last Two Decades." *Business Process Management Journal* 19 (6): 947–971. https://doi.org/10.1108/bpmj-01-2013-0003.

CHAPTER 9

Finance and Accounting—Beyond the Numbers with Self-Leadership

Darren Byrne and Dave Lees

9.1 About the Chapter

This chapter is directed to you, the reader, and in most of it we are speaking directly to you because self-development and self-leadership is a very personal and individual consideration. The purpose is to introduce you to the need to develop your "soft" skills, to outline options for how you might achieve this—including the "project" approach, and to encourage you to step onto the road of self-leadership and continual interpersonal skill development.

9.2 Introduction

Whatever your profession, unless you live on your own on Mars (and even then, you might have to be in contact with Earth), you will have to work with other people and doing so requires many skills, a lot of which might be defined as soft-skills or generic skills (Abayadeera and Watty 2016). The work environment in today's society is complex, changes constantly and requires a degree of resilience from all individuals

D. Byrne (✉) · D. Lees
University of Derby, Derby, UK

E. Conway and D. Byrne (eds.), *Contemporary Issues in Accounting*,
https://doi.org/10.1007/978-3-319-91113-7_9

to cope in building their careers (Lyons et al. 2015). Recent thinking and research in academia has shown that keys to success in organisations involve self-leadership and critical thinking skills (Ay et al. 2015), which means that, whatever your core function in an organisation, the type of skills you will need to succeed will go beyond the knowledge of your own particular speciality.

Finance and accounting specialists in particular will need to be resilient, be able to self-lead and think critically to succeed. There have been studies conducted on the skills of accounting students moving into the world of work, for example, Jackling and De Lange (2009) argued that students were not being taught the generic skills they would require with particular lack of team skills, leadership skills, verbal communication and interpersonal skills cited. Emotional Intelligence (Goleman 1995) is recognised as a career requirement—specifically for accountancy and finance (Akers and Porter 2003). Thus, being good at handling the numbers will not be enough! The question for you therefore to consider is, what do you need to do, alongside acquiring your specialist subject knowledge, to be a success in your future organisation?

To develop a practical experience, students are generally asked at University to submit something akin to a dissertation or a "big" report, project or capstone project, in order to complete their degrees. It is usually a final aspect of their degree, and it is usually the part that most students either have some trepidation about tackling or perhaps less understanding about what is required. These feelings may be derived from a lack of awareness or preparation for these types of tasks, and many students tend to focus more of their time and attention on their traditional "taught" modules, because these lie more within their comfort zone. However, the academics who develop the curriculum reason that this final task helps develop the resilience and self-leadership skills mentioned above.

Students may, for instance, have to write a "dissertation submitted in partial fulfilment of the requirements of your degree of …", or they are required to "analyse a modern-day scenario that an organisation is facing and provide recommendations within a report… ." Do these requirements sound familiar? Do they sound like finance or accounting to you? Perhaps not, but they require other aspects/abilities or "soft skills" from you with which you may not be so familiar, and maybe ones that you are not quite so aware that you have already been developing, these skills will be explored in more detail later on in this chapter.

These projects may seem somewhat removed from direct accounting and finance subject matter, but these projects are important for all the reasons we have discussed. There is precedence for this approach with other speciality subjects such as marketing, for example, Ardley and Taylor (2010) show that a project involving experiential learning is a good method of learning for students. They observed skills developed by marketing students upon their research consultancy projects, a task which they expressed was based upon "doing" rather than on other traditional methods of learning. It seemed to help in terms of skills development. Students work on real challenges and the clients actually pay for the services provided instilling some reality to this project. The project involved liaising with an organisation and the authors reported that students needed to use "negotiation, the application of numeracy, teamwork, competitive analysis, problem solving, creativity and communication" (Ardley and Taylor 2010, p. 849). The students themselves were asked to reflect upon the process; a "real-life" experience was seen to be beneficial, specifically regarding team working, interaction in the workplace, communication as well as creativity. Creativity was something recognised as an additional skill highly in demand by employers in the field of marketing. Musa et al. (2011) too demonstrated that Project Based Learning (PBL) is invaluable for students to gain key skills such as communication skills, conflict management and team-working that are applicable and necessary for the working environment.

So, what happens when you are focusing on the final task—the project? What do you need to do to put it all together? What happens when you are asked to write something yourself? What skills do you have to complete this task? What do you do? And more importantly, why do you need to do it?

We often ask students in class what skills they think are apposite for business and accounting professional careers. What skills should consultants, for instance, have at their command? Various anecdotal answers are repeatedly proposed by students starting a "project" module, including: communication skills, commercial awareness, technical knowledge and time management.

These answers are very apt and a good start, but we will add to this list still further and propose how self-leadership and other soft skills are incredibly important attributes also. But why are these skills required, how are they developed and where can a project-writing module help in this regard? We are not just working upon specific technical accounting or financial knowledge or even only with numbers or accounting concepts, these are virtues and capacities that go well beyond technical competence, these are elements that can set students, and consequently financial professionals apart. We have chosen to focus upon some of these skills developed when working towards your project that do help you in your professional career. These will be discussed later in the chapter.

9.3 What Skills Do Employers/Recruiters Want?

This section deals with skills that employers/recruiters want from budding finance and accounting professionals. A question for you, and one we will attempt to answer is, "Does a project module provide some of these sought-after elements?" A research project initiated in Australia looked into what the authors described as, "the changing skill set deemed necessary for professional accounting graduates…" (Hancock et al. 2009, p. 5). Through their research, they used interviews with employers and they found that communication, teamwork and self-management were regarded as "most desirable", thus, reflecting a little of what students thought anecdotally to be important. These themes are ever repeated throughout the literature. Hancock et al. (2009) further stated how employers would aid their own recruitment strategies by using these discriminators (i.e. proof of skills developed beyond the mere technical expectancies) to rationalise fields of candidates yet further. It can be instantly seen that employers have a view regarding what skills they want. "Problem Solving" and "Initiative & Enterprise" skills were two other non-technical skills also regarded to be expected by employers from the findings in this research.

More recently and, from a study that took a different methodology—an analysis of job adverts in Poland as basis for their study—Paszkiewicz and Gembka (2014), talk about how indispensable "soft competencies" are. They remark that even the International Accounting Education Standards Board (IAESB) cite the necessity of interpersonal and communication skills. The authors used a range of pre-researched definitions of competencies, but did not necessarily propose a new definition, other than to suggest that they observe competencies as being more aligned to the concept of human capital, and furthermore announce that this is complex.

Interestingly and rather pointedly, given the preponderance of accounting degrees that build a curriculum focused upon accreditations and maximum exemptions from professional accounting body exams, Paszkiewicz and Gembka's (2014) research infers that qualifications could soon become dated (in the eyes of employers), and that candidates who have developed the ability to exhibit these soft competencies will become more employable. This could be a revelation for some students who are so engrossed in their accounting studies that they maybe take their eye off the market to which they are aiming. These observations leave accounting programme directors and programme leaders with a stark decision about how to best prepare their students for life after graduation and employment. Modules that are able to develop deeper soft-skills will become more valuable currency is the implied opinion.

Self-leadership is one such deeper soft-skill. We argue that the development of this skill takes an ability to be self-aware and to be able to be capable of self-development. Bunney et al. (2015, p. 257) cite Bridgstock's observations (2009) that, "employability skills extend beyond a discrete list of generic skills to incorporate effective self-management and career building skills". However, Paszkiewicz and Gembka (2014, p. 8) noted the current lack of development in candidates; "the abilities of team cooperation and effective communication are among those deficit competencies which are most frequently mentioned by employers". The argument later in their research suggests that education should help provide candidates with these skills. Hancock et al.'s (2009) research introduced above had further noted that employers had the general expectation that universities should own the responsibility of developing non-technical skills, rather than leave it to be covered when in employment.

Smith and Gibson (2016) drew together some more recent observations upon this expectations gap citing a study from McKinsey where 42% of employers believed that new graduates were prepared for work and noting an even larger gap between higher education provider's and employer's opinions over whether graduates are ready to succeed at work. Webb and Chaffer found too in their 2016 survey of trainee accounting professionals that, "...a number of skills identified as important by employers fell below the satisfaction threshold in the study: oral communication, commitment to life-long learning, ethical awareness, vision and resilience" (2016, p. 362). Employers truly expect students to be "work-ready" and it is incumbent upon Higher Education establishments and employers to be aware of this discrepancy, and to converse to minimise it. Here too there may be differing views; Keevy (2016, p. 470) observed that "Certain academics alleged that pervasive skills could only be transferred while working", but that, "...the accounting profession expects academics to equip professional accountants with both technical and pervasive skills."

So again, we find that these skills are not only directly cited in studies, but are furthermore expected to have been developed before employment. The question remains, where do students develop many of these skills? Whilst technical skills and numerical reasoning are high in the agenda on an accounting degree's curricula, there still needs to be major focus on what employers want, and so a project can become a medium through which to develop these skills.

Some students may have already chosen to undertake or have completed a work placement within their degree, there are several benefits (e.g. experience and income) and students are increasingly more employable for having gained experience like this. But can they develop any further skills progress upon their return in their final college years? Surridge (2009) although recognising the value of a placement, intriguingly questions whether there is in fact any positive academic performance effect demonstrated by placement students upon their return to University for their final year, explaining how these skills don't easily transfer. This suggests that placement students may have somewhat further to travel to benefit from their placement experience to convince their ultimate employer's perspective if they do not progress in their final academic assessments. The authors recommend that placement students capitalise upon their placement experience by immediately engaging with a project module in their post-placement year in order to convert their experiences into positive skills development. However, it has been observed anecdotally by the authors and their colleagues that placement students these days do actually tend to be more focused, better prepared and more attuned to their ambition to be successful in a career by this stage of their studies. Surridge also obligingly observes Reddy and Moores' (2006, p. 557) eight benefits from the placement; "communication, time management, confidence, taking responsibility, self-presentation, making presentations, writing skills and teamwork". Finally, Bunney et al. (2015, p. 256) find that, "The new knowledge economy ... needs graduates across disciplines with flexible mindsets and transferable skill sets", but they also recognise that it is "problematic" to discover time enough on degree courses to develop generic skills, and also call for "authentic learning tasks" to be implemented to allow this to happen.

9.4 Why then Is Doing a Project Important?

Writing up a project is a focused task. Written communication skills are required and highly developed, and focused writing helps to communicate the recommendations. These written skills are difficult to develop over the course of only a 3-year accounting degree programme where the focus is more on technical and numerical abilities. Hasrati (2013) supports this discipline of writing skills in their article "Why bother about writing a Masters dissertation?", noting how self-regulated learning can help develop independence.

Bunney et al. (2015) note how a programme-wide focus on developing these types of skills is desirable. Modules such as "Academic Skills", "Project Strategy/Management" and "Employability Development" can help provide vehicles for students to develop these skills yet further. Many other modules on programmes can also help by setting innovative and developmental assignments for skills. Earlier parts of project modules typically cover areas like personal values and beliefs—see later when we discuss "authenticity" under the self-leadership section. Knowledge and awareness of practical concepts such as Corporate Social Responsibility is also generally intertwined within these modules and again this is covered under "responsibility" later. This is also where the concepts of Integrity and Professionalism can be introduced, concepts where all good accountants should have a deep awareness of through their audit knowledge and experience—but how can they exhibit and prove these virtues? We recap a model by Manz a little later in this text too, that helps you to imagine how these virtues interplay and as a backdrop for help in writing a project report.

The study mentioned earlier, developed by Hancock et al. (2009) expressed an understanding of the challenges about fitting too much into a degree programme; but this is where we argue that a "Project" module and indeed actually completing a project can tick a lot of soft-skills boxes. Imagine how one module, if sufficiently linked to other parts of the curriculum, could single-handedly allow students to develop many extra skills. This would be a curriculum-space saving solution through a stand-alone module that could also remain focused and delineated within a programme. This does not preclude the fact that some of the skills discussed and described here may not be additionally met elsewhere on the curriculum by enterprising module tutors who manage to develop innovative assessment challenges for their students, for example, presentation skills, real world exercises, case studies and similar. Students will probably find that they have been tasked and challenged upon some of these skills already by this stage.

Abayadeera and Watty (2016) introduce the concept of generic skills too within their study of Sri Lankan undergraduate accounting students. The literature supports the view that things seem to be changing in terms of student's awareness. Findings suggested that the respondents (let alone employers) themselves believed that generic skills developed upon their degree were even more important than technical skills. They depended too upon the premise discovered from their previous research, that students needed something over and above sheer technical knowledge, i.e. beyond simply handling the numbers. However, they defined generic skills as, "those capabilities required by graduate accountants for employability and career advancement" (Abayadeera and Watty 2016, p. 149), and one could imagine that technical skills might be reasonably counted within that definition too. Their study developed a list of generic skills by scouring job adverts in much the same way as Paszkiewicz and Gembka's (2014) study above had done, from a comprehension of International Education Standard 3 authored by the IAESB and from analysing previous research. This offered a list of 25 generic skills which can be found listed in their work (Abayadeera and Watty 2016, p. 157). However, their results revealed that, "undergraduates perceive that most of the skills that are important to their careers ... were not adequately developed during their undergraduate degree" (p. 165), and that there is an, "over-emphasis on technical accounting skills at a cost to generic skills" (p. 165). These results were found to be consistent with research conducted in other countries.

Other methods of developing soft skills are of course available to the academic who develops programme curricula at universities. "Case Studies" are often able to develop some very similar skills as the project, but may be less practical and immediate as a "real" project. Keevy (2016, p. 459) however discusses how these can be developed and cites Kermis and Kermis' (2010) observation regarding professional competencies; they are "necessary for a successful career, they are not sufficient", thus strengthening the importance of awareness of developing skills.

The authors' own design methodology for a "project-based" module prepared students for their engagement with organisations by using and examining case-studies within class before requiring students to derive a project proposal. A link is made with the project phase of the module by indicating that the student's engagement with a real organisation is akin to developing their own case-study and providing recommendations to the situation outlined in their "case". Keevy (2016) campaigns for the efficacy of using case-studies to develop "pervasive" skills, i.e. soft skills, and through her literature review, offers a list of competencies as identified in the South African Institute of Chartered Accountant's Competency Framework, to illustrate where case studies contribute to development of these pervasive skills (as evidenced by various authors' work from her literature review). We have adapted this table for our own use and considered where we believe competencies can be developed upon a generic "project module". These are our own observations and assumptions only, gained from assessing students' reports, observing the conduct of our students and from the reflections made by our students within the module outputs. An adaptation of this table (Keevy 2016) can be found in Table 9.1.

See if you agree. Review your own project module and consider whether your module accommodates all these skills developments? However, Keevy's research also found some respondents who did not agree that these pervasive skills were actually developed upon the programme (i.e. through case-studies) but were more clearly developed only "during practical experience". Would a practical "real" project satisfy those respondents more? Perhaps further research is required upon this aspect.

Rodrigues (2004) researched other teaching techniques, both "Active-like" and "Passive-like" activities that can be used in tuition and asked students and instructors to rate their importance. They generally found no statistically strong evidence for any activities being rated higher in terms of importance over any other aspects. However, their research did highlight that some individual students do "prefer" either Active or Passive activities, and although there were some common preferences exhibited by groups of students studying similar programmes, that it was not possible to generalise this finding to particular academic domains. Active-like activities included case studies, individual research projects, group projects and classroom discussions. The study found that these activities were not rated as important by students within this particular study, whereas students rated passive-like activities including, lectures, reading textbooks, guest speakers, videos, student

Table 9.1 Summary of the pervasive skills that can be transferred using projects

Development	*Satisfied by project?*
Ethical behaviour and professionalism	
Protects the public interest	–
Acts competently with honesty and integrity	Yes
Carries out work with a desire to exercise due care	Yes
Maintains objectivity and independence	Yes
Avoids conflict of interest	Yes
Protects the confidentiality of information	Yes
Maintains and enhances the profession's reputation	Yes
Adheres to the rules of professional conduct	Yes
Personal attributes	
Self-manages	Yes
Demonstrates leadership and initiative	Yes
Maintains and demonstrates competence and recognises limits	Yes
Strives to add value in an innovative manner	Yes
Manages change	–
Treats others in a professional manner	Yes
Understands the national and international environment	–
Is a life-long learner	–
Works effectively as a team member	Yes
Manages time effectively	Yes
Professional skills	
Obtains information	Yes
Examines and interprets information and ideas critically	Yes
Solves problems and makes decisions	Yes
Communicates effectively and efficiently	Yes
Manages and supervises	–
Understands how IT impacts a CA's daily functions and routines	–
Considers basic legal concepts	–

Source Adapted from Keevy (2016, pp. 462–464)

presentations and computer-based assignments as marginally higher in importance. However, as discussed within the article; different experiences may depend on students' own learning styles, different lecturers' abilities or delivery style, and whether guest speakers were engaging or not. Not insignificant either, is the fact that this study is now quite dated—14 years ago as we write in 2018. Anecdotal evidence from current students finds that they appreciate the discipline of Active-like activities and quite enjoy and value some of these Passive activities as well, for instance, students find that guest lecturers can be very informative, students enjoy listening and engaging with professionals who are actually "doing the job". Ultimately however, the authors observe and hear that their students find that after the initial daunting phase, doing an actual project with a client allows them to develop enormously. They reflect very positively upon their engagement with professionals at those client organisations and produce professional reports that the students can be justifiably proud of—even using the fruit of their efforts to demonstrate competence at job interviews. Rodrigues (2004, p. 181) does however recommend that, "The instructor should explain to the students why the technique is being used", and although students may, "moan and groan", it is purely a matter of helping the students to recognise that these techniques will help their development and their careers.

9.5 What Skills Will Be Derived from the Project—How Will These "Come Through" to Fruition?

Paszkiewicz and Gembka (2014, p. 10) citing Chaker (2011), declared that, "It is due to [Interpersonal skills] that an accountant can influence other people, motivate, resolve conflicts, or share obligations among co-workers in order to achieve the goals of his organization". What an amazing declaration, and perhaps one that is not so immediately recognised by many accounting students when in training or study, but this is at the heart of our observations. We argue that undertaking a project can develop many skills, which will be outlined in more detail here as we discuss effective skills.

As everyone at work is individual and unique, it is quite intuitive that even in the most closely co-ordinated and organised system of work, self-expression, self-motivation and personal performance is a matter of self-leadership. Manz (1986) and specifically Neck and Houghton (2006, p. 271) define self-leadership as "a self-influence process through which people achieve the self-direction and self-motivation necessary to perform". No-one can make an individual perform well unless that individual chooses to co-operate. The current working and economic environment point towards fewer people being employed to do as much or more work than used to be carried out by larger numbers of people, while hierarchies continue to flatten. This means that individuals in work need to take more responsibility and so self-leadership is essential because there are fewer others to "fall back on". Our environment is increasing in complexity with technology and population expansion fuelling an inexorable rise in things "to be handled" and "to know". This means in organisations, no longer can any one person be in full control at the top; responsibilities have to be devolved down to individuals in lower hierarchical positions or tasks will not get completed. Manz (1986), the originator of the academic concept of self-management (Neck and Houghton 2006), suggests that self-leadership is a purposeful process that leads to natural intrinsic rewards for the individual. Manz (2015) goes further and argues that it is the employee who, individually, chooses his or her own behaviour and response to organisational demand or guidance and thus argues (p. 133) that, "…Self-leadership… [is at] …the heart of organizational behaviour". Manz (2015) identified Authenticity, Responsibility and Expanded Capacity as three components of self-leadership. Below is an explanation of these together with an indication of how they may be developed in a project.

Authenticity is attending to your own behaviour and values which would operate to higher standards and may not necessarily be supplanted by those of a boss.

- The individual behaves congruently with personal values and beliefs.
- The individual does not forfeit these values under the pressure from a manager or the organisation.

These components can all typically be supported in a project module, whereby personal ethics and values can be introduced and assessed via reflection.

Responsibility is your own self-led behaviour and intentions with regard to a responsible outcome.

- Concern for corporate social responsibility and "the greater good" such that behaviour, in reflecting these values includes virtues such as compassion, courage and integrity.

This component is often covered in stand-alone modules that help prepare students for project modules.

Expanded capacity is developing yourself in ways that enable your personal growth towards a wider capacity for self-leadership.

- This includes adding to personal skills to achieve greater self-leadership in areas based on a wider environmental approach rather than aimed at a single self-serving purpose. This will support the achievement of the other two components.

Upon their project, students need to be mindful of the objectives, requirements and preferences of the client organisation.

These are represented in the model in Fig. 9.1.

This whole concept of the Self-Leadership High Road is valuable for you to consider regarding completion of a project because the essence of the content is to lead yourself to better things. Taking ownership for managing your own growth with high personal standards is a really positive step to take and will stand you in good stead for your future career opportunities. Be assured that employers will recognise, in their recruitment processes, those candidates who have the extra drive, values and standards to develop themselves. The components offered by Manz in Fig. 9.1 are a way of breaking the concept of self-leadership into more digestible chunks, but it would be useful to identify what the key practical skills are that are needed to be an effective self-leader. Identifying these is not so easy, as particular skill requirements and their level of

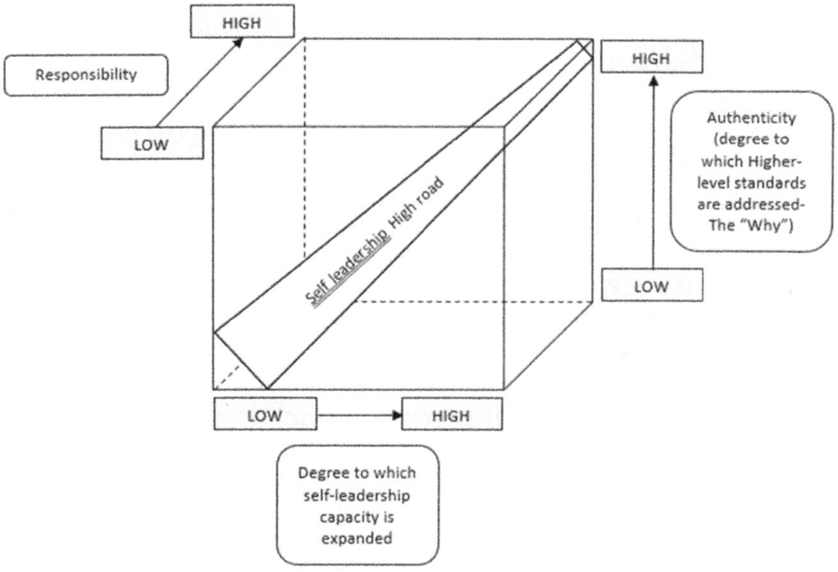

Fig. 9.1 Travelling the Self-Leadership High Road (*Source* Manz (2015, p. 134). Adapted with the kind permission of the author)

importance are very dependent on a given situation/job role. However, the recurring themes are:

- Self-discipline and self-starting… . i.e. self-leadership
- Working and communicating with others including emotional intelligence
- Creativity, Innovation and Problem Solving.

We will take each of these in order but, to discuss all of these concepts in any length is beyond the scope of this particular text, some reference and advice on what you can do to inform yourself will be made about each. For many, acquisition of these skills will be part of a work-based project.

9.6 Self-Leadership Skills

9.6.1 Self-Leadership

This is covered already by the work we discussed by Manz (2015), but there is a little more to consider. All three elements of the model of Self-leadership contribute towards understanding yourself and how you react. Control and work with these elements to develop your self-leadership and you can help your personal approach to life, work or projects significantly and effectively. Intuitively you already know a lot, but expressing what you know is not necessarily easy so there are a number of "tools" you can use to help. One type of these tools is self-assessment personality questionnaires you can use to help your self-awareness. A source for these is likely to be the careers department at your university. This is well worth a visit as you will come across these types of assessment when applying for jobs. You can find them on the internet but beware of cheap and unproven imitations, there is a lot of poor quality material published on the internet. Remember, if you know yourself and how you might react in different circumstances you will find it easier to manage yourself and respond to others more flexibly.

9.6.2 Working and Communicating with Others

As already mentioned, Hancock et al.'s (2009) report outlined how employers sought graduates with communication skills in all forms alongside team working. Many other authors report the same findings (Jones et al. 2017; Andrews and Higson 2008; Gray 2010; Jackling and

De Lange 2009). Think carefully about the circumstances in which you will be applying your financial and accounting skills and the issues will become obvious; you will be working with other people who will not necessarily have the same skills that you possess, you will have to persuade and influence your peers and your managers as well as, perhaps, managing people yourself, to at least do tasks to help you. These processes require thought and care and consideration because you will be dealing with very different personalities who will respond with different emotions, attitudes and skills to yourself, meaning that each will require a unique approach that may not match your normal style.

When embarking upon the early stages of their projects students often find that they initially find it hard to engage and liaise with professionals at their clients' organisation. Sometimes students are not quite sure how to behave and have not quite learnt the "etiquette" or "culture" at work as yet. However, this is something which applies to any person working at any organisation and this can be the source of great, and valuable, diversity and also significant conflict at times. So, you will need to:

- Be aware of your own style and approach to others and able to adjust this when required.
- Be good at communicating:
  (a) Verbally (e.g. when researching/questioning for data and instructing clients at your project organisation)
  (b) In writing via letter, email, social media, newsletter, etc. (e.g. to maintain and support progress upon projects)
  (c) In group situations (e.g. when canvassing engagement from a group of employees, or to persuade participants to complete a survey)
  (d) From a stage to groups of people (e.g. if required to disseminate findings and recommendations—perhaps at meetings).
- Be good at listening (remember that communication is a two-way process). There is a simple homily that you might hear from coaches and trainers—it's pretty kitsch but worth a mention—remember that you have two ears and one mouth … . if you communicate in that proportion you will get it about right! Listening means *really* listening, that is not only hearing but responding and acting appropriately with self-discipline and responsibly as a result.
- Be good at using your emotional intelligence (EI) (Goleman 1995, 1999) to understand and react to others. An effective starting place

for this subject is to read the works of Daniel Goleman as referenced at the end of this chapter. Many of you will have heard about the Intelligence Quotient (IQ) and will have some appreciation of what it is. You might come across individuals who are super-bright and have really high IQ and yet can seem to have little common sense or little idea of how to relate to other people. It can be argued that what they need is more EQ. EQ requires understanding of emotional components of behaviour and interpersonal interactions. Akers and Porter (2003) highlight the importance of IQ and in particular EQ. They highlight five key areas of additional skills development that EQ can bring; Self-awareness, Self-regulation, Motivation, Empathy and Social Skills, collectively referred to as behavioural skills. Reuven Bar-On (2018) an expert in EI, hosts a website (http://www.reuvenbaron.org) which has produced a good self-assessment questionnaire for EI, so this is worth a visit. EQ has been extensively written about in the literature, but one could argue that it is still not at the forefront of finance and accounting professional skills development. This subject deserves more discussion but, once again, this is beyond the scope of the current text.

9.6.3 Creativity, Innovation and Problem Solving

Aspects of these last three skills in our discussion have been found to be debatable; how much is innate to the individual and how much can be learned? We think that, whatever the balance, there are at least some aspects that can be learned and practiced. One certainty is that employers look for these skills and will often test for them in recruitment and selection processes. Logically speaking almost every job will need all three aspects, so they are something to be considered and explored. Seek to practise these employable skills whenever you can.

9.7 Conclusion

We have had the pleasure of supervising many student's projects over the last few years; students have demonstrated the knowledge and abilities that they have learnt upon their degree programme and proven how they have developed. Most students have adapted, and applied models, techniques or theory learnt to real organisations and thought more about strategic outcomes. Many have found that they have developed many of the skills that we have discussed in this chapter along the way.

Students are challenged to apply their degree knowledge to various real situations and to develop themselves, they also demonstrate their competence and professionalism alongside many other skills as we have described.

The Chartered Institute of Management Accountants (CIMA) also recognise the need for "soft skills" in its membership. They have published a Competency Framework (2014), identifying four knowledge areas. "Technical skills" and "business skills" are two of these areas, but "people skills" and "leadership skills" are also included. CIMA define influence, negotiation and decision making, communication and collaboration and partnering under "people skills". Are these skills/competencies all developed on a traditional financial accounting module? Maybe not always or specifically. Are they skills that are developed upon a project-based module? We believe so. Leadership includes: "sharing of ideas that align with the organisational strategy", "advise others on how to perform, improve and succeed", "support, implement and monitor", "inspired, encouraged and valued" and "recognise the need for change and embrace new ways" (CIMA 2014, pp. 56–60).

A well-designed project-based module will afford you much time spent with a tutor whose expertise and experience may be able to guide you subtly—but they will not tell you what to do; Smith and Gibson (2016, p. 42) say that the instructor should guide "...the process as a coach". You are applying your knowledge and making recommendations based on tuition that you have received throughout your degree. Engage with the organisation and develop communication skills by "doing it". Smith and Gibson (2016, p. 42) also find that, "Most business students make it clear they prefer 'hands-on' learning", and that projects can help participants to make new contacts and to enable them to extend their networking opportunities.

Does that sound like something worthwhile achieving?

Great—do it! Enjoy the experience.

References

Abayadeera, Nadana, and Kim Watty. 2016. "Generic Skills in Accounting Education in a Developing Country: Exploratory Evidence from Sri Lanka." *Asian Review of Accounting* 24: 149–170. https://doi.org/10.1108/ara-03-2014-0039.

Akers, Michael D., and Grover L. Porter. 2003. "Your EQ Skills: Got What It Takes?" *Journal of Accountancy* 195 (3): 65–70.

Andrews, Jane, and Helen Higson. 2008. "Graduate Employability, 'Soft Skills' Versus 'Hard' Business Knowledge: A European Study." *Higher Education in Europe* 33 (4): 411–422. https://doi.org/10.1080/03797720802522627.

Ardley, Barry C., and Nick Taylor. 2010. "The Student Practitioner: Developing Skills Through the Marketing Research Consultancy Project." *Marketing Intelligence & Planning* 28: 847–861. https://doi.org/10.1108/02634501011086454.

Ay, Ferda Alper, Abdullah Karakaya, and Kasim Yilmaz. 2015. "Relations Between Self-leadership and Critical Thinking Skills." *Procedia—Social and Behavioral Sciences* 207: 29–41. https://doi.org/10.1016/j.sbspro.2015.10.147.

Bar-On, Reuven. 2018. "Motivation Quotient Inventory™." http://www.reuvenbaron.org/wp/?s=questionnaire. Accessed 14 Mar 2018.

Bunney, Diane, Elaine Sharplin, and Christine Howitt. 2015. "Generic Skills for Graduate Accountants: The Bigger Picture, a Social and Economic Imperative in the New Knowledge Economy." *Higher Education Research & Development* 34 (2): 256–269. https://doi.org/10.1080/07294360.2014.956700.

CIMA. 2014. "CGMA Competency Framework." https://www.cgma.org/Resources/Tools/DownloadableDocuments/competency-framework-complete.pdf. Accessed 28 Jan 2018.

Goleman, Daniel. 1995. *Emotional Intelligence: Why It Can Matter More Than IQ*. New York: Bantam Books.

Goleman, Daniel. 1999. *Working with Emotional Intelligence*. New York: Bantam Books.

Gray, F. Elizabeth. 2010. "Specific Oral Communication Skills Desired in New Accountancy Graduates." *Business Communication Quarterly* 73 (1): 40–67. https://doi.org/10.1177/1080569909356350.

Hancock, Philip, Bryan Howieson, Marie Kavanagh, Jenny Kent, Irene Tempone, and Naomi Segal. 2009. *Accounting for the Future: More Than Numbers: A Collaborative Investigation into the Changing Skill Set for Professional Accounting Graduates Over the Next Ten Years and Strategies for Embedding Such Skills into Professional Accounting Programs*, vol. 1. Western Australia: University of Western Australia. https://eprints.usq.edu.au/6333/5/Hancock_Howieson_Kavanagh_etal_v1_2009_PV.pdf. Accessed 16 Mar 2018.

Hasrati, Mostafa. 2013. "Why Bother About Writing a Masters Dissertation? Assumptions of Faculty and Masters Students in an Iranian Setting." *Asia Pacific Education Review* 14: 445–465. https://doi.org/10.1007/s12564-013-9273-x.

Jackling, Beverley, and Paul De Lange. 2009. "Do Accounting Graduates' Skills Meet the Expectations of Employers? A Matter of Convergence or

Divergence." *Accounting Education* 18: 369–385. https://doi.org/10.1080/09639280902719341.

Jones, Michael, Cindi Baldi, Carl Phillips, and Avinash Waikar. 2017. "The Hard Truth About Soft Skills: What Recruiters Look for in Business Graduates." *College Student Journal* 50: 422–429.

Keevy, Monique. 2016. "Using Case Studies to Transfer Soft Skills (also Known as Pervasive Skills) Empirical Evidence." *Meditari Accountancy Research* 24 (3): 458–474. https://doi.org/10.1108/medar-04-2015-0021.

Lyons, Sean T., Linda Schweitzer, and Eddy S.W. Ng. 2015. "Resilience in the Modern Career." *Career Development International* 20 (4): 363–383. https://doi.org/10.1108/CDI-02-2015-0024.

Manz, Charles C. 1986. "Self-leadership: Toward an Expanded Theory of Self-influence Processes in Organizations." *Academy of Management Review* 11: 585–600. https://doi.org/10.5465/amr.1986.4306232.

Manz, Charles C. 2015. "Taking the Self-leadership High Road: Smooth Surface or Potholes Ahead?" *Academy of Management Perspectives* 29: 132–151. https://doi.org/10.5465/amp.2013.0060.

Musa, Farida, Norlaila Mufti, Rozmel Abdul Latiff, and Maryam Mohamed Amin. 2011. "Project-Based Learning; Promoting Meaningful Language Learning for Workplace Skills." *Procedia Social and Behavioral Sciences* 18: 187–195. Accessed 3 July 2017.

Neck, Christopher P., and Jeffery D. Houghton. 2006. "Two Decades of Self-leadership Theory and Research Past Developments, Present Trends, and Future Possibilities." *Journal of Managerial Psychology* 21 (4): 270–295. https://doi.org/10.1108/02683940610663097.

Paszkiewicz, Aleksandra, and Sylwia Silska Gembka. 2014. "The Role of Soft Competencies in the Accountant's Work—Results of Empirical Research From Poland." https://www.researchgate.net/profile/Sylwia_Silska_Gembka/publication/308695804_The_Role_of_Soft_Competencies_in_the_Accountant%27s_Work_-_Results_of_Empirical_Research_from_Poland/links/57eba9ef08ae5a3c9e6354ab/The-Role-of-Soft-Competencies-in-the-Accountants-Work-Results-of-Empirical-Research-from-Poland.pdf. Accessed 31 Jan 2018.

Reddy, Peter, and Elisabeth Moores. 2006. "Measuring the Benefits of a Psychology Placement Year." *Assessment & Evaluation in Higher Education* 31 (5): 551–567. https://doi.org/10.1080/02602930600679555.

Rodrigues, Carl A. 2004. "The Importance Level of Ten Teaching/Learning Techniques as Rated by University Business Students and Instructors." *Journal of Management Development* 23 (2): 169–182. https://doi.org/10.1108/02621710410517256.

Smith, P.P., and L.A. Gibson. 2016. "Project-Based Learning in Colleges of Business: Is It Enough to Develop Educated Graduates?" *New Directions for Teaching and Learning* 145: 41–47. https://doi.org/10.1002/tl.20173.

Surridge, Ian. 2009. "Accounting and Finance Degrees: Is the Academic Performance of Placement Students Better?" *Accounting Education* 18 (4–5): 471–485. https://doi.org/10.1080/09639280802008498.

Webb, Jill, and Caroline Chaffer. 2016. "The Expectation Performance Gap in Accounting Education: A Review of Generic Skills Development in UK Accounting Degrees." *Accounting Education* 25 (4): 348–367. https://doi.org/10.1080/09639284.2016.1191274.

CHAPTER 10

The Future of Accountancy—Beyond the Numbers

Elaine Conway

10.1 Introduction

The pace of change in the modern world is constantly increasing through rapid technological developments and it will undoubtedly impact the accounting profession (ICAEW 2017a). However, it is not the only profession to be affected by the advances of technology, law is also facing challenges. Susskind (cited in Harbison 2017) provides the example of the 60 million disputes resolved annually on the eBay e-mediation platform, which operates without the use of any traditional lawyers. A review of recent professional accounting articles is unanimous on the impact that technology will have. For example, Pitter (2018) expects that robotics will eliminate forty percent of basic accounting work by 2020; Gottschalk (2017) agrees that as machine learning and artificial intelligence mature, they will carry out administrative accounting tasks more efficiently than humans do currently; a view to which Susskind (as interviewed in Harbison 2017) also subscribes. Technology-driven change is also is a recurring topic throughout the chapters in this book. Arguably, accountants are not strangers to change, given the number

E. Conway (✉)
Derby Business School, University of Derby, Derby, UK

E. Conway and D. Byrne (eds.), *Contemporary Issues in Accounting*,
https://doi.org/10.1007/978-3-319-91113-7_10

of regulations, standards and guidance which are constantly evolving in response to changes in the economic and social environment. Therefore, they should look to embrace the future opportunities which may arise from the adoption of new ways of working.

10.2 The Accountant of the Past, Present and Future

Consider these two vignettes of an accountant:

> The typical accountant is a man, past middle age, spare, wrinkled, intelligent, cold, passive, non-committal, with eyes like a cod-fish; polite in contact but at the same time unresponsive, calm and damnably composed as a concrete post or a plaster of Paris cast; a petrification with a heart of feldspar and without charm of the friendly germ, minus bowels, passion or a sense of humor. (19th century thinker, Elbert Hubbert, cited in Ketz 2017)

Fast forward to 2027 and to the future accountant; a 'millennial' accountant—someone born in the years between the early 1980s and the end of the millennium—also referred to as 'Generation Y' (Welker 2017). Unlike the Hubbert vignette, the millennial accountant is a multitasker, highly connected (if a little prone to distractions!), tech-savvy and expects rapid rewards. They can demonstrate great flexibility, but insist on a reasonable work-life balance and are sensitive to the environment and civic responsibilities; they like to collaborate and are very transparent in their professional relationships (Abbot 2013; Welker 2017).

Indeed, consider the accountant of the future's 'typical' day: it starts with her (note the change of gender from the Hubbert vignette!) running diagnostics on client data stored in the cloud, then she interacts with an Artificial Intelligence-enabled (AI) assistant to assure data security and various other interactive 'bots' and AI to carry out routine tasks, leaving her to meet, help train and advise clients in collaboration with other professionals, such as a labour economist and a tax partner. Throughout her 'typical' day, she continually monitors client accounting data and reviews security protocols on blockchains. She ends her day with a video conference to a potential client in Buenos Aires. To create his vignette, Hood (2017) solicited the predictions of more than a hundred accounting professionals about what an accountant might expect to be doing in 2027. It echoes many of the points raised in Chapter 7 of this book on challenges facing the auditors of the future.

In many ways, some of technological capabilities behind this scenario are already theoretically possible, albeit not at a sufficiently mature or robust state to fully implement as yet. The academic background of Hood's theoretical accountant was in computer programming, not accountancy and that speaks volumes for the skill sets of the future accountant, certainly in an accounting or auditing firm.

However, despite the fact that technology will undoubtedly drive the most radical and disruptive transformation in the accounting profession over the next decade as discussed at length in Chapter 3 of this book, initially, much of this will be focused on taking out the mundane, routine data collection and analysis work. Whilst potentially a threat for those people who may have sought those kinds of jobs, the accountant of the future will have to provide a different kind of value to his or her organisation, whether as an accountant in industry or within an audit firm. As the authors in this book have indicated, there are nonetheless other changes which are already happening which affect accountants, such as risk management around sustainability and long-term resource supply as discussed in Chapter 2. Stakeholders beyond the traditional providers of capital expect much more from organisations: they demand greater transparency and standards of ethics and more explanation about the responsibilities of business towards their wider environment and society. This has created a plethora of new reports such as Sustainability, Environmental and Corporate Social Responsibility reports to which many accountants are expected to contribute.

The increasing pressure on scarce natural resources, accompanied with an ever-increasing human population may also necessitate a transition to a different business model, such as one derived from circular economy principles as expounded on in Chapter 3. This will require considerable re-evaluation of the value-drivers in the business in order to design out waste, recycle, reuse and revalue materials and goods across their life cycle. For accountants, it will require new approaches to product costing and pricing and considerable discussion with customers to create a better understanding of 'remanufactured versus new' goods.

Increased globalisation and consumer power are intrinsic drivers to multinational firms having to be cognisant of the need for an appropriate, ethical and forward-thinking Corporate Tax Strategy (CTS) as discussed in Chapter 5. It is now no longer socially acceptable for firms to avoid tax by shifting profits around the world to benefit from low tax rates—the emphasis is on paying a 'fair share of tax' which is socially responsible. This globalisation of tax planning, reporting and disclosure requirements has been in part driven by evidence of large-scale tax avoidance, inappropriate transfer pricing and money laundering which has emerged through high profile data 'leaks' to the international press such as the Panama papers (Islam 2017).

Equally, shareholders and other stakeholders demand more transparency and disclosure from organisations on business, social and environment matters (Islam 2017; ACCA 2016). Chapter 6 discussed how, in the face of such stakeholder but also legislative and regulatory pressures, organisations are increasingly expected to 'tell their story' through more narrative reporting about their total impacts on the environment and society. Firms will need to report more frequently on a greater range of issues and perhaps more importantly, demonstrate the clear links between financial and non-financial reporting (ACCA 2016) within the context of the organisation's strategy. This is likely to increase the amount of firms adopting new forms of corporate reporting as discussed in Chapter 6, such as integrated reporting.

This increased emphasis on more explanatory narrative and non-financial information is also discussed in Chapter 8. Whilst specifically much of the discussion centred on UK Local Government, the points raised in this chapter are valid for all organisations, profit-making or not. It is vital to understand how value is created within the particular firm and to devise a meaningful performance measurement system with appropriate targets, using tools such as the Balanced Scorecard (Kaplan and Norton 1992) to support improvements both financially and non-financially. Whilst some of the internal data may not be divulged externally to wider stakeholders and shareholders, it is essential for management to understand their key performance indicators in order to deliver value in the long term.

The role of the auditor as discussed in Chapter 7, will be radically impacted by technology in the long run, and there is already considerable engagement with Cloud Computing, Big Data, Artificial Intelligence and blockchain by the Big 4 auditing firms (ACCA 2016; O'Dwyer and Owen 2005; Arrowsmith 2017; ICAEW 2017a, b; Harbison 2017). Whilst these changes are likely to be evolutionary rather than revolutionary, as there are still many issues to resolve with some of the technologies around access and security, auditors should be actively involved with the design and delivery of these technologies in conjunction with data technologists and programmers. As the more mundane tasks become increasing digitalised, this eventually will lead the role of the auditor away from compliance and towards more consultancy, and improving the quality of audit work. It will require an understanding of the wider issues of businesses and their industries and good evaluation skills to advise clients of the best courses of action.

Given the plethora of changes which the future accountant will have to address, it is perhaps their own personal self-management and leadership to be able to manage multiple tasks, find value and then transfer insights to businesses and clients which will be of critical importance. Chapter 9 discussed the softer side of the accounting skill set which is the area of greatest impact beyond the technological skills which the future accountant will need. By having technologies such as AI and blockchain to 'crunch the numbers', the future accountant will need to be more customer-facing and seek ways in which to add additional value to the organisation through collaborative working with others both internal and external to their own organisation (e.g. those with whom blockchains may be shared or other specialists such as logistics experts and data analysts). Of course, many accountants already act as intermediaries between functional departments in many firms; the difference in the future will be that this negotiating and explaining role will take on more importance as everyone will have access to the same data in real time on any device they need—even those in 'offshore' teams overseas (Nixon 2016). Indeed it is expected that Cloud Computing will become the norm even in small- and medium-sized enterprises (SMEs) as people expect data to be accessible on mobile devices as well as on desktop computers (Nixon 2016). Hence there will be fewer conversations about where the data has come from and more discussions about its meaning and value for decision-making.

The important issue to grasp amidst all this change and transition to a more digitally supported profession is that despite the increasing technology around us, we are human and should regard technology as a tool to do the tasks which it can do better than us (ICAEW 2017a). We should reserve the higher level (and arguably more rewarding) activities to humans, which exploit the unique skills that humans possess and which machines cannot yet (and doubtless never will) fully replace. As an accountant, it is important to exercise the intrinsically human skills and attributes of judgement, ethics, morals and humanity, demonstrate a consideration for different contexts (hence the support for more principles, rather than rules-based standards) and make measured responses to the evidence at hand.

That said, accountants will need to have more specialised and higher level skills in order to support this process: skills of data analytics, cybertechnology, but underpinned with critical thinking and impressive interpersonal and communication skills (Pitter 2018; Ketz 2017). This is so they are capable of advising and consulting more in their roles rather than purely 'crunching the numbers'. Indeed, Nixon (2016) predicts that 80% of accounting firm revenues in the future will consist of business advisory services, rather than compliance and audit work, which will become a commodity and become very low-cost (Nixon 2016). The most repetitive tasks likely to be replaced by technology are: invoice processing and matching, analytics calculations and bank reconciliations; later, with more machine learning capability, risk assessments and forecasting could be delegated to computers (Marr 2017).

ACCA (2016) have assessed what skills are likely to be needed in the future; it refers to them as Professional Quotients (PQ) and it considers that future accountants will need to have a combination of these PQ in order to fit their current and prospective roles as their careers develop. These PQ are designed to reflect specific competences and skills over seven areas (ACCA 2016):

- Technical skills and ethics (TEQ): The standard skills required to carry out the necessary day-to-day accounting tasks to high levels of integrity, ethics, scepticism and independence;
- Experience (XQ): The comprehension of customer expectations and the ability to respond to them to add value to the customer;
- Intelligence (IQ): The ability to learn and apply knowledge to solve problems;
- Digital awareness (DQ): The knowledge and application of both existing and emerging technologies in a professional context to support practice and strategy;
- Creativity (CQ): The ability to learn and apply knowledge in different situations, to connect information and create new ideas;
- Emotional intelligence (EQ): The ability to acknowledge and respect personal emotions in the self and others to employ and manage them to best advantage; and
- Vision (VQ): The ability to extrapolate existing trends to spot emergent trends and to evaluate them creatively.

ACCA acknowledge that the mix of these PQ will vary according to individual, industry, job roles and locations, and that some will gain in importance whilst others may decline over time. It is keen to stress that all of these will need to be underpinned by strong ethical standards, independence and a sense of professional scepticism (ACCA 2016).

Educators will need to look carefully at their curricula to ensure that they are able to support this wide variety of skills (Islam 2017) and professional bodies will need to incorporate them within their syllabuses to provide employers with the assurance that newly trained accountants are indeed future-ready.

10.3 The Way Ahead

In conclusion, there is a clear expectation that all professional accountants in the future will have to look 'beyond the numbers' (Islam 2017; ACCA 2016). As ACCA remark:

> They will need to collaborate and partner with people in other parts of the business and outside the business; interpret and explain the numbers; provide insight and information; help organisations to achieve short-term goals and longer-term objectives; think and behave more strategically and become more involved in decision-making than before. (ACCA 2016, p. 10)

Adopting the common themes which have emerged throughout this book, the traits and skills of the future accountant could be expressed using the acronym "accountant":

A Accountable
C Collaborative
C Considerate
O Outcomes-focused
U Unafraid of change
N Negotiator
T Transformative
A Assurance aware
N Numerate
T Technology confident

In order to ensure good career progression, it will not be sufficient to rely on the technical accounting knowledge which has been the mainstay of accounting education in the past. To future-proof one's career, an accountant will need to be much more externally facing, picking up on emerging trends, such as the ones highlighted in this book, across the spectrum of tax, audit, corporate reporting, performance management, business models, sustainability, corporate social activities, environmental and social issues, business intelligence and technology. More collaborative working, increasingly globally, will require knowledge of emerging trends on an international scale regarding culture, demographics, politics, law and international relations (ACCA 2016). This knowledge, combined with strong interpersonal skills of relationship building, negotiation and self-leadership will create a really strong and valued member of any future organisation.

The world of accounting is set to become eminently less transaction-driven and more value-focused with the most amazing tools available to sweep away many of the more tedious tasks and provide insights previously unimaginable. Accountants are not going to be replaced by machines anytime soon! These are exciting times to be an accountant!

References

Abbot, Lydia. 2013. "8 Millennials' Traits You Should Know About Before You Hire Them|LinkedIn Talent Blog." LinkedIn Talent Blog. https://business.linkedin.com/talent-solutions/blog/2013/12/8-millennials-traits-you-should-know-about-before-you-hire-them.

ACCA. 2016. "Drivers of Change and Future Skills," 1–88. www.accaglobal.com.

Arrowsmith, R. 2017. "AICPA and WSBA Partner to Drive Blockchain Adoption." *Accounting Today*. https://www.accountingtoday.com/news/aicpa-and-wsba-partner-to-drive-blockchain-adoption.

Gottschalk, Kim. 2017. "5 Things You Need to Know About the Future of Accounting." *Accounting Web*. https://www.accountingweb.com/practice/growth/5-things-you-need-to-know-about-the-future-of-accounting.

Harbison, Andrew. 2017. "End of the Accounting Profession?" *CA Today*. ICAS. https://www.icas.com/ca-today-news/the-end-of-the-accounting-profession-as-we-know-it.

Hood, D. 2017. "A Day in the Life of the Future Accountant." *Accounting Today*. https://www.accountingtoday.com/opinion/nov-1-2027-a-day-in-the-life-of-the-future-accountant.

ICAEW. 2017a. "Artificial Intelligence and the Future of Accountancy," 1–16. https://www.icaew.com/-/media/corporate/files/technical/information-technology/technology/artificial-intelligence-report.ashx?la=en.

ICAEW. 2017b. "Blockchain and the Future of Accountancy." ICAEW. https://www.icaew.com/en/technical/information-technology/technology/blockchain/blockchain-and-the-accounting-perspective.

Islam, Muhammad Azizul. 2017. "Future of Accounting Profession: Three Major Changes and Implications for Teaching and Research|IFAC." IFAC Global Knowledge Gateway. https://www.ifac.org/global-knowledge-gateway/business-reporting/discussion/future-accounting-profession-three-major.

Kaplan, Robert S., and David Norton. 1992. "The Balanced Scorecard: Measures That Drive Performance." *Harvard Business Review* 70 (1): 71–79.

Ketz, J. Edward. 2017. "Your Future in the Accounting Profession|Accounting Today." *Accounting Today*. https://www.accountingtoday.com/opinion/your-future-in-the-accounting-profession.

Marr, Bernard. 2017. "Machine Learning, Artificial Intelligence—and the Future of Accounting." *Forbes.com*. https://www.forbes.com/sites/bernardmarr/2017/07/07/machine-learning-artificial-intelligence-and-the-future-of-accounting/#2c1199d52dd1.

Nixon, Rob. 2016. "12 Predictions on the Future of the Accounting Profession." *Accountex*. http://www.accountex.co.uk/12-predictions-on-the-future-of-the-accounting-profession/.

O'Dwyer, Brendan, and David L. Owen. 2005. "Assurance Statement Practice in Environmental, Social and Sustainability Reporting: A Critical Evaluation." *The British Accounting Review* 37 (2): 205–229. https://doi.org/10.1016/j.bar.2005.01.005.

Pitter, Amy. 2018. "Job Disruption Is Quickly Coming to Accounting, Too|Accounting Today." *Accounting Today*. https://www.accountingtoday.com/opinion/job-disruption-is-quickly-coming-to-accounting-too?utm_campaign=accountingtechnology-mar192018&utm_medium=email&utm_source=newsletter&eid=64feb67490c8babba0a42bc4766215b2.

Welker, Bryce. 2017. "How to Find Success in the Future of Accounting|Inc.com." *Inc.com*. https://www.inc.com/young-entrepreneur-council/the-future-accountants-are-you-ready.html.

Index

E. Conway and D. Byrne (eds.), *Contemporary Issues in Accounting*,
https://doi.org/10.1007/978-3-319-91113-7

Made in the USA
Monee, IL
12 September 2026

62974220R00125